The Security-Development Nexus

The Security-Development Nexus

Peace, Conflict and Development

Edited by
RAMSES AMER, ASHOK SWAIN
and JOAKIM ÖJENDAL

ANTHEM PRESS
LONDON · NEW YORK · DELHI

Anthem Press
An imprint of Wimbledon Publishing Company
www.anthempress.com

This edition first published in UK and USA 2013
by ANTHEM PRESS
75–76 Blackfriars Road, London SE1 8HA, UK
or PO Box 9779, London SW19 7ZG, UK
and
244 Madison Ave. #116, New York, NY 10016, USA

First published in hardback by Anthem Press in 2012

British Library Cataloguing-in-Publication Data
A catalogue record for this book is available from the British Library.

Library of Congress Cataloging-in-Publication Data
The Library of Congress has cataloged the hardcover edition as follows:
The security-development nexus : peace, confl ict and development /
edited by Ramses Amer, Ashok Swain and Joakim Öjendal.
p. cm.
Includes bibliographical references.
ISBN 978-0-85728-351-1 (hardback : alk. paper)
1. Peace-building–Case studies. 2. Human security. 3. Security,
International. I. Amer, Ramses. II. Swain, Ashok. III. Öjendal,
Joakim.
JZ5538.S42 2012
355'.033–dc23
2011048731

ISBN-13: 978 1 78308 065 6 (Pbk)
ISBN-10: 1 78308 065 5 (Pbk)

This title is also available as an ebook.

CONTENTS

LIST OF TABLES AND FIGURES

Tables

Figures

LIST OF EDITORS AND CONTRIBUTORS

Editors

Ramses Amer is an associate professor in peace and conflict research, and a senior research fellow with the Department of Oriental Languages, Stockholm University, Sweden; guest research professor at the National Institute for South China Sea Studies, Haikou, Hainan, China; and a research associate, Swedish Institute of International Affairs, Stockholm. Major areas of his research include security issues and conflict resolution in Southeast Asia and the wider Pacific Asia, and the role of the United Nations in the international system. His most recent books are *Conflict Management and Dispute Settlement in East Asia* (Ashgate, 2011), co-edited with Keyuan Zou; *International Relations in Southeast Asia: Between Bilateralism and Multilateralism* (Singapore: Institute of Southeast Asian Studies, 2010), co-edited with N. Ganesan; *The Democratization Project: Opportunities and Challenges* (Anthem Press, 2009) and *Globalization and Challenges to Building Peace* (Anthem Press, 2007), both co-edited with Ashok Swain and Joakim Öjendal.

Ashok Swain is Professor of Peace and Conflict Research at Uppsala University, Sweden. He also serves as the director of Uppsala Centre for Sustainable Development. He received his PhD from the Jawaharlal Nehru University, New Delhi in 1991. He has been a MacArthur Fellow at the University of Chicago, as well as a visiting fellow at the UN Research Institute for Social Development, Geneva; the University Witwatersrand, South Africa; the University of Science, Malaysia; the University of British Columbia; and the University of Maryland. He has written extensively on new security threats and international water sharing issues. His publications include *The Environmental Trap: The Ganges River Diversion, Bangladeshi Migration and Conflicts in India* (Uppsala: Deptartment of Peace and Conflict Research, 1996),

International Fresh Water Resources: Conflict or Cooperation (with Peter Wallensteen, Stockholm: Stockholm Environment Institute, 1997), *Managing Water Conflict: Asia, Africa and the Middle East* (Routledge, 2004) and *Struggle Against the State* (Ashgate, 2010). His edited books include *Education as Social Action* (Palgrave MacMillan, 2005) and *Islam and Violent Separatism* (Kegan Paul, 2007). He is co-editor (with Ramses Amer and Joakim Öjendal) of *Globalization and Challenges to Building Peace* (Anthem Press, 2007) and *The Democratization Project: Opportunities and Challenges* (Anthem Press, 2009).

Joakim Öjendal is a professor in peace and development studies at the School of Global Studies, University of Gothenburg, Sweden. He has inter alia co-edited (with Mona Lilja) a volume on reconstruction, *Beyond Democracy in Cambodia: Political Reconstruction in a Post-Conflict Society* (NIAS Press, 2009), a volume on democratization (with Ashok Swain and Ramses Amer), *The Democratization Project: Opportunities and Challenges* (Anthem Press, 2009), and (also with Swain and Amer) *Globalization and Challenges to Building Peace* (Anthem Press, 2007). Recently he was the co-editor (with Maria Stern) of a thematic issue of *Security Dialogue* on the 'Security-Development Nexus'. Currently Öjendal is editing a volume on the state of the art of local governance and decentralization.

Contributors

Ruben de Koning is a researcher with the Armed Conflict and Conflict Management Programme of the Stockholm International Peace Research Institute (SIPRI), Sweden. His research interests include inter-state border disputes, small-arms violence and rebel movements in the context of natural resource scarcity and abundance. His present work focuses on the artisanal mining sector and its association with conflicts in the Democratic Republic of the Congo. Prior to joining SIPRI he worked at the United Nations Development Programme (UNDP) and at the Center for International Forestry Research (CIFOR). Recent publications include: *Controlling Conflict Resources in the Democratic Republic of the Congo* (Stockholm International Peace Research Institute Policy Brief, July 2010); *Soldiers and Traders in War and Peace: The Resilience of Conflict Resources in DRC* (Swedish Defence Research Agency, 2009); *Forest Related Conflict: Impacts, Links and Measures to Mitigate* (Rights and Resources Initiative, 2008); 'Resource–Conflict Links in Sierra Leone and the Democratic Republic of the Congo' (*SIPRI Insights on Peace and Security* 2008/2) and 'Greed or Grievance in West Africa's Forest Wars?' (in W. de Jong et al. (eds), *Extreme Conflict and Tropical Forest*, Springer, 2007).

Sofie Hellberg is a PhD candidate in peace and development research at the School of Global Studies, University of Gothenburg, Sweden. Hellberg is affiliated to the Centre for Civil Society, School of Development Studies, University of KwaZulu-Natal, South Africa. During spring 2011 she was a visiting academic research fellow at the School of Environment and Development, University of Manchester. Her PhD dissertation on water and water service delivery in eThekwini Municipality, South Africa starts from the notion of biopolitics and looks into how instruments of policy implementation are restricting and/or facilitating certain ways of life, and explores the subjectivities that are being produced in these hydropolitical power relations. Hellberg's research interests revolve around biopolitics and power, water and water service delivery, as well as the nexuses between environment and development and between security and development.

Roland Kostić is a researcher at the Hugo Valentin Centre at Uppsala University, Sweden. Since 2002 Mr. Kostić has carried out various assignments and produced a number of academic and policy papers relating to post-conflict peacebuilding and reconciliation in the Balkans. He has also authored reports commissioned by such bodies as the Swedish Ministry of Foreign Affairs, Swedish International Development Cooperation Agency and the United Nations Research Institute for Social Development. His research interests include social psychology, group mobilization and attitudes, transitional justice and international peacebuilding. His most recent publication, 'Yugoslavs in Arms: Guerrilla Tradition, Total Defence and the Ethnic Security Dilemma' (co-authored with T. Dulić) was published in *Europe-Asia Studies* in September 2010.

Florian Krampe is a doctoral candidate at Uppsala University in the Department of Peace and Conflict Research and the Uppsala Centre for Sustainable Development, Sweden. In his research Krampe is interested in climate change and environmental factors and their relation to armed conflict, peacebuilding and post-conflict reconstruction. Krampe's expanded interest covers reconciliation in southern Africa and Afghanistan, sociological perspectives on armed conflict, peacebuilding and reconciliation, as well as ethics and violence. He has published on new wars theory and the case of Bosnia and Herzegovina, applying a sociological perspective. He has also published and presented papers on post-conflict developments in southern Africa.

Marlène Laruelle is a senior research fellow with the Central Asia-Caucasus Institute and Silk Road Studies Program, a joint centre affiliated with Johns Hopkins University's School of Advanced International Studies, Washington DC and the Institute for Security and Development Policy, Stockholm. Her main areas of expertise are nationalism, national identities, political philosophy,

intellectual trends and geopolitical conceptions of local elites in Russia and
Central Asia. Her English-language publications include *Russian Eurasianism.
An Ideology of Empire* (Woodrow Wilson Press/Johns Hopkins University Press,
2008); *In the Name of the Nation. Nationalism and Politics in Contemporary Russia*
(Palgrave, 2009); and as editor, *Russian Nationalism and the National Reassertion of
Russia* (Routledge, 2009).

Nhi Phan is presently affiliated to the Department of Peace and Conflict
Research, Uppsala University, Sweden as a guest researcher. She received an
Erasmus Mundus Euroculture MA from Uppsala University in 2009. She has
also worked as a lecturer and researcher at Hue University, Vietnam during
2006–7. Her research interests include diasporas and their role in peace and
development as well as broader migration issues in the international system.

Sébastien Peyrouse is a senior research fellow with the Central Asia-
Caucasus Institute and Silk Road Studies Program, a joint centre affiliated
with Johns Hopkins University's School of Advanced International Studies,
Washington DC and the Institute for Security and Development Policy,
Stockholm. His research originally focused on the impact of the Russian/
Soviet heritage in the five Central Asian republics. His main areas of expertise
are political systems in Central Asia, Islam and religious minorities, and
Central Asia's geopolitical positioning toward China, Russia and South Asia.
In English, he has published *China as a Neighbor: Central Asian Perspectives and
Strategies* (Central Asia-Caucasus Institute, 2009) with Marlène Laruelle, and
'The Economic Aspects of the Chinese-Central-Asia Rapprochement' (*Silk
Road Papers*, Central Asia-Caucasus Institute, 2007).

Maria Stern is an associate professor in peace and development studies
at the School of Global Studies, University of Gothenburg and at the
Gothenburg Centre for Globalization and Development. Her current
research includes an extended project on gender in the armed forces
(and security system reform) in the DRC with Maria Eriksson Baaz and,
(with Joakim Berndtsson) a project on security privatization. She is the
guest co-editor (with Joakim Öjendal) of a special issue on the Security-
Development Nexus Revisited, *Security Dialogue*. She is also co-editor of
Feminist Methodologies for International Relations (Cambridge University Press,
2006) the author of *Naming Security – Constructing Identity* (Manchester
University Press, 2005). She has co-authored (with Maria Eriksson Baaz)
the report, *The Complexity of Violence* (Sida/NAI, 2010). Her articles have
appeared in leading journals, including *Alternatives, Journal of Modern African
Studies, International Journal of Peace Studies, International Studies Quarterly,*

Review of International Studies, *Security Dialogue* and *Journal of International Relations and Development*.

Zou Keyuan is Harris Professor of International Law at the Lancashire Law School of the University of Central Lancashire (UCLan), United Kingdom. He specializes in international law, in particular law of the sea and international environmental law. Before joining UCLan, he worked at Dalhousie University (Canada), Peking University (China), University of Hannover (Germany) and National University of Singapore. He has published over fifty refereed English-language papers in nearly thirty international journals. His most recent single-authored book is *China-ASEAN Relations and International Law* (Chandos, 2009). He is a member of the editorial boards of the *International Journal of Marine and Coastal Law*, *Ocean Development and International Law*, *Journal of International Wildlife Law and Policy*, *The Polar Journal* and *Chinese Journal of International Law*, and is a member of the advisory board of the *Chinese Oceans Law Review*.

Malin Åkebo is a PhD student at the Department of Political Science, Umeå University, Sweden. Her dissertation concerns the role of cease-fires in peace processes in protracted intra-state conflicts, which is part of the project designed to focus on cases in the Asian region. She is the author of: 'The role of external actors in managing peace processes in Asia: an overview of attempts in Aceh, Mindanao and Sri Lanka', in Ramses Amer and Keyuan Zou (eds), *Conflict Management and Dispute Settlement in East Asia* (Ashgate, 2011).

ACKNOWLEDGEMENTS

The inspiration for this edited volume began at the 2009 Conference of the Swedish Network of Peace, Conflict and Development Research (PCDRNET) on the topic 'Development and Security Nexus' held in Stockholm on 6–7 November 2009. The workshop was hosted by the Department of Oriental Languages, Stockholm University through its Center for Pacific Asia Studies (CPAS).

In this volume seven revised papers from the conference have been included together with the keynote address as well as an introductory chapter; in addition one commissioned chapter is included. Contributors have followed a tight schedule in revising their contributions and in responding to various queries and comments.

As editors, we would like to acknowledge the early expression of interest by Anthem Press. We greatly appreciate each chapter contributor for her/his contributions to this edited book and their close cooperation with us during the editing period as well as various comments emanating from participants in the original workshop and conference.

The editors' work on this volume has been made possible through the financial support of the Swedish International Development Cooperation Agency (Sida) – the main sponsor of the PCDRNET – whose support we gratefully acknowledge.

Ramses Amer, Ashok Swain and Joakim Öjendal
Stockholm, Uppsala and Gothenburg
July 2011

Chapter 1

RESEARCHING THE SECURITY-DEVELOPMENT NEXUS THROUGH A MULTI-DISCIPLINARY APPROACH

Ramses Amer, Ashok Swain and Joakim Öjendal

Introduction

Following a global flurry of 'new wars' and 'new conflicts' in the post–Cold War era (Kaldor 2007; Keen 2008), a lot of rethinking has been done (and certainly will be done) on the causes of violent conflict in the global system. After a decade dominated by, inter alia, '9/11', the unstable and violent African development context and the relatively sustainable peace (and very successful development) in East Asia, reflections on the relations between development and security (and vice versa) became unavoidable. In policy documents (e.g., UN 2004; OECD 2007; DFID 2005; European Council 2003, 2008; UNDP 2005), as well as in academic circles (Buur, Jensen and Stepputat 2007; Chandler 2007, 2008; Duffield 2001, 2007; Paris and Sisk 2007), the 'development-security nexus' was coined as a concept and emerged as a hotly contested topic. Unsurprisingly, the policy world was jumping to 'new solutions', with reductionist conclusions, whereas research remained more sceptical. For instance, irrespective of whether we listen to the 'new' United States foreign policy articulated by Colin Powell or by General Petraeus, to the secretary-general of the United Nations and to the International Commission on Intervention and State Sovereignty on 'Responsibility to Protect' (UN 2009; ICISS 2001), or the European Union's 'European Security Strategy' (European Council 2008), the attention is increasingly on how conflicts of various sorts can be prevented through greater focus on 'development'. The nexus became a commodity over which intellectual ownership was as unclear as important. Voices critical of the good intentions (Duffield 2010) as well as the clarity of the concept (Stern and Öjendal 2010) emerged, and the idea is struggling with credibility. In this light, in this edited book we offer an intellectual contribution in order to further the debate through both conceptual, theoretical and case study analyses from a multi-disciplinary approach.

Although the nexus between security and development has come onto the policy agenda explicitly after 9/11, the idea has been influencing international development policy for some time. Even the Marshall Plan and Truman Doctrine were products of this. In the post–Cold War period, the definition of security has been redefined to include people's security. The United Nations Development Programme's 1994 Human Development Report argued for human security as 'freedom from fear' and 'freedom from want' (UNDP 1994). The recent political priority of emphasizing the nexus has led to the securitization of development policy, and rich countries allocate large portion of their aid to countries and regions perceived as a risk to their security interests. In the post-9/11 period, the US aid policy has been open and obvious in this regard, but the EU donors have also increasingly joined the trend to allocate most of their aid strategically. There is no doubt that this securitization trend of the aid policy has further reduced the already limited resources available for the development to the poor countries. However, the predicament is much more complex than this.

As development and security are relational concepts, many question whose security and whose development this nexus is concerned with. Short-term security considerations of rich and powerful countries increasingly override the long-term developmental challenges of poor regions. This approach also poses challenges for long-term engagements necessary for sustainable peace. There are also huge coordination gaps between different agencies and their policies in connecting development and security. There is a certain move towards policy standardization, but as Chandler (2006) and Paris (2004) argue, that coordination is in most cases limited to rhetoric only. Besides the lack of coordination among relevant agencies, the policies driven by the nexus approach also suffers from a huge disparity between policy and implementation, an absence of real local involvement, and a scarcity of resources. Moreover, the security-development nexus has led, to a certain extent, to a conceptual chaos.

The rationale behind this edited book is to use a multi-disciplinary perspective to address the discussion of different positions on what the security-development nexus necessitates. In the context of the book, several academic disciplines are brought together – peace and conflict, peace and development, international relations, international law and political economy. All contributors have their academic background in one or more of these disciplines. The majority of the contributors come from peace studies and its two main sub-fields, peace and conflict and peace and development.

The main theme of this edited book draws from the 2009 Conference of the Swedish Network of Peace, Conflict and Development Research (PCDRNET) on the topic 'Development and Security Nexus' held in Stockholm, Sweden on 6–7 November 2009. The contributions to the book are revised and updated versions of the keynote address and selected papers presented at the conference. In addition, one chapter has been commissioned and this introductory chapter has been added.

A Multi-disciplinary Approach

As noted above, the security-development nexus can be researched through a number of academic disciplines, and in this book the various contributors address the nexus from several relevant academic disciplines. The majority of the contributors come from peace studies.

Being a relatively young academic discipline, peace studies draws on other more established disciplines including international relations, international law and political economy in the context of global, regional, and other forms of inter-state disputes and conflicts, as well as from political science, sociology and anthropology in the context of intra-state disputes and conflicts. Peace studies seeks to explain and understand factors that cause disputes and conflicts. It also seeks to study and develop various approaches to resolve and manage potential and existing disputes and conflicts. The approaches range from actions of international and regional organizations through frameworks, principles and mechanisms to various forms of actions including peacekeeping. Peace studies is also concerned with factors that hamper conflict management and disputes settlement as in, for example, so-called spoilers and their impact on peace processes and the implementation of peace agreements (e.g., Stedman 1997). The role of third parties is of particular relevance in peace studies and this can be seen in the study of both negotiation and mediation as, for example, in the research on 'ripeness' (e.g., Zartman 2001), as well as in the study of various forms of interventionism (e.g., Amer 1994). Peace studies also addresses the linkage between regime types and conflict behaviour, e.g., 'democratic peace' and 'liberal peace' (e.g., Richmond 2007). If peace studies historically has been focusing to a large extent on 'from war to peace' the introduction of, and interest for, the 'security-development nexus' turns this on its head and suggests an increased focus on (preventing the passage) 'from peace to war'. As such, it is an important piece in the puzzle of understanding the full circle of conflict cycles from causes of conflicts to post-conflict developments.

In this edited book a number of these dimensions of peace studies are highlighted in the context of the study of the links between security and development. The starting point is an exploration of the conceptual dimensions of the security-development nexus in Chapter 2. This chapter also links the book to both the existing scholarly literature in the field (e.g., *Security Dialogue* 2010; *Third World Quarterly* 2009) and to the policy debates relating to the linkages between security and development. The linkages are also explored through two case studies of the Democratic Republic of the Congo (DRC) and South Africa, with Chapter 9 dealing with trade and exploitation of minerals in the DRC and Chapter 10 dealing with water management through a case study of eThekwini Municipality in South Africa. Also related is the broad human security dimension which is examined in Chapter 7 through a study of the Central Asian region. In Chapter 3, key dimensions of 'liberal peace' are addressed through a case study of Kosovo. The role of external parties in intra-state conflicts is addressed through the analysis of the cases of Aceh and Sri Lanka in Chapter 6. Chapter 4 examines the rise of China and the possible impact that will have on the existing international order. Both Chapters 4 and 5 address issues relating to interventionism – in particular, the principle on non-interference and the prohibition of the threat or use of force in inter-state relations – through analyses of the foreign policy of China and an analysis of the principles governing the Association of Southeast Asian Nations (ASEAN).

The multi-disciplinary approach can clearly bee seen through the different approaches utilized by the contributors to the book. Chapter 4, dealing with the rise China, applies a purely international law approach to the problematic, and Chapter 5 also addresses some dimensions through the international legal tradition but combines it with some aspects on peace and conflict, in particular those dealing with interventionism. Taken as whole, this edited book displays how multi-disciplinary peace studies really is and how broad the methodological, theoretical and conceptual approaches encompassed under the umbrella of peace studies are.

The contributions to the book display the complexities of the linkages between security and development at both the inter-state and intra-state levels, and the book also addresses the conceptual discourse relating to the nexus. This is complemented by both theoretical testing on relevant case studies and by in-depth empirical case studies. Taken as whole, the contributions make the edited book both conceptually, theoretically and empirically relevant in the context of the scholarly debate and study of the security-development nexus. It is also of relevance for the broader policy debate on the linkages between security and development at global, regional and national levels in the international system.

Geographical Focus and Case Studies

The edited book is not intended to deal with one specific geographical area; consequently, the book deals with cases from a wide section of the world, notably Africa, Asia and Europe. The two chapters dealing with African cases focus on the DRC and South Africa. Four chapters address Asian cases: one chapter deals with China specifically; one with China and ASEAN; one with the cases of Ache (in Indonesia) and Sri Lanka; and one with Central Asia as a whole. The two chapters dealing with European cases focus on Kosovo and Sweden (specifically, the Vietnamese diaspora).

The cases are studied from different perspectives in the respective chapters. One dimension is the international involvement in intra-state disputes both through international intervention, as with Kosovo, and through international mediation, as with Ache and Sri Lanka. Another dimension concerns foreign policy and international security relating to inter-state relations, as with China and ASEAN.

Structure of the Book

The edited book is structured in the following way. Chapter 2 by Maria Stern and Joakim Öjendal is a conceptual exploration of the security-development nexus. Chapter 3 by Roland Kostić, Florian Krampe and Ashok Swain assesses liberal state-building and environmental security in the context of the case of Kosovo. Chapter 4 by Zou Keyuan assesses the rise of China in the context of the existing international order. Chapter 5 by Ramses Amer investigates the linkages between some key dimensions of the Charter of the United Nations and the issue of security with specific reference to Pacific Asia. Chapter 6 by Malin Åkebo deals with the international dimensions of the peace processes in Aceh and Sri Lanka with a focus on the role of intermediaries. Chapter 7 by Marlène Laruelle and Sébastien Peyrouse assesses the challenges of human security and development in Central Asia. Chapter 8 by Ashok Swain and Nhi Phan explores the role of diasporas in peacebuilding through the case of the Vietnamese diaspora in Sweden. Chapter 9 by Ruben de Koning examines the nexus between development and security in the DRC through the study of the exploration and tracing of minerals. Finally, Chapter 10 by Sofie Hellberg studies the linkage between water management and the security-development nexus through a case study of eThekwini Municipality in South Africa.

Main Findings

The chapters included in this edited book deal with issues relating to the linkages between security and development from various perspectives and through various approaches providing relevant findings for a broader understand of the complexities of the security-development nexus in today's world.

In Chapter 2 'Exploring the Security-Development Nexus', Maria Stern and Joakim Öjendal observe that it is now beyond doubt that attention to the 'security-development nexus' has become commonplace in national and global policy-making; yet it remains underexplored *how* 'the nexus' is differently imbued with meaning and ultimately employed. In their chapter Stern and Öjendal suggest one possible framework for mapping the multiple understandings which underlie specific articulations of 'the nexus' in order to reveal the ways in which meaning may shift in different (yet seemingly similar) discourses. To this end, Stern and Öjendal draw upon familiar stories about development and about security and offer a brief reading of ways in which 'the nexus' is articulated in policy texts. This framework also provides insights into what such articulations may imply for the policy agenda.

In Chapter 3, 'Liberal State-Building and Environmental Security: The International Community Between Trade-Off and Carelessness', Roland Kostić, Florian Krampe and Ashok Swain note that several studies show that environmental stress is one of the main catalysts of societal insecurities that can escalate to armed conflict. Current international peacebuilding efforts, resting on the premises of liberal peace, strive to ameliorate such conflicts and address societal insecurities in the post-conflict situation. However, the focus on democratization, human rights, rule of law institution and capacity building means that the issue of environmental stress often remains unaddressed, thus creating new casus belli. The authors take Kosovo as a case in point to illustrate how the efforts of a complex peacebuilding operation aiming to provide conditions for durable peace can lead to an increasing environmental stress. As a result, the effects are development-induced displacement and pollution caused, for example, by the extensive opencast mining for lignite. The authors argue that environmental and societal security needs have to be addressed simultaneously to reduce the danger of recurring conflicts.

In Chapter 4, 'The Rising China and Maintaining the International Order: Some Reflections', Zou Keyuan notes that with the rise of China, people around the world are wondering whether this rising power would change the existing international order, which is a result of the order reconstruction after World War II with the establishment of the United Nations and its associated specialized intergovernmental organizations. Zou argues that as a member, China is bound by the Charter of the United Nations, including its legal principles, and must carry out its corresponding obligations. The chapter discusses and assesses China's practices in international affairs including the maintenance of international peace and security in three aspects: fighting against terrorism and other international crimes, humanitarian intervention and international disarmament. It also examines China's role in the promotion of a new order for the environment and economy in two aspects: the establishment of both an international climate change regime and a new international economic order. Finally, the chapter examines China's approaches to international dispute settlement. Some conclusions are drawn from relevant observations that, although the rising China is no doubt playing a more active and on some occasions critical role in international affairs, it is not yet a global power which can direct the course of change in the international order. Zou observes that China is a maintainer and supporter of the existing international order rather than a challenger – and much less an overthrower – of the current order. This can be seen from Chinese statements made within the United Nations system that the authority of the charter must be maintained and that 'defending the authority of the Charter is essential for maintaining the rule of law at the international level' (Duan 2007, 187). However, working within the current international order does not mean that China is contented with the international system in all aspects. Due to its rise as an economic power, China is demanding a bigger say in international financial and banking affairs as discussed above, and even attempted to call for the establishment of a new international economic order. Zou argues that history shows that China's foreign policy is subject to changes and adjustments from time to time. The author concludes that if China is accommodated satisfactorily in the current international economic order, it is very likely that it will drop its call for a new order and live within the existing one. Zou also argues that if China demands a bigger and more vigorous say, it should consider whether it is ready to assume more responsibilities in world affairs. He observes that this is a real challenge to China in assuming its global responsibilities and there may be several benchmarks against which to observe China's readiness in this regard.

In Chapter 5, 'Non-use of Force, Non-interference and Security: The Case of Pacific Asia', Ramses Amer investigates the links between some key dimensions of the Charter of the United Nations and the issue of security. This is done through an examination of two key norms of the charter: the prohibition of the threat or use of force in inter-state relations and the principle of non-interference in the internal affairs of states. The empirical application of these principles and their impact on regional security in the Pacific Asia region is examined through the study of the foreign policy of China and through the study of the principles governing ASEAN. Amer notes that both China and ASEAN pursue policies that favour the principle of non-interference in the internal affairs of other countries, they also pursue policies that adhere to the prohibition of the threat or use of force, and both China and ASEAN are committed to the peaceful settlements of disputes. Amer argues that although recent practice indicates a more flexible stand on interventionism on China's part, China would not tolerate any such action directly affecting it and strongly reacts when its national interests are threatened by actions carried out elsewhere in the international system. The author also notes that as in the case of China, the individual member states of ASEAN display more flexible policies towards interventionism and to peacekeeping outside the region.

In Chapter 6, 'International Dimensions of Peace Processes in Aceh and Sri Lanka: The Role of Intermediaries in the 2000s', Malin Åkebo deals with two Asian cases. The chapter addresses the international dimensions of peace processes in intra-state conflicts in the Asian region by focusing specifically on the involvement of external actors in managing peace attempts in Aceh and in Sri Lanka. It aims to map out the main external actors and their involvement in the peace processes, focusing on developments in the 2000s. It begins with a brief background to the Asian context, focusing on conflicts and conflict management in intra-state conflicts in this region and then focuses upon the above two cases, starting with a background description to the conflicts, which is followed by an overview of important peace attempts and the main external actors involved in these attempts. Åkebo observes that although the selected conflicts have to a large extent been internally driven, the peace processes have experienced external third-party involvement. However, these involvements required the consent from the primary conflicting parties, who accordingly have to a large extent determined the features of the efforts. Furthermore, the author notes the importance of facilitation rather than mediation in the external involvement.

In Chapter 7, 'The Challenges of Human Security and Development in Central Asia', Marlène Laruelle and Sébastien Peyrouse examine the intersection of human security challenges in the Central Asian region (Kazakhstan, Kyrgyzstan, Uzbekistan, Tajikistan and Turkmenistan): narcotics traffic and the criminalization of the state apparatus; pauperization of rural populations; challenging water management and food security; threats to literacy and health care systems; and large migration flows. The multiplicity and overlapping nature of these challenges make for a particularly tense social and political situation, as demonstrated by the recent violent events in Kyrgyzstan in June 2010. These all serve to demonstrate the importance of a holistic approach at the micro, meso and macro levels, combining historical, sociological, political and economic analyses in order to articulate these human security issues.

In Chapter 8, 'Diasporas' Role in Peacebuilding: The Case of the Vietnamese-Swedish Diaspora', Ashok Swain and Nhi Phan examine the impact that globalization has had on how diaspora communities interact with their homelands, particularly in the context of post-conflict situations.

According to most of the existing body of research, diasporas are predisposed to political radicalism and the fomenting of violence within their homelands. However, the chapter explores and analyses the constructive impacts of the Vietnamese-Swedish diaspora group as a critical agent of social, political and cultural change in peacebuilding and reconstruction processes in Vietnam.

In Chapter 9, 'Tracing Minerals, Creating Peace: The Security-Development Nexus in the DRC', Ruben de Koning notes that war in the DRC is often considered as a means for armed groups to control resources-extraction areas and trade networks. In its response, the international community focuses on measures that block 'dirty' trade of resources that finance illegal armed groups, and formalize and facilitate 'clean', legal trade that presumably does not. De Koning notes that this approach fails to recognize that militarized systems of control established during war persist in the post-war context. As a result, regular forces are as much involved as irregular ones, and legal trade may still fuel conflict at the production level. The chapter illustrates the persistence and complexity of militarized networks of resource control with the case of the Nyunzu territory in northern Katanga where the Congolese National Army is deeply involved in the extraction and trade of coltan – a metal that together with cassiterite and gold constitute the main 'conflict minerals' in the eastern DRC today. The case demonstrates different forms of military profiteering, sometimes involving loot seeking but usually involving locally negotiated forms of access, in return for security provision. While higher state and military authorities do little to hold soldiers and field commanders to account, the increasing presence of civil state authorities and other civil actors at mining sites helps to reduce military presence and moderate its behaviour. The formalization of the artisanal mining sector can give further impetus to this process. The chapter also looks at governance arrangements in artisanal copper mines in the Kambove territory in the south of the province. The second case shows that although military elements are absent, other state and non-state security services are often drawn in to enforce economic operators' claims to artisanal production. The author concludes that to make mineral trade truly 'conflict free' security sector reform and development efforts need to meet at the production level.

In Chapter 10, 'Water Management and the Security-Development Nexus: The Governing of Life in eThekwini Municipality, South Africa', Sofie Hellberg notes that during the last decades water has increasingly become a critical issue in global and local governance, raising questions about human and environmental security and about states' and individuals' right to fresh water and to development. Global water challenges include a shrinking availability of water per capita, due to pollution, population growth, urbanization and industrialization – problems that are further amplified by the unpredictability of climate change. At the same time there is an urgent need to reduce the proportion of people living without access to safe drinking water. Hellberg outlines that there has been an increasing recognition of water issues as a global concern and the subsequent need for mechanisms for conserving and distributing water. She also notes that a consensus has emerged for a more conservationist approach to water management and for a change in our perceptions and handling of water resources. These efforts are developed under the heading of 'Integrated Water Resource Management' (IWRM) and are set to promote management of water that is more efficient, equitable and sustainable. Hellberg discusses global water issues in relation to development and security and the security-development nexus. This is done through a biopolitical lens that explores how water management in an IWRM regime can be understood as a technique of governing subjects, life and lifestyles. To illuminate this, Hellberg studies the case of eThekwini Municipality in South Africa. Hellberg's chapter provides a critical reading of efforts to create a water secure world and problematize the human dimension of the human right to water.

Overall, a number of key dimensions of peace studies are highlighted in this book regarding the linkages between security and development. The starting point is the exploration of the conceptual dimensions of the security-development nexus. After the introduction, a chapter follows that in the broadest possible way introduces the debate, and serving to position 'the nexus' in such a way that it opens up for a wide range of cases studies. The case studies – including Kosovo, China, ASEAN, Ache and Sri Lanka, Central Asia, Vietnam, the DRC and South Africa – illuminate the wide variety of content the nexus can evoke. Each case study either starts in a security concern and involves development concerns, or highlights development dilemmas and introduces the security dimension.

This edited volume has, thanks to its multi-disciplinary approach and the various level of analysis (from conceptual, to global, to inter-state, to intra-state, to local), generated new insights and knowledge about the complexities of issues relating to the nexus between security and development. To be able to talk about 'the nexus' – in the singular and with a pretence of overall consensus on its meaning – will need a lengthy academic debate, and a concerted effort at precision and function. Until then, we have learnt to be cautious about over-interpreting to what extent the contents of 'the nexus' are as commonly shared and understood as is sometimes assumed.

Hence, the contributions to the book display the complexities of the linkage between security and development at both the inter-state and intra-state levels. The book has also addressed the conceptual discourse relating to the nexus. This has been complemented by both theoretical testing on relevant cases studies and by in-depth empirical case studies, which in themselves provide a rich reflection of contemporary dilemmas in each case. Taken as a whole, the contributions make the edited book both conceptually, theoretically and empirically relevant in the context of the scholarly debate and study of the security-development nexus. The findings and observations are also of considerable relevance for the policy-making community.

References

Amer, Ramses. 1994. 'The United Nations' Reactions to Foreign Military Interventions'. *Journal of Peace Research* 31(4): 425–44.

Buur, Lars, Steffen Jensen, and Finn Stepputat. 2007. *The Security-Development Nexus: Expressions of Sovereignty and Securitization in Southern Africa*. Uppsala: Nordic Africa Institute (NAI).

Chandler, David. 2006. *Empire in Denial: The Politics of State-Building*. London: Pluto Press.

_____. 2007. 'The Security-Development Nexus and the Rise of "Anti-Foreign Policy"'. *Journal of International Relations and Development* 10(4): 362–86.

_____. 2008. 'Review Essay: Human Security: The Dog That Didn't Bark'. *Security Dialogue* 39(4): 427–438.

DFID. 2005. *Fighting Poverty to Build a Safer World: A Strategy for Security and Development*. London: Department for International Development. Online: http://webarchive. nationalarchives.gov.uk/+/http://www.dfid.gov.uk/documents/publications/ securityforall.pdf (accessed 27 January 2011).

Duan Jielong. 2007. 'Statement on the Rule of Law at the National and International Levels'. *Chinese Journal of International Law* 6(1): 185–8.

Duffield, Mark. 2001. *Global Governance and the New Wars*. London: Zed Books.

_____. 2007. *Development, Security and Unending War: Governing the World of Peoples*. Cambridge: Polity Press.

_____. 2010. 'The Liberal Way of Development and the Development–Security Impasse: Exploring the Global Life-Chance Divide'. *Security Dialogue* 41(1): 53–76.

European Council. 2003. *A Secure Europe in a Better World: A European Security Strategy*. Brussels: Council of the European Union. Online: http://www.consilium.europa.eu/uedocs/ cmsUpload/78367.pdf (accessed 27 January 2011).

_____. 2008. *Report on the Implementation of the European Security Strategy: Providing Security in a Changing World*. Brussels: Council of the European Union. Online: http://www. consilium.europa.eu/uedocs/cms_data/docs/pressdata/en/reports/104630.pdf (accessed 27 January 2011).

ICISS. 2001. *The Responsibility to Protect: Report of the International Commission on Intervention and State Sovereignty*. Ottawa: International Commission on Intervention and State Sovereignty. Online: http://responsibilitytoprotect.org/ICISS%20Report.pdf (accessed 29 September 2011).

Kaldor, Mary. 2007. *New and Old Wars: Organized Violence in a Global Era*. San Francisco: Stanford University.

Keen, David. 2008. *Complex Emergencies*. Cambridge: Polity Press.

OECD. 2007. *The OECD DAC Handbook on Security System Reform (SSR): Supporting Security and Justice*. Paris: Organisation for Economic Co-operation and Development.

Paris, Roland. 2004. *At War's End: Building Peace After Civil Conflict*. Cambridge: Cambridge University Press.

Paris, Roland and Timothy D. Sisk. 2007. *Managing Contradictions: The Inherent Dilemmas of Postwar Statebuilding*. New York: International Peace Academy.

Richmond, Oliver P. 2007. 'The Problem of Peace: Understanding the "Liberal Peace"'. In A. Swain, R. Amer and J. Öjendal (eds), *Globalization and Challenges to Building Peace*, 17–37. London, Chicago and New Delhi: Anthem Press.

Security Dialogue. 2010. Special Issue: The Security-Development Nexus Revisited. *Security Dialogue* 41(1).

Stedman, Stephen J. 1997. 'Spoiler Problems in Peace Processes'. *International Security* 22(2): 5–53.

Stern, Maria and Joakim Öjendal. 2010. 'Mapping the Security-Development Nexus: Conflict, Complexity, Cacophony, Convergence?' *Security Dialogue* 41(1): 5–31.

Third World Quarterly. 2009. Special Issue: War, Peace and Progress: Conflict, Development, (In)Security and Violence in the 21st Century. *Third World Quarterly* 30(1).

UN. 2004. *A More Secure World: Our Shared Responsibility: Report of the High-level Panel on Threats, Challenges and Change*. United Nations Department of Public Information. Online: http://www.un.org/secureworld/ (accessed 27 January 2011).

———. 2009. 'Implementing the Responsibility to Protect: Report by the Secretary-General'. United Nations (A/63/677) General Assembly, 12 January. Online: http://www.un.org/Docs/journal/asp/ws.asp?m=A/63/677 (accessed 27 January 2011).

UNDP. 1994. *Human Development Report 1994: New Dimensions of Human Security*. United Nations Development Programme. New York and Oxford: Oxford University Press. Online: http://hdr.undp.org/en/reports/global/hdr1994/ (accessed 27 January 2011).

———. 2005. *Human Development Report 2005: International Cooperation at a Crossroads: Aid, Trade and Security in an Unequal World*. New York: United Nations Development Programme. Online: http://hdr.undp.org/en/reports/global/hdr2005/ (accessed 27 January 2011).

Zartman, I. William. 2001. 'Preventive Diplomacy: Setting the Stage'. In I. William Zartman (ed.), *Preventive Negotiation. Avoiding Conflict Escalation*, 1–18. Carnegie Commission on Preventing Deadly Conflict, Carnegie Corporation of New York. Lanham, MD: Rowman & Littlefield.

Chapter 2

EXPLORING THE SECURITY-DEVELOPMENT NEXUS[1]

Maria Stern and Joakim Öjendal

Development and security are inextricably linked. A more secure world is only possible if poor countries are given a real chance to develop. Extreme poverty and infectious diseases threaten many people directly, but they also provide a fertile breeding ground for other threats, including civil conflicts. Even people in rich countries will be more secure if their Governments help poor countries to defeat poverty and disease be meeting the Millennium Development goals. (UN secretary-general Kofi Annan, UN 2004, vii)

Wars kill development as well as people. The poor therefore need security as much as they need clean water, schooling or affordable health […] DFID, working with poor people and their government and international partners, can help build a more secure future for us all. (DFID 2005)

Introduction

The 'security-development nexus' enjoys many guises. Perhaps most frequently, policy makers proffer the 'nexus' as description of, and solution to, the pressing and interrelated problems commonly understood to belong under the rubrics of security and development. References to the 'nexus' therefore often appear in the form of apparently self-evident approaches for addressing or treating extremely complex issues (such as, for example, the connections between poverty, armed conflict and sexual and gender-based violence).[2] These approaches are usually painted in broad sweeping brushstrokes and receive little further explanation or justification of what is meant by security-development. Furthermore, remedial policies designed to 'cure' security-development problems are often conceived from within distinct spheres of 'development' or 'security', and the effectiveness of such policies are often assessed through either 'security' or 'development' metrics – at best ambiguously defined. Furthermore, as has been argued in myriad ways in debates over external interventions more generally, the long-term 'success' (defined, usually loosely, according to the inherent logics of the interventions) of many policies implemented in the name of security/development (such as those aimed at stemming sexual violence and redressing its effects in contexts of armed conflict) remain dubious indeed.[3]

This chapter therefore will probe into the meanings given to, or implied by, the 'security-development nexus'. It will do so through mapping six possible stories of 'security-development' (which in turn build upon six familiar accounts of security, and of development.) It will proceed as follows: In the next section we will pause to critically consider how the 'security-development nexus' has been evoked and explored in both academic research and among policy makers and explain more fully what we mean by a 'nexus'. We then briefly reflect upon our methodology. In the ensuing section we re-tell a narrative about development and then one about security, to be followed by a discussion of the nexus (or, nexuses, as it turns out) that emerge through our accounts. The conclusion returns to reflect upon the elusive but paramount importance of how the nexus is understood, and to touch on questions of methodology for studying it.

'Development and security are inextricably linked'

As UN secretary-general Kofi Annan boldly states, 'development and security are inextricably linked'. It is, by now, beyond doubt that attention to the 'security-development nexus' has become commonplace in national and global policy-making (e.g., UN 2004; OECD 2007; DFID 2005; European Council 2003, 2008; UNDP 2005). The 'security-development nexus' has also become the focus of key think-tanks (IPA 2004 , 2006; CIDSE 2006), and figures increasingly prominently in university based research (e.g., Buur, Jensen and Stepputat 2007; Call 2008; Chandler 2007, 2008; Duffield 2001, 2007; Paris and Sisk 2007; Picciotto 2007; Klingebiel, ed. 2006; Uvin 2002, 2008).

In the emerging literature – including in the official 'report industry' – there is a seeming consensus that security and development are interconnected, and that their interrelationship is growing in significance given the evolving global political-economic landscape.[4] The notion of a 'nexus' seems to provide a possible framework for acutely needed progressive policies designed to address the complex policy problems and challenges of today. Furthermore, and perhaps most importantly, an ever growing amount of economic resources and political will is being poured into the 'security-development nexus' and the attendant revamping of national and multilateral institutions and actions designed to address this nexus. Hence it matters. Security policies include explicit references to development and poverty reduction in the globalized fight against terrorism (e.g., European Council 2003, 2); the UN Millennium goals include direct references to providing peace and security for peoples all over the globe. The Organisation for Economic Co-operation and Development handbook on security sector reform, or SSR, (OECD 2007, 3) and the 'white paper' from the Department for International Development (DFID 2009, forward) provide some of the most recent examples of the assumed interconnections between security and development as a taken-for-granted point of departure.

Yet, what does Kofi Annan (and others, e.g., OECD 2007, 2) mean by the claim that security and development are inextricably linked; that there *is* a security-development nexus, even if its meaning is surely not 'a fixed reality'(Duffield 2010)? And, importantly, what can and/or should be done, by whom and for whom in the name of such a security-development nexus?

Understanding, responding to, or enacting a security-development nexus (hereafter, 'the nexus') promises to be a daunting project. One quick foray into current academic debates reveals how notions of both 'security' and 'development' emerge from disparate ontologies, refer to many different empirical realities and processes, and evoke much contestation over meaning (Uvin 2008; Chandler 2007; IPA 2006). On the one hand, the terms can be seen as the tools of scholars and policy analysts to *describe* and *analyse* macro processes in international affairs and to generate knowledge; on the other, they are used by actors applying these concepts to *prescribe* processes and *determine* outcomes. Importantly, as critical scholars have convincingly argued, they can also be seen as discursive constructions which create the reality they seem to reflect, and thus serve certain purposes and interests. Surely, the power of definition over 'development' and 'security' also implies the power to define not only the relevant field of interest, but also the material content of practices, the distribution of resources and subsequent policy responses (cf. Chandler 2007).

Indeed, beyond a recognition of the meshing of processes and domains commonly understood as 'security' and 'development', consensus around what is meant by 'the nexus' rapidly comes tumbling down. These domains remain frustratingly separated in the institutional bodies and organizational structures designed to 'provide' development and 'ensure' security and in the enactment of security and development at particular and localized sites (Jensen 2010; Orjuela 2010; cf. Öjendal and Lilja 2009). Such disconnection renders the call for a concerted attention to 'the nexus' all the more resounding and compelling. Yet, the political purchase that the naming of this 'nexus' occasions warns us to heed caution in our embrace of 'the nexus' as policy premise or goal (Chandler 2007; Duffield 2007a, 2007b).

In the realm of policy, the echoes of the harmonious plea for attention to 'the nexus', resonate as confusion, lack of conceptual clarity and ideological divisions at best, and as rhetorical facades, interest politics and shallow political correctness at worst (see footnote no. 3; cf. Chandler 2008). Academic discourses have not – in spite of the high stakes – adequately addressed this term, 'nexus'.[5] Rather, the relation between development and security has been described as one marked by distance and 'antipathy' (Shaw 2006), where the two fields have been seen to be mutually 'agnostic' (Uvin 2008). Indeed, Duffield's statement made already in 2001 that, as an intellectual project the 'security-development' terrain is comparatively novel, remains salient (Duffield 2001).[6]

Hence, whereas 'consensus' – or even the semblance of clarity and attendant claims to knowledge of the a priori ontology of these 'essentially contested terms' (Gallie 1956) – should not be expected or even desired in intellectual debates, it remains nonetheless underexplored *how* 'the nexus' is differently experienced, imbued with meaning and ultimately employed. We therefore echo Chandler's concern that:

> Rather than clarity, the security-development nexus sets up a framework where any external regulatory or interventionist initiative can be talked up by the proposing government or institution as being of vital importance. (Chandler 2007, 368)

Our unease deepens as we note a widespread discourse emerging *as if* there were a broad agreement on both the content of these concepts as well as the consequences of creating policy which reflects a (certain) understanding of 'the nexus'. And as always, national/global policy proceeds *as if* we collectively understood the context and consequences of the workings of a 'security-development-nexus' or, alternatively, as if it (as a desirable policy goal) were a recognizable and simple thing to achieve. Here we find a dual dilemma that provides the impetus for this chapter: there is a curious absence of attempts to probe evocations of 'the nexus' in order to discern the possible meanings attributed to it, and secondly, the familiar uneasy relationship between intellectual enquiry and policy formulation becomes particularly fraught in such evocations.[7]

The 'Security-Development Nexus': What is a Nexus Anyway?

The complexity of 'the nexus', and the ways in which it is represented and produced through both development and security discourses, enjoys a long history. As Duffield (2010) and Hettne (2010) separately but convincingly argue, historically, the intermingling of strategies of security and development have been commonplace in policy debates and implementation (see also Buur, Jensen and Stepputat 2007; Uvin 2008). Indeed, attention to 'security' was a pinnacle of much 'development' strategy during the colonial era; similarly, the Marshall Plan offers an example of 'development' concerns as central to Western security policies. However, contrary to the contemporary scene, none of this was carried out *in the name of a nexus*, or in an explicit articulation of the connections between the two.[8]

Contemporary expressions of (in)security and (under-)development, however, spill over the well-worn frameworks for their understanding. In tracing the macro-history of the evolution of the security-development dynamic on the European scene, Hettne (2010), for instance, helps us to see how the entrenched 'grids of intelligibility' (Dillon 2004) for understanding security-development have evolved. Additionally, other recent work in a special journal issue on the security-development nexus (*Security Dialogue* 2010) offers detailed accounts of how contemporary articulations of 'the nexus' play out in the politics of aid, the control and outlawing of migration, and the shift in focus to the security of people living within states (Duffield 2010); the policies and practices in the war on gangs in a South African township (Jensen 2010); and the local, both contradictory and mutually reinforcing, experiences of people in Colombo, Sri Lanka (Orjuela 2010).

To be clear: in this chapter, we do not argue for filling the idea of a nexus with a particular content or form that shall accurately describe reality or prescribe desirable futures. Instead we see 'the nexus' as representing a many-stranded point of suture. Hence *a nexus can be understood as a network of connections between disparate ideas, processes or objects; alluding to a nexus implies an infinite number of possible linkages and relations*. As noted above, the aim of this chapter is quite limited: we suggest a critical (fledgling) framework for mapping multiple understandings which arguably underlie specific articulations of 'the nexus'. To this end, we draw upon familiar accounts of different understandings of 'development' and 'security', which derive both from the policy world and from the realm of academic debate, as well as from their inevitable intermingling. Ultimately, this guide may hint at what such articulations may imply for the policy agenda. Before we delve into our development and security stories, however, we turn briefly to a discussion of our methodology.

A Note on Methodology: Narratives and Map-Making

Any account of the vast fields that encompass considerations and practices of development and security will undoubtedly be partial; the politics of inclusion/exclusion and framing involved in delimiting or mapping any field, for instance, are well debated (e.g., Salter 2007). Following the move in critical scholarship which makes explicit how authoritative knowledge is constructed and meaning is imposed through credible, comprehensible narratives, we refer to our brief accounts of development and security as narratives (see Butler 2004, 4–5; Zalewski 2006). The stories we relay, however, are not whimsical tales but instead rely on familiar accounts of the concepts and practices – such as the ones that are retold in various forms in basic (Western academic) textbooks – on development theory or security studies. These overarching narratives are made up of sub-plots (e.g., the dominant realist story about state security and the counter-story about human security) which include a whole array of elements. They 'answer', for instance, what it (i.e., 'security' or 'development') is about; who it concerns; what its referents are; who acts; what its prescriptions for action are; and finally its desired end result.

In our account, we re-jig the familiar overarching narratives about development and security in order to clearly show the similarities of their sub-stories and thus lay the groundwork for mapping different accounts of the nexus. We do so through identifying and briefly introducing the following six story-lines (or approaches): (1) Development/Security as Modern (Teleological) Narrative; (2) Broadening, Deepening and Humanizing Development/Security; (3) Development/Security as Impasse/Impossible; (4) Post–Development/Security; (5) Development/Security as Technique of Governmentality; and (6) Development/Security as Globalized. We do not, however, trace the ways in which each of these approaches has grappled historically with related security/development issues (such as the connections between poverty and conflict or peace and prosperity (Hettne 2010)).

Our six parallel accounts each of development and security might at times seem to belong to different orders, logics or grammars, often blending description, prescription, strategy and critique. However, when read together these accounts – although surely dog-eared and limited – may offer a useful guide for better discerning how and when shifts in meaning occur in different (yet seemingly similar) discourses about 'the nexus'. We therefore then mesh these parallel development/security narratives together into six (less familiar, but nonetheless recognizable) accounts of 'the nexus' – for example, 'Security-Development as Modern (Teleological) Narrative'. By making explicit what reading our parallel accounts may imply for filling the 'nexus' with meaning we point to the multitude of meanings possible in the many different ways in which 'the nexus' is used (and critiqued). This elaboration, we believe, places in sharp contradistinction the (sometimes) facile evocation of 'the nexus' in ever widening policy-circles.

Importantly, it becomes overly clear – though not empirically proven – that our map must contain many more than these six accounts of 'the nexus'; the seemingly incompatible stories of various ontologically and epistemologically different accounts of development/security in this 'nexus' are ridiculously plentiful, even infinite. In inviting the reader to probe the myriad meanings of 'the nexus' already discursively available, we fundamentally challenge the seeming consensus of the nexus as imminent promise: something given, clear and shared.

We turn now to the development and security stories which serve as the building blocks for our ensuing mapping of nexuses.

Stories about Development

Development as Modern (Teleological) Narrative

As a deeply historical concept, 'development' has been understood as a process of biological evolution, signifying the ultimate fulfillment of the process of becoming what 'one' is supposed to be (Nisbet 1980). 'Development', as it were, became a key strategy for state-building in the post-colonial societies in which there was an urgent need for both economic growth and political consolidation (Simon 1999). Unfettered belief in modernization through 'development' as a quick route away from prevailing 'under-development' followed suit (Rostow 1962; de Janvry and Kanbur 2006). The state was the sovereign key actor and 'guarantor' of development (measured in economic terms). Importantly, through development so understood, nation-states were to be invented, established, secured, and evolved along a linear trajectory of 'progress', following the path forged by Europe. The political and economic elites were the necessary drivers of this process, and 'trickle-down' was the hope for the rest. As such, development was not only driven by the state, but also served to constitute the state. However, the post-colonial world in the 1960/70s did not realize this modernist dream, but rather social and political problems proliferated, unavoidably calling into question the teleology of 'development'.

Broadening, Deepening and Humanizing Development

At least two distinctly different counter-narratives came to challenge the mainstream story, serving to broaden, deepen and humanize development: first, it was countered by a Marxist/structuralist fundamental critique, focusing on the international power structures in combination with the prevailing capitalist mode of production. This critique was theoretically explained through 'world system theory' (Wallerstein 1974) and more concretely through 'dependencia' (Prebisch 1950; Frank 1967). These schools forcefully emphasized the structurally exploitative nature of the capitalist world system and its negative impact on third world development. Hence there was, it was argued, a necessity for poor third world countries to 'delink' and develop through self-sufficiency. Hence, the story of (mainstream) development was reversed, but remained teleological, state-centric and elite-driven. At the other end of the spectrum, we saw a 'participatory revolution' emphasizing the significance of 'reconnecting' to the true 'subjects' of development, namely the poor, the local, the grassroots and the voiceless. To 'put the last first' (Chambers 1983), 'small is beautiful', 'appropriate technology' (Schumacher 1973), and later, 'empowerment' (Friedman 1992) became common calls. These alternative development approaches looked both 'inwards' and 'backwards' for (true) development. The shift in focus from state-centric development to 'human' development is perhaps the most profound and durable impact that can be traced to these critiques of the dominant development narrative (Pietersee 2000).

Development as Impasse

The dented credibility of the mainstream story of development and its neo-liberal decade of the 1980s, including the infamous structural adjustment programs, did anything but rescue mainstream 'development'. Consequently, it was profoundly questioned, from another angle, by critics arguing the 'impasse' of development theory and practice (Booth 1985; cf. Schurman 1993). According to this story-line, both mainstream and alternative development had been tried and did not work; furthermore, it was ineffective and possibly harmful. The supposedly desired state of development did not appear desirable. This idea of 'impasse' was triply fed by the actual failure of development to alleviate poverty in the third world; the broad post-modernist critique of development as instrument of colonial power and the portrayal of the 'third world' as homogenous; and, finally, by the obvious over-belief in the state as the agent and referent in the development process, in the wake of emerging globalization (Schurman 1993, 2000).

Post-Development

The critique of the grand idea of 'development' was further deepened in the post-modernism/post-colonialism pulse. 'Development' (as process or thing) had no inherent substance and/or, as discursive practice, it was imperialistic and reproduced colonial attitudes and power relations. Focus was placed on what was *done* in the name of development, rather than on what form of development was desirable. A school of 'post-development' emerged (Escobar 1995; Rahnema 1997; Esteva 1992), claiming that the idea of 'development' de facto made substantial, from-within progress impossible, *dis*empowered people, and *dis*rupted existing local power structures, thus creating instability and conflict. As such, 'development' was counterproductive (like in the above account), ethically corrupt, and served to uphold differences and hierarchies. 'Development' was seen as the reason for, and guardian of, inequalities between people and societies, not the solution to them.

Development as Technique of Governmentality

In reaction (in part) to the recent shift in development policy away from a traditional neo-liberal trend and towards a call for stronger institutions and more responsible regulation (Craig and Porter 2006; cf. Bello 2005; cf. Hettne 2010; World Bank 1997), as well as the focus on bolstering 'failed/fragile' states (OECD 2007) in the wake of the Global War on Terror, critics of the politics of aid and development called attention to how 'development' has become a technique of governmentality;[9] of disciplinary and biopolitical control (Sylvester 2006). In Duffield's words (2010), understanding development and under-development biopolitically means understanding them 'in terms of how life is to be supported and maintained, and how people are expected to live, rather than according to economic and state-based models.' Read this way, practices of development, ostensibly designed to 'uplift' first states, (and later societies and peoples) are techniques of government (broadly understood) which separate lives worth living from those that are expendable, dangerous, or insufficient and unacceptable because of their incompleteness (Buur, Jensen and Stepputat 2007; Dillon 2007; 2008, 310). This approach asks questions about the ways in which human lives are regulated (by whom and for what purposes), and the violence and marginalization that such regulation entails.

Globalized Development

Globalization has challenged the traditional idea of development, both in terms of 'global governance' narratives and those more critical narratives that embrace a just and environmentally sustainable global domain as the desirable goal of development. The global (good) governance discourse holds that (neo-liberal) globalization works through processes such as trade, migration, aid-flows and foreign direct investments, but, importantly, fails because of feeble attempts at regulation on a global scale (cf. Risse-Kappen 1995). For many, 'global development' is understood as a process which undermines state authority and its capacity to govern and 'uplift' lives in any particular territory. Hence, as (the idea of) 'global governance' gains momentum, global 'regimes' (human rights, sustainable development, etc.) are vigorously pursued, and issues previously thought of as geographically appearing (only) in the developing world are seen as global (hence common) concerns (Hettne 2009). 'Development', according to a slightly different line of critique, fuels environmentally unsustainable change, mobility, and the restructuring of (g)local power structures, thus exacerbating the vulnerabilities (such as poverty and gender-based violence) of those most at risk, triggering conflicts, and even bringing imminent planetary environmental catastrophe (Cerny 1999; Anderson 1999; Junne and Verkoren 2004).

Stories about Security

Security as Modern (Teleological) Narrative

Global politics (and the field of international relations which studies it) is predominantly about (state) security – its procurement, its maintenance, its promise. Or so we are led to believe. In the grammar of modern politics, the state is understood as 'the foundation of freedom, democracy and the good society' (Neocleous 2008, 4). The dominant and oft-told story of the state, the international system of states and survival is a story about emergence: becoming (secure) and fulfilling the promise of achieved security (Dillon 2008; Dillon and Lobo-Guerrero 2008). It can therefore be seen as a modern – even teleological – narrative of progress: insecurity (in the past) necessitates the promise of security (now) and the ultimate achievement of security and all that security implies (in the future). In short, in modern political imagination, 'security' has traditionally revolved around the principle of modern state sovereignty. If the state is not 'secure', then political order unravels and ultimately citizens, and all other possible 'referents of security' are imperilled. State survival – traditionally through military means – trumps any other aspect of politics, either nationally or in the international state system. Although security is always ultimately deferred, and new threats inevitably arise, security is represented as an imminent promise (Dillon 1996).[10] Inevitable danger and threat require the continual enactment of security measures that will ultimately end insecurity and enable the 'good society' to flourish and develop.[11]

Although it has weathered much critique, and undergone numerous revisions (such as the addition to this story of other means for achieving (state) security, i.e., economic power, diplomacy, etc.), its basic logic still dominates the agenda in the worlds of security policy and academia. 'Security' remains a necessary and fundamentally 'good' thing, and it shall be maximized

(Bigo 2001), even as it is parsed into different sectors (e.g., the economic sector, the environmental sector, etc. (Buzan, Wæver and Wilde 1998)).

Broadening, Deepening and Humanizing Security

The meaning of security has nonetheless been fiercely contested, both within policy circles and academia. Much of the contention has been about deepening or widening security beyond the state to include different threats and referent 'objects' (e.g., Brundtland 1989; King and Murray 2001; Palme Commission 1982). This move has coincided with an increasingly accepted truism in both policy and academic circles that the nation-state system lacks the tools with which to contend with today's threats – including terrorist networks, gender-based violence, violent 'ethnic' discrimination, global pandemics or climate change. The multiplicity of security providers and the increasing privatization and commodification of security services dislocate 'security' as a (national) public good further from the modern sovereign state (Zedner 2009).

Perhaps most significant has been the shift in focus from state security to 'human security' as a sorely needed venue for highlighting the particular vulnerabilities of peoples who suffer violence from representatives of the state, as well as other forms of violence and injustices. Although it is also the subject of much debate and critique (for being alternately too wide, narrow, empty, etc.), 'human security' provides a language for addressing different experiences of (in)security for its advocates.[12] Feminist analyses of security as deeply gendered run as a strand throughout all of these moves to deepen, widen and humanize security, raising vital questions of voice, identity, power and location (cf. Ackerly Stern and True 2006).

Security as Impossible

In concert with the appeal to look elsewhere for the sources and experiences of, and solutions to insecurity for referents other than (or in addition to) the state, a line of critique emerged which explicitly focused on how security measures employed by the state (but also by groups of people, and individuals) often create ripples of violence and fear, and produce more insecurity – both for those whom security measures aim to protect as well as others.[13] Variations of this critique coincide in the argument that security measures designed to secure states, humans and societies, instead (or also) cause harm to people, cultures and the natural environment.[14] Furthermore, security measures increase fear and a sense of impending danger; the prescribed order, stability or 'fortress' is inherently precarious and in need of reinforcing (Campbell 1998; Dillon 1996).

Post-Security

Moreover, enquiries into the practice of security as dangerous and productive of relations of violence and fear resonated with another avenue of critique, here summarized as *post-security*. In line with the 'discursive turn' in social science more generally, scholars criticized the notion of security as a thing, condition or state of being which could be attained. 'Securitization' (and calls for de-securitization), are the most familiar and well-accepted re-conceptualizations of security as discursive practice (Buzan, Wæver and Wilde 1998; Wæver 1995). Additionally, critical scholars argued that security, as master narrative, substantiates the political body in the name of which it is ostensibly operating: be it 'the state' or 'the culture' or 'women'; in so doing, 'security' produces the very subject it purports to secure (Campbell 1998; Dillon 1996; Stern 2005). The political power of security as imagined above derives from the (im)possibility (Pin-Fat 2000) of its promise, and the attendant perpetual production of danger and fear.

Security as Technique of Governmentality

In response to the violence and control which accompanies security and securing (so blatant, for example, in the recent War on Terror), critics have addressed security as a technique of governing danger and contingency. Security in these readings, is seen as a technique of sovereign power which produces certain sorts of subjects and involves oppression, regulation, violence, control, policing and surveillance of life itself (Buur, Jensen and Stepputat 2007; Dillon and Lobo-Guerrero 2008; Duffield 2010; Huysmans 2006.) As such, securing practices serve as counter-insurgency tactics against challenges to the accepted neo-liberal order (Duffield 2007b; Jensen 2010). Such avenues of thought, for instance, place familiar ways of framing the trade-offs between liberty and security under critical scrutiny, arguing that they are written with a shared underlying – violent – grammar (Dillon and Reid 2009; Huysmans 2004; Jabri 2007; Walker 2006). The idiom of risk avoidance (through insurances) commodifies the contingency that living necessarily entails, and serves as a technological device to 'secure' (certain) forms of life and render others not worthy of insuring (Aradau, Lobo-Guerrero and van Munster 2008; Duffield 2010; *Security Dialogue* 2008).

Globalized Security

The increasing appeal of human security in global policy discourse coincided with a widely adopted move to speak of the globe (or the international community) as the appropriate realm through which to guarantee (global) security and human rights. Security is thus globalized. This move reflects the growing ontology of globalization as a way of making sense of – and ultimately waylaying – global dangers attendant to the modern human condition, via, among other vectors, the notion of risk management (Beck 2006). Global environmental sustainability, including the mitigation of the causes and effects of global warming and natural disasters, has become perhaps the most pressing globalized security concern. Furthermore, the concept of human security as global offers a platform from which an idea of a transnational humanitarian responsibility for human welfare could be translated into policy such as 'the Right to Protection' (Glasius and Kaldor 2006; ICISS 2001).

Mapping 'the Nexus'

Taking seriously the above stories allows us to critically reassess the oft-implied pretence of consensus around 'the nexus' as a move which (intentionally or unintentionally) glosses over differences and obfuscates the complexity, the politics and the ethical implications of the practices enabled through the naming of 'the nexus'.

In the next few paragraphs we will mesh our 'parallel' stories, creating some common narratives with unquestionably overlapping tangents. Other narratives (such as the combination: 'Security as Modern (…)'–'Development as Broadening (…)') which criss-cross seemingly incompatible accounts of security/development will be left unexplored, but will be alluded to in our cursory reading of this chapter's opening citations in the next section. Our intention here is to make *some* sense in the cosmology of possible and de facto usages, and to help us see the very many ways security-development is imbued with meaning (and therefore, again, to suggest that we need to heed caution in swallowing facile references to 'the nexus' without proper rumination).

The Security-Development Nexus as Modern (Teleological) Narrative

As we show above, 'security' and 'development' (traditionally understood) have been imbued with meaning through linear modernist discourses that reflect European experience and resonate with colonial logics. Security and development are spatially located in a certain and bounded geographical space – usually the state, but also increasingly the region (e.g., the EU) – and temporally located, through a certain historical trajectory, in relation to other geographical spaces (Bhaba 2004; Hutchings 2008; Jabri 2006; Walker 2006). Read through this common story, the promise of security depends upon the successful (and sure-footed) march towards progress and modernity and the forms of modern life that inhere in this trajectory, and vice versa (see discussion in Duffield 2010). When spatially located *within* the same place (the state), 'the nexus' emerges as the juncture through which the conditions of and for security mutually reinforce those for development and progress; this is *internal* confluence. Here, for instance, economic growth, democratization and social welfare (i.e., conditions of development) require a state to have considerable domestic control, a strong defence and high levels of political legitimacy (i.e., conditions of security), and again the reverse logic holds. 'The nexus', so understood, ideally creates a double bind where security and development mutually reinforce each other. However, in contexts where neither security nor development (understood according to the story-line above) is attainable, the mutuality crumbles. In most of the 'developing world', these preconditions have not been met, rendering 'the nexus' dysfunctional. Most of the policy community nevertheless maintains this variation of 'the nexus' as a recipe for the mutual achievement of security and development as a primary policy goal (see OECD 2008).

'The nexus' also refers to a relation of implication across borders – or, in other words, a link from there to here, then to now. In this sense, 'the nexus' bridges the spatial and temporal (e.g., developing countries as 'lagging behind' those more 'developed') divergence that is implied when the (in)security and continued development of one state (e.g., the US) is implicated in the security and – much 'failed' – development of another (e.g., the Democratic Republic of the Congo). Emphasis is placed on the bridge occurring between (our future) security (as paramount and located in one place – the North) and development (over/down/back there/then). However, both of these – 'the nexus' as *internal* confluence, and as spatiotemporal *bridge* – are compatible.

The Security-Development Nexus: Deepened, Broadened, Humanized

In contrast, we can identify the 'counterpoint' or 'alternative' to these dominant stories. Such alternative narratives ostensibly provide an escape route from the prevailing (and predetermined) notions of 'what and how one is supposed to become' secure and developed. Read this way, 'the nexus' reflects a conjoining of challenging views on what the foundation for a good, safe and just society might be. This nexus might rely upon a more cyclical temporality as it gazes backwards in time to find the genuine, the good and the (truly) desirable state of living; of security and safety achieved – for humans, women, cultures, or for the natural environment. Or it may involve another form of forward trajectory than that embarked upon by (neo-)liberal security-development, such as one that attends to the localized experiences (fears, desires, needs, etc.)

of vulnerable peoples. (See Duffield 2010 for the further fleshing out of the notion of neo-liberal development and Orjuela 2010 for an exploration of particular local dynamics.) This re-conceived 'security-development' (be it in relation to human or environmental issues) challenges – indeed negates – the mainstream idea of determinism in what it is one is supposed to be or become. In this logic, 'the nexus' can perhaps be best illustrated as the merging of human development and human security – as intricate and complex ambitions in idealist and normative combinations.

The Security-Development Nexus as Impasse / Impossible

In contradistinction to the above conceptualization of security-development as an accurate reflection of a desired reality, one can see critics of both development as 'impasse' and security as 'impossible' as coinciding in their belief that these concepts/practices are both mutually constitutive and misconceived, and increasingly so (see Duffield 2010 and Jensen 2010 for different variations of such a critique.) For a plethora of reasons within each these fields, so-called real development and security remain perpetually out of reach. Efforts at achieving development breed underdevelopment, more poverty and disenfranchisement. Security carries with it insecurity, violence and threat, as in, for instance, the theater of the 'new wars' (Kaldor 2007). The ways in which they merge (such as in the ways in which development breeds poverty and dependence and therewith, increasing ripples of violence) as they are currently pursued in (global) policy are at best meaningless and futile for the real betterment of peoples' lives and safety; at worst they create the security-development problem they are expected to solve, in direct contrast to the 'recipe' proposed in the above story of 'The Nexus as Modern (...)'. According to the 'Impasse/Impossible' account, 'the nexus' as currently articulated and implemented is empty, impossible and harmful; the policies enacted in its name achieve little – if anything – desirable, and instead cause harm and occasion the wasting of time and money.

Post–Security-Development

This account is similar to the 'Impasse/Impossible' account above, but places more emphasis on the 'nexus' as linked discursive practices that produce certain realities and are thus the tools of power. The enactment of these practices often fulfils those interests that are implicated in their motivating rationale. They are mutually constitutive and are written out of a similar (if not the same) modern neo-liberal (post-colonial) logic in which sovereignty (of the individual and of the state) privileges certain subjectivities (see Duffield 2010; Jensen 2010). Practices and discourses of security-development, so understood, reproduce spatiotemporally defined relations of inequality, injustice, harmful mechanisms of inclusion and exclusion, violence, and insecurity and danger. According to this account, security and development are both impossible and inherently oxymoronic in themselves as well as in combination (i.e., in the 'nexus'). They become self-perpetuating and impossible promises as well as vectors for those with vested interests to protect. This is scary and intimidating for the rest of us; hence this nexus should be refused, critiqued and avoided (e.g., Neocleous 2008).

Security-Development as Technique of Governmentality

Security and development are seen as mutually reinforcing idioms and techniques of biopower through which subjectivity, imagination and ultimately life are governed. Biopolitics is necessarily about the governing and regulation of (the development of) life, through, for instance, interrelated efforts aimed at 'improving' life, the management of contingency and the exclusion of 'the dangerous' (Buur, Jensen and Stepputat 2007, 15; Dillon and Lobo-Guerrero 2008, 266). According to this line of critique, 'the nexus' emerges as the site in which counter-insurgency (understood broadly) plays out (Duffield 2007a, 2007b; Jensen 2010). Hence, a biopolitical reading of 'the nexus' might enquire into, for instance, the politics of aid, humanitarian assistance, the good governance agenda, as well as the localized and globalized technologies and practices which enact the Global War on Terror. Such readings make visible and trace the ways in which techniques of 'security/development' counter the insurgency against sovereign biopower – through controlling, disciplining, 'uplifting' and regulating the 'dangerous', the unruly, the subalterns and the voiceless (Duffield 2010; Jensen 2010). Understood this way, the discursive use and concrete enactment of 'the nexus' (through both technologies and policies) seemingly evacuate the political question of the ethics of 'governing the other' (and life itself) and technologize (or in other words, depoliticize) the (bio)politics of security-development.

Globalized Security-Development

This 'nexus' is written out of a similar logic to that of 'Security-Development: Deepened, Broadened, Humanized', but one which is also embedded in an ontology of globalization; one which no longer relies on 'methodological territorialisation' (Hettne 2010; Scholte 2005, 27). In short, the pervasive modern representation of the world as being made up of distinct social, political, cultural spaces bounded by territory has had to fundamentally change to better reflect the empirical reality of a globalized world in which such distinctions blur. 'Globalization' therefore demands the rephrasing of perennial questions about the organization and experience of political, cultural, social and individual life, as well as the structures and institutions designed to govern society and interact with the natural world. Uncertainty and contingency, as well as subjectivity, belonging, accountability and responsibility, are globalized. Understood through this prism, 'the nexus' acts as a vector for representing (and addressing holistically) the interrelated and mutually constitutive global human survival issues such as global climate change, global food security, natural disasters, global energy and water crises, gender-based violence, as well as the threats and risks associated with violent conflict and acts of terrorism. As such, it is the ultimate arena.

Ridiculous and Representative? Stories Aplenty...

Parsing 'development' and 'security' into the (separate) sub-stories told as precursors to the above six security-development stories invites the drawing of a (ridiculous) anti-figure designed to represent and allude to the multitude of possible narratives about nexuses.

As noted above, we have briefly fleshed out only six accounts – the six that possibly 'make sense' from an ontological/epistemological point of view (these

Figure 2.1. Possible 'nexuses'?

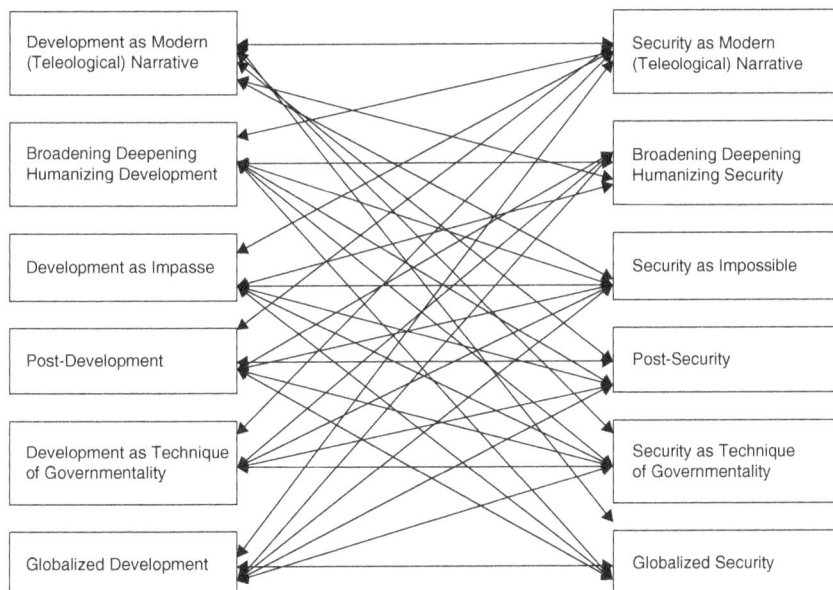

appear as the horizontal lines above) – of the myriad possible stories about the 'nexus' represented in this anti-figure. However, the policy world, like all other fields of knowledge, does not adhere to ontological or epistemological consistency; policy documents are peppered with seemingly incompatible stories (these are illustrated aplenty by the diagonal lines drawn above). Many even seem to make good policy sense.

In the following paragraphs we briefly return to the citations that opened this chapter in order to exemplify how the above map (with its supply of readily available narratives about 'the nexus') could be employed in an attempt to trace how security and development, and 'the nexus' between them, shift and slide in meaning even in these short citations – and in our critical reading of them. We are aware that the 'boxes' used to connote the distinct approaches indubitably leak and change form; other 'boxes', neither inscribed nor imagined here, surely inform the articulation and practice of 'the nexus' in disparate contexts. We nonetheless use these boxes as tools of analysis.

We address *A Secure World* (UN 2004) more fully and then touch on the citations by the UK Department for International Development (DFID) as a point of contrast.

> Development and security are inextricably linked. A more secure world is only possible if poor countries are given a real chance to develop. Extreme poverty and infectious diseases threaten many people directly, but they also provide a fertile breeding ground for other threats, including civil conflicts. Even people in rich countries will be more secure if their Governments help poor countries to defeat poverty and disease by meeting the Millennium Development goals. (UN secretary-general Kofi Annan, UN, 2004, vii)

This citation states clearly that development and security are linked. It is implied here that security and development are known and knowable processes, conditions or states of being which intersect. What is implied by 'security' and 'development', though not explicit, takes shape through the ways in which they are evoked in the text. References to 'a more secure world' draw upon the framing of 'Globalized Security-Development', which arguably lend legitimacy and urgency to the call for 'giving the poor countries a real chance to develop' (understood through the 'Modern (…)' narrative?) as the only viable way out of the implied 'insecure' world in which we now live.

The scary image is cultivated in the following sentence: 'Extreme poverty [...]', which arguably draws upon the 'Broadening, Deepening, Humanizing' discourse in its depiction of human insecurities and symptoms of human under-development or arrested development. The sentence then shifts to the 'Modern (Teleological) Narrative' as source for presenting the scenario of 'other threats' (terrorism?), civil conflicts, and the violence and destruction they wreak.

Importantly, drawing upon the story of 'the nexus' as told through 'Post Security-Development' allows us to discern how the ghosts of a colonial past must be exorcised from the promise of a more secure world for it to be credible. Furthermore, such a lens reveals how the depiction of a 'fertile breeding ground for [...] threats' evokes the image of the political body/ society as an infested wound, which must be cured of its 'germs' for it to be secure.

'Security as Technique (…)' helps us see how efforts to reduce poverty and mitigate disease, as well as the very identification of poverty and disease as a breeding ground for threat, controls the population implied in the text and discerns the life that is possible and desirable in this potential breeding ground (Elbe 2008). Such efforts ensure that these threats do not spread to healthier (less fertile) grounds in distant and safer places, such as the 'rich' countries alluded to in the next sentence.

The text continues: 'Even people in rich countries will be more secure' if these unhealthy breeding grounds are cured. Here, development as written through the 'Modern (Teleological) Narrative' is again evoked as it is clear that the relevant political-economic unit is the state and that certain 'countries' are richer (and further developed) along the path to wealth, prosperity, stability and security than those poorer countries in the developing world. The solution to underdevelopment-insecurity lies in development assistance. If the rich governments help the poor countries along this path (by defeating poverty and disease), the text promises us, then *even people* in these rich countries will be more secure.

Whispers of warning derived from the 'Security-Development as Impasse/ Impossible' narrative resound from this claim and invite us to wonder how further development assistance will help eradicate poverty and the threats it supposedly breeds. Furthermore, the fear that human development (imbued with meaning through the 'Broadening, Deepening, Humanizing' discourse) is being subsumed, even thwarted by its securitization (identified as such through a 'Post–Security-Development' reading) also urges us (as critics) to question how the alleviation of poverty and disease *there* has become a counter-insurgency strategy *here*. Reading through, 'Security as Technique of Governmentality' suggests that framing the alleviation of poverty and disease *there* as a threat to security *here* (a spatiotemporal bridge in the 'Modern (Teleological) Narrative') enables us to employ techniques to control and discipline all of us both *here* and *there* (Bigo 2001).

We now draw attention also to the citation from the DFID document (DFID 2005, 3), because few documents are as explicit as this on the one-to-one connection between (in)security and development.

> Wars kill development as well as people. The poor therefore need security as much as they need clean water, schooling or affordable health […] DFID, working with poor people and their government and international partners, can help build a more secure future for us all. (DFID 2005)

The constellation of meanings of 'the nexus' that emerges here is slightly different from that in the UN passage above. The fabulous first sentence, 'wars kill development as well as people', first gains meaning through the evocation of the 'Modern (Teleological) Narrative', where development as a known process can be 'killed' or arrested. It then swiftly moves on to draw upon the 'Broadening, Deepening, Humanizing' discourse in references to the poor, and then shifts back to the 'Modern (Teleological) Narrative' when separating security from, for instance, clean water. It then returns to the 'Modern (Teleological) Narrative' in making sense of the agents who will 'build a more secure future' (including the DFID), to finally glide into a 'Globalized Security' story, in its call for secure future 'for us all'.

Reading critically through the lenses offered by the 'Post–Security-Development' and the 'Security-Development as Technique (…)' perspectives foretells another story. It allows us to glimpse, for instance, at how 'poor people' are being situated and represented in this text. Poor people, the text implies, are dangerous and threaten the security of us all. They therefore should be controlled by 'development' and (assumedly) good governance. Hence its 'Globalized Development' approach appears as a means to a 'Security-Development as Technique of Governmentality' end, mixing the seemingly altruistic common concern of universal poverty alleviation with a narrow imperative to control the 'wretched of the earth'.

Conclusion: The Significance of Identifying 'the Nexus(es)'

The above (critical) cursory reading does not leave us much wiser as to what 'the nexus' is, should be, or does. Importantly, however, it may hopefully open avenues of critique for assessing what is being done in the name of 'the nexus' by exploring how different narratives imbue it with meaning, even in the same policy text. With this in mind, this chapter has tried to achieve three things: First, it has drawn attention to the claims that there is an empirically real and growing 'nexus', which is reflected in the increased usage of the term 'development-security nexus'. Although timely, we aver that this borders on the banal: 'the nexus', however conceived, reflects a reality that resonates in the experiences and imaginations of many; it is being used to 'describe' a growing realm.

Second, and perhaps more intriguingly, the 'content' or form of 'the nexus' is not clear. It is therefore open for all kinds of (illicit) use under the guise of progressive and ethically palatable politics. We believe that we have, in this chapter, illustrated that different discourses imbue 'the nexus' with different meanings, and hinted at how (in)security and (under-)development are being *produced as problems* through a broader assemblage of logics that render certain discourses intelligible. Yet, a focus on the discursive realm, while important, surely engages too little with the underlying cartographies of power that inform readings and help determine effect. Indeed, in an effort to 'uncover' the different ways in which the nexus is imbued with meaning, there is always a risk that one inadvertently reinforces and naturalizes the ways in which the nexus serves the interests of power (see Reid-Henry 2011). As 'the nexus' is being and can be used as a 'recognizable' and seemingly comprehensible narrative, various processes can be pursued in the name of (more or less) (in)compatible combinations of security-development, as delineated above.

Despite this, we have not made a claim as to what 'the nexus' could, should or has entail(ed) in any particular site because, in part, we have not yet conducted a thorough and systematic empirical investigation of its actual usage in distinct contexts – either through a full-bodied analysis of its discursive construction or through a reading of *how* it is being practised – or of its effects. Surely, interrogating (and mapping) the different narratives that make sense of 'the nexus' also implies calling into question the practices that emerge through such discourses. Hence, in our above reading (and writing) of the 'stories aplenty' about 'the nexus', we hope eventually also to provide some tools for further inquiry into the practices and effects of security-development in distinct sites.

Third, therefore, in concluding this chapter our attention is drawn to the need to engage in the difficult – and often overlooked – questions of methodology: how can we creatively study the different ways in which 'the nexus' is being practised, negotiated and resisted in distinct sites – and to what effect?[15] We have only touched upon this last point in this chapter. While we have engaged in a mapping exercise as an initial methodology, we are aware that no map could ever serve as a definitive or complete tool for understanding the world 'out there', or for doing anything about the vast injustices and violence that distinct security-development problems (or solutions) produce. The trick, as we see it, is to develop an approach that allows for attention to the logics that underwrite prevailing discourses about security-development;

the ways in which security-development is being imbued with meaning in these discourses; the ways in which the nexus means 'different things at different scales of action' (Reid-Henry 2011, 101) and to different people – in all spaces of the globe; the shifting politico-economic interests among and between different actors; the ways in which 'the nexus' is being negotiated, resisted and reformed in distinct sites; and its various effects on the lives of people and the planet. Incorporating all of these aims into a viable research agenda, one that takes seriously the methodological implications of its theoretical framework, is not an easy – or maybe even a doable – task. Nonetheless, it is one that should, we believe, remain as a guidepost in our further critical scrutiny of the politics of 'the nexus'.

At the very least, this chapter illustrates a multitude of ways in which 'security' and 'development' can be (and are being) understood, combined and ultimately enacted, for purposes of understanding our emerging world, or for purposes of shaping it (*Security Dialogue* 2010). There should be no doubt, however, that for the foreseeable future, the way we perceive, pursue and produce 'the nexus' will be of crucial importance.

Notes

1 The majority of this chapter has been published elsewhere (Stern and Öjendal 2010); portions have even been published in Stern and Öjendal (2011). We thank the editors at *Security Dialogue* and Sage Publications for the permission to reprint this work here. We would also like to thank the Department of Research Collaboration – SAREC, Swedish International Development Cooperation Agency (Sida) for their support. We are also indebted to three anonymous reviewers, the editors at *Security Dialogue*, and our colleagues in Peace and Development Research (Sofie Hellberg in particular) for their comments on drafts and earlier versions of this chapter.

2 See for example, the implementation report of 2008 of the European Union Security strategy. Under the heading, *Security-Development Nexus*, it reads: 'As the ESS and the 2005 Consensus on Development have acknowledged, there cannot be sustainable development without peace and security, and without development and poverty eradication there will be no sustainable peace. Threats to public health, particularly pandemics, further undermine development. Human rights are a fundamental part of the equation. In many conflict or post-conflict zones, we have to address the appalling use of sexual violence as a weapon of intimidation and terror. Effective implementation of UNSCR 1820 on sexual violence in situations of armed conflict is essential' (EC 2008, 8). See also the revised Cotonou Partnership Agreement of 2010, which states: 'The parties acknowledge that without development and poverty reduction there will be no sustainable peace and security, and without peace and security there can be no sustainable development'. Later, the same article then states that 'relevant activities shall also include [...] support for addressing the problems of child soldiers and of violence against women and children'(Cotonou Working Group 2010).

3 The fine words cited in the implementation report of the EU security policy and the Cotonou Partnership Agreement (above footnote) appear rather empty when

applied to a particular 'security-development problem'. An example can be found in the difficulty of addressing sexual violence in the DRC. The protracted conflict in the DRC and the central role that both the national armed forces and the different militia groups play in the continuation of massive human rights abuses against the civilian population have received worldwide attention, the massive amounts of rape particularly so. Calls for a comprehensive effort to halt the widespread violence – in particular sexual violence against women and girls – have become frequent among governments, NGOs and at the highest echelons of the UN. Many of the pleas and ensuing remedial polices to end SGBV (sexual and gender-based violence), as well as the widespread violence more generally, frame SGBV as both a security and a development problem – as a problem which resides at the heart of the security-development nexus. However, in practice, these domains remain parsed and interventions are funded, organized and implemented in the seemingly distinct zones of 'security' (such as defence reform), humanitarian assistance and development assistance. Furthermore, a plethora of actors identify different curative strategies, aimed at diverse 'root causes' at different scales of action in order to end sexual violence and/or to mitigate its effects. Aid from both individual states and NGOs earmarked for combating sexual violence and attending to its victims pour into the Eastern Congo. Numerous external 'security' actors (such as the US, MONUSCO and EUSEC) engage in SSR efforts. Vital coordination of efforts is lacking. Rapes continue, people suffer, and little seems to help those most vulnerable. See Eriksson, Baaz and Stern (2010; 2011) for further discussion of these points.

4 A flood of 'new' research aimed at reflecting this complex reality has emerged, e.g., works which explore 'peacebuilding' (Doyle and Sambanis 2006), 'complex emergencies' (Keen 2008), 'new' patterns of localized warfare with globalized borders (Kaldor 2007a; Cerny 1999), 'post-conflict reconstruction' (Junne and Verkoren 2004), human security (Chandler 2008), 'intervention' (e.g., Chesterman 2007), and the like.

5 There is of course an impressive and diverse literature within several disciplines on these underlying issues, for instance, Chandler (2008); Duffield (2007) *Security Dialogue* (2008); Hardt and Negri (2000); Hettne (1995); and Inayatullah and Blaney (2004). However, here we are zeroing-in on the increasing, and explicit usage of the term.

6 Recently the 'nexus' has been more frequently and deeply addressed in terms of terrorism and counter insurgency. See *Third World Quarterly* (2009).

7 The International Peace Academy (IPA)'s program on the 'security-development nexus' illustrates the difficulty of combining an explicit and careful analysis of the ways these concepts and practices are imbued with meaning with the demands for recommendations that the urgent need for policy transformation and even intervention oblige (IPA 2004, I, 17; IPA 2006, 2).

8 Duffield (2001) spoke of the Development-Security terrain, and the notion of a security-development nexus was used explicitly as a distinct concept by Uvin (2002), and later primarily discussed by IPA (2004, 2006); It has also figured in numerous other works such as Klingebiel, ed. (2006), Chandler (2007), and Buur Jensen and Stepputat (2007). For further discussion, see also *Journal of International Development* (2006) and *Third World Quarterly* (2009).

9 See Foucault (2004).

10 See NSS (2002, 2006); EC (2003) for telling examples.

11 As this story is contingent upon danger and threat always looming, its main plot is also dependent on a sub-plot which is relies on a repetitive or even cyclical temporality: new threats keep emerging (Hutchings 2008, 14).

12 See discussions in *Security Dialogue* (2004, 2008) for a good overview.

13 See also Ackerly, Stern and True (2006); Hansen (2000); *Security Dialogue (2004)*; Sjöberg (2009).

14 Ibid.

15 We are grateful to Simon Reid-Henry (2011) for his thoughtful review essay of a previous version of this chapter, Stern and Öjendal (2010).

References

Ackerly, B., M. Stern and J. True (eds). 2006. *Feminist Methodologies for International Relations*. Cambridge: Cambridge University Press.

Anderson, Mary. 1999. *Do No Harm*. London: Lynne Rienner.

Aradau, Claudia, Luis Lobo-Guerrero and Rens van Munster. 2008. 'Security, Technologies of Risk, and the Political'. *Security Dialogue* 39(2–3): 147–54.

Beck, Ulrich. 2006. *Cosmopolitian Vision*. London: Polity Press.

Bello, Walden. 2005. *Deglobalization: Ideas for a New World Economy*. London: Zed Books.

Bhabha, Homi. 2004. *The Location of Culture*. New York: Routledge.

Bigo, Didier. 2001. 'Internal and External Securit(ies), the Mobius Ribbon'. In M. Albert, D. Jacobson and Y. Lapid (eds), *Identities, Borders, and Orders*, 91–136. Minneapolis: Minnesota University Press.

Booth, D. 1985. 'Marxism and Development Sociology: Interpreting the Impasse'. *World Development* 13(7): 761–87.

Brundtland, Gro Harlem. 1987. *Our Common Future: The World Commission on Environment and Development*. Oxford: Oxford University Press.

Butler, Judith. 2004. *Precarious Life: The Powers of Mourning and Violence*. New York: Verso.

Buur, Lars, Steffen Jensen and Finn Stepputat. 2007. *The Security-Development Nexus: Expressions of Sovereignty and Securitization in Southern Africa*. Uppsala: Nordic Africa Institute (NAI).

Buzan, Barry, Ole Wæver and Jaap de Wilde. 1998. *Security: A New Framework for Analysis*. Boulder, CO: Lynne Rienner.

Call, Charles T. 2008. 'The Fallacy of the "Failed State"'. *Third World Quarterly* 29(8): 1491–1507.

Campbell, David. 1998. *Writing Security: United States Foreign Policy and the Politics of Identity*. Manchester: Manchester University Press.

Cerny, Philip G. 1999. 'Globalization, Governance and Complexity'. In A. Prakash and J. A. Hart (eds), *Globalization and Governance*, 188–212. New York and London: Routledge.

Chambers, Robert. 1983. *Rural Development: Putting the Last First*. Harlow Essex: Longman.

Chandler, David. 2007. 'The Security-Development Nexus and the Rise of "Anti-Foreign Policy"'. *Journal of International Relations and Development* 10(4): 362–86.

———. 2008. 'Review Essay: Human Security: The Dog That Didn't Bark' *Security Dialogue* 39(4): 427–438.

Chesterman, Simon. 2007. 'Ownership and Practice: Transfer of Authority in UN Statebuilding Operations'. *Journal of Intervention and State Building* 1(1): 3–26.

CIDSE. 2006. *CIDSE Study on Security and Development: A CIDSE Reflection Paper*. Brussels: International Cooperation for Development and Solidarity.

Cotonou Working Group. 2010. *Second Revision of the Cotonou Agreement: Agreed Consolidated Text, 11 March 2010*. Brussels.

Craig, David and Doug Porter. 2006. *Development Beyond Neoliberalism? Governance, Poverty Reduction and Political Economy*. London: Routledge.

de Janvry, Alain and Ravi Kanbur. 2006. *Poverty, Inequality, and Development: Essays in Honor of Erik Thorbecke*. Springer.

DFID. 2005. *Fighting Poverty to Build a Safer World: A Strategy for Security and Development*. London: Department for International Development.

———. 2009. *Eliminating World Poverty: Building Our Common Future*. London: Department for International Development.

Dillon, Michael. 1996. *Politics of Security*. London and New York: Routledge.

———. 2004. 'Correlating Sovereign and Biopower'. In Jenny Edkins, Véronique Pin-Fat and Michael Shapiro (eds), *Sovereign Lives: Power in Global Politics*, 41–61. London: Routledge.

Dillon, Michael and Luis Lobo-Guerrero. 2008. 'Biopolitics of Security in the 21st Century'. *Review of International Studies* 34(2): 265–92.

Dillon, Michael and Julian Reid. 2009. *The Liberal Way of War: Killing to Make Life Live*. London: Routledge.

Doyle, Michael and Nicholas Sambanis. 2006. *Making War and Building Peace: United Nations Peace Operations*. Princeton: Princeton University Press.

Duffield, Mark. 2001. *Global Governance and the New Wars*. London: Zed Books.

———. 2007a. *Development, Security and Unending War: Governing the World of Peoples*. Cambridge: Polity Press.

———. 2007b. 'Development, Territories, and People: Consolidating the External Sovereign Frontier'. *Alternatives: Global, Local, Political* 32(2): 225–46.

———. 2010. 'The Global Life-Chance Divide'. *Security Dialogue* 41(1): 53–77.

Elbe, Stefan. 2008. 'Risking Lives: AIDS, Security and Three Concepts of Risk'. *Security Dialogue*. 39(2–3): 177–98.

Eriksson Baaz, Maria and Maria Stern. 2010. *The Complexity of Violence: A Critical Analysis of Sexual Violence in the Democratic Republic of Congo (DRC)*. Stockholm: Sida/Nordic Africa Institute (NAI).

———. 2011. 'Whores, Men and Other Misfits: Undoing "Feminization" in the Armed Forces in the DRC' *African Affairs* 110(441).

European Council. 2003. *A Secure Europe in a Better World: A European Security Strategy*. Brussels: Council of the European Union.

———. 2008. *Report on the Implementation of the European Security Strategy: Providing Security in a Changing World*. Brussels: Council of the European Union.

Escobar, Arturo. 1995. *Encountering Development: The Making and Unmaking of the Third World*. Princeton: Princeton University Press.

Esteva, Gustavo. 1992. 'Development'. In W. Sachs(ed), *The Development* Dictionary, 6–25. London: Zed Books.

Foucault, Michel. 2004. *Security, Territory, Population: Lectures at the Collège de France, 1977–1978*. New York: Palgrave.

Frank, Andre Gunder. 1967. *Capitalism and Underdevelopment in Latin America: Historical Studies of Chile and Brazil*. Monthly Review Press.

Friedman, Jonathan. 1992. *Empowerment*. Oxford: Blackwell.

Gallie, W. B. 1956. 'Essentially Contested Concepts'. *Proceedings of the Aristotelian Society* 56: 167–98.

Glasius, Marlies and Mary Kaldor. 2006. *A Human Security Doctrine for Europe: Project, Principles, Practicalities.* London: Routledge.

Hansen, Lene. 2000. 'The Little Mermaid's Silent Security Dilemma and the Absence of Gender in the Copenhagen School' *Millennium* 29(2): 285–306.

Hardt, Antonio and Michael Negri. 2000. *Empire.* Cambridge, MA: Harvard University Press.

Hettne, Björn. 1995. *Development Theory and the Three Worlds.* London: Longman Press.

_____. 2009. *Thinking about Development: Historical Discourses of Theory and Practice - Towards Global Social Theory.* London: Zed Books.

_____. 2010. 'History of the Development–Security Nexus'. *Security Dialogue* 41(1): 31–53.

Hoogensen, Gunhild and Svein Vigeland Rottem. 2004. 'Gender Identity and the Subject of Security' *Security Dialogue* 35(2): 155–71.

Hutchings, Kimberly. 2008. *Time and World Politics: Thinking the Present (Reappraising the Political).* Manchester: Manchester University Press.

Huysmans, Jef. 2004. 'A Foucaultian View on Spill-over. Freedom and Security in the EU'. *Journal of International Relations and Development* 7(3): 294–318.

_____. 2006. *The Politics of Insecurity. Fear, Migration and Asylum in the EU.* London: Routledge.

ICISS. 2001. *The Responsibility to Protect: Report of the International Commission on Intervention and State Sovereignty.* Ottawa: International Development Research Council.

IPA. 2004. *Strengthening the Security-Development Nexus.* New York: International Peace Academy.

_____. 2006. *Building Partnerships for Crisis Prevention.* New York: International Peace Academy.

Jabri, Vivienne. 2007. *War and the Transformation of Global Politics.* London and New York: Palgrave Macmillan.

Jensen, Steffen. 2010. 'War on Gangs, Counterinsurgency and Citizenship' *Security Dialogue* 41(1): 77–99.

Journal of International Development. 2006. Special Section on Policy Arenas, *Journal of International Development* 18(1): 51–150.

Junne, Gerd, and Willemijn Verkoren (eds). 2004. *Postconflict Development. Meeting New Challenges.* London: Lynne Rienner.

Kaldor, Mary. 2007. *New and Old Wars: Organized Violence in a Global Era.* San Francisco: Stanford University Press.

Keen, David. 2008. *Complex Emergencies.* Cambridge: Polity Press.

King, Gary and Christopher L. Murray. 2002. 'Rethinking Human Security'. *Political Science Quarterly* 116(4): 585–610.

Klingebiel, Stephan (ed.) 2006. *New Interfaces between Security and Development: Changing Concepts and Approaches.* Bonn: Deutsches Institut für Entwicklungspolitik.

Liedman, Sven-Erik. 1997. *I skuggan av framtiden* [In the Shadow of the Future]. Stockholm: Bonnier Alba.

Neocleous, Marc. 2008. *Critique of Security.* Montreal: McGill-Queens University Press.

Nisbet, R. 1980. *History of the Idea of Progress.* London: Heineman.

OECD. 2007. *The OECD DAC Handbook on Security System Reform (SSR): Supporting Security and Justice.* Paris: Organisation for Economic Co-operation and Development.

_____. 2008. *Concepts and Dilemmas of State Building in Fragile Situations: From Fragility to Resilience.* Paris: Organisation for Economic Co-operation and Development.

Öjendal, Joakim and Mona Lilja, (eds). 2009. *Beyond Democracy in Cambodia: Political Reconstruction in a Post-Conflict Society.* Copenhagen: NIAS Press.

Orjuela, Camilla. 2010. 'The Bullet in the Living Room', *Security Dialogue* 41(1): 99–120.

Palme Commission. 1982. *Common Security: A Program for Disarmament: The Report of the Independent Commission on Disarmament and Security Issues.* Stockholm: Tidens.

Paris, Roland and Timothy D. Sisk. 2007. *Managing Contradictions: The Inherent Dilemmas of Postwar Statebuilding.* New York: International Peace Academy.

Pietersee, Jan N. 2000. 'After Post-Development'. *Third World Quarterly* 21(2): 175–91.

Pin-Fat, Véronique. 2000. '(Im)possible Universalism: Reading Human Rights in World Politics'. *Review of International Studies* 26(4): 663–74.

Prebisch, Raul. 1950. *The Economic Development of Latin America and its Principal Problems.* New York: United Nations.

Rahnema, Majid. 1997. 'Towards Post-Development: Searching for Signposts, A New Language and New Paradigm'. In M. Rahnema and V. Bawtree (eds), *The Post-Development Reader*, 337–404. London: Zed Books.

Reid, Julien. 2004. 'War, Liberalism, and Modernity: The Biopolitical Provocations of "Empire"'. *Cambridge Review of International Affairs* 17(1): 63–79.

Reid-Henry, Simon. 2011. 'Spaces of Security and Development: An Alternative Mapping of the Security-Development Nexus'. *Security Dialogue.* 42(1): 97–104.

Risse-Kappen, Thomas. 1995. *Bringing Transnational Relations Back In: Non-State Actors, Domestic Structures and International Institutions.* Cambridge: Cambridge University Press.

Rostow, W. W. 1962. *The Stages of Economic Growth: A Non-Communist Manifesto.* Cambridge: Cambridge University Press.

Salter, Mark B. 2007. 'On Exactitude in Disciplinary Science: A Response to the Network Manifesto' *Security Dialogue* 38(1): 113–22.

Scholte, Jan A. 2005. *Globalization: A Critical Introduction.* London: Palgrave.

Schumacher, E. F. 1973. *Small is Beautiful: A Study of Economics as if People Mattered.* London: Blonde & Briggs.

Schurman, Frans J. (ed.) 1993. *Beyond the Impasse: New Directions in Development Theory* London: Zed Books.

Security Dialogue. 2004. 35(3).

———. 2008. 39(2–3).

———. 2010. Special Issue: The Security-Development Nexus Revisited. *Security Dialogue* 41(1).

Shaw, Timothy Sandra J. MacLean and David R. Black. 2006. 'Introduction: A Decade of Human Security: What Prospects for Global Governance and New Multilateralism'. In S. J. MacLean, , D. R. Black and T. Shaw (eds), *A Decade of Human Security: Global Governance and New Multilateralisms.* Aldershot, Hampshire and Burlington, VT: Ashgate.

Simon, David. 1999. 'Development Revisited: Thinking About, Practising and Teaching Development after Cold War', in A. Närman and D. Simon (eds), *Development as Theory and Practice.* London: Longman.

Sjöberg, Laura. 2009. *Gender and International Security: Feminist Perspectives.* London: Routledge.

Stern, Maria. 2005. *Naming Security: Constructing Identity.* Manchester: Manchester University Press.

Stern, Maria and Joakim Öjendal. 2010. 'Mapping the Security-Development Nexus: Conflict, Complexity, Cacophony, Convergence?'. *Security Dialogue* 41(1): 5–31.

———. 2011. 'Mapping Security–Development: A Question of Methodology?'. *Security Dialogue* 42(1): 105–10.

Sylvester, Christine. 2006. 'Bare Life as a Development/Postcolonial Problematic'. *The Geographical Journal.* 172(1): 66–77.

Third World Quarterly. 2009. Special Issue: War, Peace and Progress: Conflict, Development, (In)Security and Violence in the 21st Century. *Third World Quarterly* 30(1).

UN. 2004. *A More Secure World: Our Shared Responsibility: Report of the High-level Panel on Threats, Challenges and Change*. United Nations Department of Public Information.

UNDP. 1996. *Human Development Report 1995*. United Nations Development Programme. New York: Oxford University Press.

_____. 2005. *Human Development Report 2005: International Cooperation at a Crossroads: Aid, Trade and Security in an Unequal World*. New York: United Nations Development Programme .

Uvin, Peter. 2002. 'The Development/Peacebuilding Nexus: A Typology and History of Changing Paradigms'. *Journal of Peacebuilding and Development* 1(1): 1–20.

_____. 2008. 'Development and Security: Genealogy and Typology of an Evolving International Policy Area'. In Hans Günter Brauch et al. (eds), *Globalization and Environmental Challenges: Reconceptualizing Security in the 21st Century*, 151–65. Springer.

Walker, R. B. J. 2006. 'Lines of Insecurity: International, Imperial, Exceptional'. *Security Dialogue* 37(1): 65–82.

Wallerstein, Immanuel. 1974. *The Modern World-System, vol. I: Capitalist Agriculture and the Origins of the European World-Economy in the Sixteenth Century*. New York and London: Academic Press.

World Bank. 1997. *World Development Report*. Washington.

Wæver, Ole. 1995. 'Securitization and Desecuritization'. In Ronny Lipschutz (ed.), *On Security*, 46–86. New York: Columbia University Press.

Zalewski, Marysia. 2006. 'Distracted Reflections on the Production, Narration and Refusal of Feminist Knowledge in IR'. In B. Ackerly, M. Stern and J. True (eds), *Feminist Methodologies for International Relations*, 42–62. Cambridge: Cambridge University Press.

Zedner, Lucia. 2009. S*ecurity (Key Ideas in Criminology)*. London: Routledge.

Chapter 3

LIBERAL STATE-BUILDING AND ENVIRONMENTAL SECURITY: THE INTERNATIONAL COMMUNITY BETWEEN TRADE-OFF AND CARELESSNESS

Roland Kostić, Florian Krampe and Ashok Swain

Introduction

Since the early 1990s the international community has been increasingly adopting liberal state-building as part of a wider liberal peacebuilding strategy for addressing the plethora of problems facing post-conflict societies (Chandler 2006; Chesterman 2005; Kostić 2007; MacGinty 2006; Paris 2004). In that sense, liberal state-building is viewed as a peacebuilding measure with the aim to construct or reconstruct the institutions of governance capable of providing citizens with physical and economic security (cf. Paris 2004; Richmond 2006).[1] One of the guiding assumptions has been that the presence of strong state institutions would facilitate macro-economic growth and provide economic and societal security of its citizens (Paris 2004).[2] Such measures, in combinations with strong state institutions and functioning infrastructure, are supposed to bring economic well-being that would in return strengthen the legitimacy of the state among its citizens by means of democratic elections, thus bringing about political moderation and societal integration in previously fragmented societies (Paris 2004).

However, while it has been shown that this type of liberal state- and nation-building fails short of bringing societal integration in multiethnic societies (Kostić 2007, 2008), it does not include in its framework of analysis the environmental problems of post-conflict societies. Economic development projects such as large hydro projects or opencast mining for lignite – as an element of a broader state-building exercise – lead to environmental stress for the communities, and can further exacerbate inter-communal incompatibilities (Swain and Krampe 2011). Thus, it has been argued that a 'failure to respond to the environmental needs of war-torn societies can greatly complicate the already difficult tasks of peace, reconciliation, political institutionalization and economic reconstruction' (Conca 2006, 1).

While environmental factors are unlikely a direct cause of conflicts, it is indisputable that the destruction of the environment has severe consequences for societies. Several studies (Gleditsch 1998; Homer-Dixon and Blitt 1998; Lee 2009; Percival and Homer-Dixon 1998; Swain 1993) show that environmental stress is increasing societal insecurity. Recently, the debate on climate change and its effects on conflicts has extended the argumentation further (Barnett and Adger 2007; Brown, Hammill and McLeman 2007; Detraz and Betsill 2009; Lee 2009; Nordas and Gleditsch 2007; Raleigh and Urdal 2007; Trombetta 2008), thus moving focus away from the study of the effects of environmental factors on society. However, to understand the specific effects of climate change on society, one first needs to understand the general effects of environmental stress on society. We understand the interaction between environment and society as reflexive. In the specific context of armed conflict, Wallensteen and Swain (1997) identify (a) environmental destruction as the repercussion of conflict and (b) environmental destruction as the cause of conflict itself. In this chapter we first highlight the relationship between environmental stress and peacebuilding processes in post-conflict societies and introduce a theoretical model explaining the reflexivity of these two causal directions, i.e., how they are interrelated and mutually reinforcing. Subsequently the theoretical model is applied to examine the suitability and sustainability of the external state-building project in Kosovo. We are particularly interested at the strategies that are adopted in the field of energy production within a wider framework of liberal state-building in Kosovo. The guiding question for this investigation is whether the actors participating in the peacebuilding process have the capacity to address and provide environmental security as well as to resolve the issues of societal security for communities in Kosovo.[3] The case study of state-building in Kosovo is used to highlight the complexities of sustaining a peaceful post-conflict situation within the framework of the existing peacebuilding model. Moreover, it emphasizes that environmental and societal security requirements have to be addressed simultaneously to reduce the risk of recurring conflicts. The expectation is that through a better understanding of the interaction between societal and environmental security, further valuable conclusions can be drawn about the capacity and limitations of the prevailing models for building peace in the aftermath of civil wars.[4]

Peacebuilding in Times of Liberal State-Building

Liberal state-building is the dominant Western-centric approach to the resolution of contemporary intra-state conflicts and focuses particularly on the re-creation of the state's capacity to govern, the democratization of societies and the generation of macro-economic growth in post-conflict societies (Chandler 2006; Chesterman 2005; Kaldor 2006; Kostić 2007; MacGinty 2006; Paris 2004; Richmond 2007). As many authors argue, it was the post–Cold War confidence in the Western liberal model as the ultimate form of human government that has led to its adoption as the optimal way of reconstructing societies that have fallen victim to the perils of internal strife and intolerance (Atwood 1994; MacGinty 2006; Mandelbaum 2002). Accordingly, attempts to create durable peace[5] include measures to create a particular type of government based on the liberal norms of democracy, market economy and the Western concept of the civic nation-state.

However, these state-building projects commonly fail to take into account aspects of the environment and the sustainable use of natural resources in the reconstruction phase of post-conflict societies. Many have raised their own concerns about this lack of attention to environmental issues in state-building strategies (Conca 2006; Conca and Dabelko 2002; Matthew, Brown and Jensen 2008; UN Peacebuilding Commission 2008; Wallensteen and Swain 1997). For peace to endure, it is vital to balance social, economic and environmental factors in development policies, with particular focus on sustainable development (Adams 2006; Ott 2003; UN General Assembly 2005).[6]

Unquestionably, following the end of the Cold War the number of conflicts has been in decline, and researchers have observed an increase in the number of peace settlements since 1995 (Harbom and Wallensteen 2005). At the same time, durable outcomes of many state-building initiatives launched by external parties at the onset of peace settlements remain highly uncertain. Part of the reason lies in the focus of external parties on resolving the immediate 'situational stability', while less emphasis is being placed on long-term peacebuilding strategies and their outcomes. The urgency of the identity, economic and social issues facing post-conflict societies and a confidence in the liberal peace model among the key actors engaging in peacebuilding projects leads to the promotion – often unilaterally – of specific policies to remedy these problems. In the field of economics, the policies are best summarized in terms of a mixture of modernization and neo-liberal market policies consisting of (a) the privatization of the industrial sector, (b) the creation of conditions for external investments, and (c) urbanization. These measures, in combination with the creation of strong state institutions and a functioning infrastructure, are supposed to bring economic well-being that would in return, through elections, generate legitimacy of the state with its citizens, thus eventually bringing political stability and societal integration (Paris 2004).

Liberal peacebuilders reproduce the same logic of the liberal theory which dominated the thinking of American academics and policy makers regarding state- and nation-building in the 1960s (Jahn 2007a, 2007b; Kostić 2007), and which predicted that modernization, in the form of increased urbanization, industrialization, education, communication and transport would lead to an increased social mobilization and assimilation of local communities (Deutsch 1966, 150). The argument was that the assimilation of different ethnic groups is a 'simple' matter of social engineering (Deutsch 1966, 164), which 'the states could consciously direct or at least influence and which will determine what they are to become' (Rivkin 1969, 11). The approach generously borrows from a simplified model of the civic nation-building experience of parts of Western Europe and United States, whereby nationalism comes before nations; nations do not make states and nationalism, but the other way around (Gellner 1983, 55; Hobsbawm 1990, 10). This approach is flawed, as it clearly ignores the existence of an alternative model of nation-building whereby, as Hroch (1993) explains, ethno-national communities organized themselves into national movements in order to achieve all the attributes of fully fledged nations. As a result, liberal peacebuilders fail to account for the effects of the external

Figure 3.1 The reflexive relationship between environmental and societal security

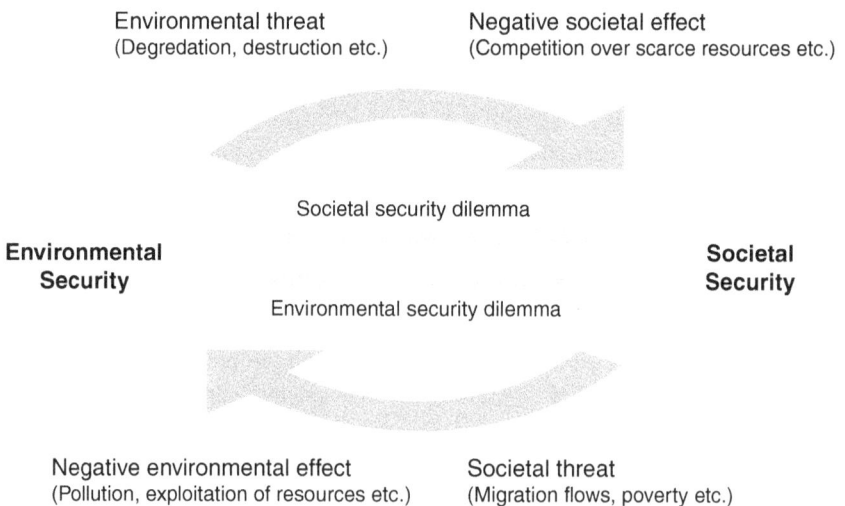

Environmental threat
(Degredation, destruction etc.)

Negative societal effect
(Competition over scarce resources etc.)

Societal security dilemma

**Environmental
Security**

**Societal
Security**

Environmental security dilemma

Negative environmental effect
(Pollution, exploitation of resources etc.)

Societal threat
(Migration flows, poverty etc.)

impositions on the securitization of existing ethno-national identities among recipient communities, i.e., their societal security. Secondly, they do not take into account the interactions between societal security and environmental stress caused by the economic policies of liberal state-building.

The Model of Societal and Environmental Security

Environmental and societal security exist in a reflexive relationship (see Figure 3.1). The model illustrates how environmental insecurity is leading to societal insecurity, and societal insecurity is causing environmental insecurity. The following section describes the theoretical model, starting off with the link from societal to environmental insecurity before describing the upper part of the model, i.e., the effect of environmental insecurity on societal insecurity.

Societal Security

The Copenhagen School developed the concepts of societal security and the societal security dilemma in order to take into account the concerns of a group experiencing a threat to its identity. One of the key notions of the approach is that group identity can be securitized. In general terms, a society is defined as a collective of people who have a clear sense of common identity and a common tradition, culture, collective memory, belief system and social structures (Bar-Tal 2000, xvi). Based on this understanding of society, societal security is defined as a 'security of the community to sustain traditional patterns of language, culture, association, and religious and national identity and custom, albeit within an acceptable framework of evolution' (Wæver 1993, 43). Conceptually, the societal security dilemma is based on the notion that if a group loses its identity – that is, if the group identity cannot be internalized and externalized by its members and passed on to future generations – it ceases to exist (Roe 1999, 193; 2005, 43). The main units of analysis for societal security are 'politically significant ethnonational and religious entities'. Hence, societal security primarily concerns the maintenance of significant ethno-national groups. As Roe puts it, a threat to an ethno-national or religious group exists when a group is convinced that the group's identity is put in danger, regardless of whether this is objectively established or not (Roe 2005, 48). The threats to a community can range from the suppression of its rights of expression to interference with its ability to reproduce itself across generations. In other words, the threat may include a range of measures such as 'forbidding the use of language, names and dress, through to the closure of places of education and worship, to the deportation or killing of members of the community' (Wæver 1993, 43). At the non-violent end of the scale, threats to the reproduction of an ethno-national community can occur through the application of repressive measures against the expression of communal identity, that is, if the institutions that reproduce language and culture are prohibited to operate, and as a consequence, the identity cannot be transmitted effectively from one generation to another (Wæver 1993, 43). As a result, without a sense of collective identity, the ethnic group as a self-conscious body may cease to exist.

Environmental Security

Environmental security has been defined as 'freedom from environmental danger/conflicts' (Swain 1997, 32). Increasing environmental insecurity in recent times emphasizes the need for a broader view on security, and confirms that state-centred security policies are not sufficient. The 'transnational element' (Graeger 1996) of environmental threats is a main foundation of environmental security analysis today (Beck 1987, 2007; Detraz and Betsill 2009). While the devastating effects of environmental disasters are unquestioned, there is a debate over whether environmental threats should be included on the security agenda of states. Two perspectives were discussed in the 1990s: (1) including the environment on the security agenda will reduce political space for action through militarizing it (Graeger 1996, 111); and to the contrary, (2) including environment will widen political space and demilitarize the security agenda (Ullman 1983, 133–4). Today the term environmental security has reached the international security debate. Thus, the elaborations by Detraz and Betsill (2009) give guidance in making an important distinction in the environmental discourse: environmental conflict versus environmental security. The authors differ between environmental conflict, which they argue addresses mainly traditional 'hard' security concerns and is consequently state centred, and environmental security, which, on the other side, is associated with the broad human security aspect and thus lies beyond state borders.

Societal Security as a Result of Environmental Elements and Scarcity

The relationship between environmental threats and societal security is frequently addressed in debates on how climate change will cause conflict; however, it needs further clarification. While we do not believe that environmental degradation itself can cause war, we find that environmental threats, following environmental degradation and destruction, have severe negative societal effects which create situations that can promote the salience of disputes. In combination with institutional mismanagement and the political will for conflict, these conditions might culminate in armed conflict.

For example, natural resource scarcity due to droughts, etc. causes resource competition and/or leads to population migration, enhancing resource stress in other areas. This has been seen in the Sahel region of Africa, where the weakness of governments prevented the good governance of scarce resources, indirectly supporting migration and the salience of conflicts all over the region. Natural disasters as well can destroy natural resources or make them unusable, which can have a severe impact on society, creating opportunities for political actions. Resource depletion limits development and leads to a loss of livelihood. Thus, economic factors like poverty are major concerns that decrease security and increase the likelihood of conflict (Ohlsson 2000).

Theoretically one can say that negative environmental development and emerging environmental stress can play an important role in the appearance of a societal security dilemma. Environmental degradation – leading to scarce resources, causing migration and further leading to resource competition and economic stress – poses a direct threat to the individuals' and groups' identity.

This becomes evident when looking at environmentally induced migrations. The loss of living space and livelihood due to environmental stress could lead to the migration of affected people (Swain 1996). All through human history, people have been forced to flee their homes because the land on which they live could no longer sustain them. Deforestation, desertification and drought significantly affected the populations of the past. However, severe destruction of the environment is becoming a potential problem that could cause new mass migrations, and has already become a major issue of concern for the international community. Though major research attention and media coverage can be attributed to the visibility of South/North migration and East/West migration, most of the ongoing movements occur from rural to urban areas within developing countries, or from one developing country to another.[7] The world's largest trans-border migration is taking place in Africa, Asia and Latin America. In South Asia alone, about thirty-five to forty million people have crossed international borders within the region in recent years.

The cities in less developed regions are swelling every year: 914 million of the world's poorest people moved from rural areas into urban zones alone between 2000 and 2010 – more than 91 million per year in this time frame. By 2010, 45 per cent of the population (2.5 billion people) of the less and least developed regions will be living in urban areas. Cities in these regions are already surrounded by shanty suburbs which contain millions of inhabitants, a high proportion of whom are without jobs (UN DESA – Population Division 2009).

Today the crisis of environmentally forced population migration ranks as one of the foremost security problems. These migrants have, however, been viewed as a peripheral concern. Yet their sheer size has brought them as one of the most important items on the global political agenda today, and climate change is likely to increase environmentally induced forced migration. Transnational migrants pose a structural threat to the host country by increasing demands on its scarce natural resources, but could also be framed as a possible societal threat to the receiving societies. Migrants taking advantage of their location and engaging in opposition against the home state government, as in the Chad-Darfur region, potentially strains the relations between host and home countries. But environmental migration not only generates conflict among states; it further induces a situation of latent violent conflict among domestic communities. Their change of residence brings an increased demand for food and other basic necessities of life, which put new burdens on the host society. The resulting scarcity encourages the 'sons of the soil' to organise against the migrants to protect their interests.

Environmental Insecurity as Result of Armed Conflict

The effects of armed conflict are multiple, from social, political, economic as well as environmental perspectives. Studies show that conflicts create severe ecological damage to the environment through direct impact: for example, detonated bombs and unexploded explosives may make fields and water unusable; military vehicles compress the soil severely and make cultivating the land difficult; and the use of chemical weapons directly affects the health of the environment in the conflict zones. But armed conflict has further, indirect effects on the environment: conflict-induced migration results in displaced people in refugee camps leading to social stress, and also to ecological stress.

When armed conflicts lead to severe negative environmental effects, environmental insecurity is the logical consequence. In the face of such environmental threats, members of securitized communities get trapped in a 'first strike situation': they start securing the scarce resource before members of other competing communities in order to secure the survival and reproduction of their own community. In that regard, the community could be described as facing an environmental security dilemma. The environmental security dilemma occurs when the actions a community – who seeks to secure its own environmental resources and survival – securitizes the resources and thus securitizes the existence of other groups, which, consequently, may put all parties into a situation where they face an environmental security dilemma due to environmental stress and a shortage of resources. This insecurity is mutually reinforcing for all affected groups and can spur ethnic mobilization and adversarial political actions and, in the worst case scenario of conflict escalation, even military actions.

The above theoretical and empirical evidence reflects the complexity of the challenges at hand, particularly when considering durable peacebuilding in the aftermath of such conflicts. Reconciling the priorities of energy production, sustainable development and environmental security within the existing state- and nation-building models presents a particular puzzle to international interveners. This study explores the sustainability of energy projects in Kosovo, which are being promoted by the international community as a part of a durable state-building strategy. The main aim is to examine whether the solutions regarding energy production are sustainable in terms of long-term development and state-building, particularly when considering their connections to environmental and societal security. To that end, the links between environmental and societal security are being explored in the case of post-war Kosovo. Two questions guide the investigation: (a) What kinds of energy solutions are being promoted as a part of comprehensive state-building? (b) What are the impacts of the adopted energy policies on environmental and societal security?

Peacebuilding and the Environment: A Case Study of Kosovo

Background of the Kosovo Conflict and Building Peace Thereafter

Although the region of Kosovo has been traditionally one of the economically less developed areas in the Balkans, it has a symbolic significance for both the Albanian and Serbian populace. The roots of the Serbian Orthodox Church have their origins in the province; and the monastery in Peć was the first residency of the Serb patriarch. Furthermore, the Battle of Kosovo between the Christian armies of the Balkans lead by Serbian nobility and the Ottoman Empire in 1389 has a prominent place in the Serbian national narrative (Bakic-Hayden 2004).

After the Balkan war in 1912,[8] Serbia was given sovereignty over Kosovo, which had been the part of the Ottoman Empire since the fifteenth century. After World War II, Kosovo, although formally a part of the Socialist Republic of Serbia, was one of two autonomous provinces within the Socialist Federal Republic of Yugoslavia (SFRY), which included six republics.[9] After the political struggles in the 1960s, the Albanian majority in Kosovo was granted extensive autonomy in 1974 and became a de facto equal member of the federation. Slobodan Milošević, president of the Republic of Serbia, limited Kosovo's autonomy in 1989 (O'Neill 2002).

Ibrahim Rugova, one of the 1989 founders of the Lidhjes Demokratike të Kosovës (Democratic League of Kosovo, LDK), was elected president of the self-declared Republic of Kosovo in 1992, and proclaimed a peaceful separation from Serbia.[10] The Albanian paramilitary forces (Kosovo Liberation Army, UÇK), believed to be founded in 1994, started the first violent attacks on the Croatian Serb refugee camps and police forces in 1996 (Kaufman 2002; O'Neill 2002). The escalation occurred with the background of the EU-US failure to include the question of Kosovo in the Dayton peace negotiations, and the subsequent lifting of international sanctions and international recognition of FR Yugoslavia.[11] In 1998, the conflict escalated into a war between the police forces of Serbia and the UÇK, who by then received the US support as Albanian freedom fighters, despite their previous appearance on the US list of terrorist organizations (Uppsala Conflict Data Program 2010).

By 1998, the West increased its involvement as the violence escalated and thousands of internally displaced civilians sought shelter in the hills of Kosovo. The Serbian authorities were compelled to sign a ceasefire and agreed to a partial retreat, monitored by observers from the OSCE (Organization for Security and Co-operation in Europe) according to an agreement negotiated by the US mediator, Richard Holbrooke. As soon as the Serb troops retreated, the UÇK assumed the control of the roads and key junctions, which eventually provoked the military re-deployment of the Serbian government's troops. The ceasefire did not hold as the fighting resumed in December 1998. The Račak massacre in January 1999 in particular brought fresh international attention to the Kosovo conflict. Within weeks, an international conference was convened, and by March had prepared a draft agreement of the Rambouillet Accords. The accords, based on the principle 'take it or leave it', called for the restoration of a broad autonomy of Kosovo and the deployment of NATO peacekeeping forces, along with their right to enter Serbian territory, use resources without due compensation, and freedom from prosecution for the crimes committed on the territory of Serbia during their deployment (Magnusson 1999). The Serbian party found the terms unacceptable, refused to sign the draft, and tried to negotiate certain revisions that were not accepted by the US.

In response to the failure of the Rambouillet conferences, NATO unilaterally conducted its military operation, 'Allied Force', between 24 March and 10 June 1999. By bombing Yugoslavia, the operation aimed to force Milošević to withdraw his forces from Kosovo, but also to undermine his regime in Belgrade. The NATO military action was not authorized by the Security Council of the United Nations and was therefore contrary to the provisions of the United Nations Charter. Despite being branded a humanitarian intervention with the goal of preventing human rights abuses, the NATO attacks elicited major retaliatory actions by the Serbian forces and paramilitaries, and resulted in a further massive population displacement in Kosovo. During the conflict, some eight hundred thousand ethnic Albanians fled or were forcefully driven from Kosovo. After three months of attacks the Serbian government and NATO signed the Kumanovo ceasefire, and NATO-led Kosovo Force (KFOR) troops were deployed in the province with the backing of the newly passed UN resolution 1244. As KFOR was deploying, the returning Albanians retaliated against Kosovo Serbs and Roma causing an exodus of some two hundred thousand from the province.[12] The Uppsala Conflict Data Program (UCDP) estimates the number of battle-related deaths to be between two and seven thousand for the years 1998 and 1999.[13] The formal status of Kosovo was left undecided until it met the basic international standards of governance, and in the mean time, the province was put under the administrated of the United Nations Interim Administration Mission in Kosovo (UNMIK), which was supposed to assist it in the task.

United Nations Interim Administration Mission in Kosovo

On 10 June 1999, the UN Security Council passed UN Security Council Resolution 1244, which placed Kosovo under transitional UN administration (UNMIK) and authorized KFOR, the NATO-led peacekeeping force. Resolution 1244 provided that Kosovo would have autonomy within the Federal Republic of Yugoslavia, and affirmed the territorial integrity of Yugoslavia, which has been legally succeeded by the Republic of Serbia. Among other things, Resolution 1244 called upon UNMIK to perform basic civilian administrative functions; promote the establishment of substantial autonomy and self-government in Kosovo; facilitate a political process to determine Kosovo's future status; coordinate the humanitarian and disaster relief of all international agencies; support the reconstruction of key infrastructure; maintain civil law and order; promote human rights; and assure the safe and unimpeded return of all refugees and displaced persons to their homes in Kosovo (UNSC 1999).[14] In the early stages, the international community called for the creation of democratic institutions in Kosovo, which would have to fulfill the standards of democratic governance, respect human rights, ensure the safe return of displaced Serbs, as well as facilitate the safety and freedom of movement of the remaining Serbs in Kosovo before the discussion on the province's final status was to be opened.

Despite the ample assistance of the international administration, the elected Kosovo authorities struggled on a number of issues. Faltering infrastructure, donor-dependency, corruption, the trafficking of drugs and humans, unemployment rates of some 45 per cent and occasional attacks on Serb minorities constantly reminded Kosovo's politicians and population about the difficulty of fulfilling the standard criteria for the discussion on the future status of the province. The slow pace and shortcomings only added to the frustration of Kosovo's Albanian leaders and Albanian population, which culminated in the orchestrated attacks of Kosovo Albanian groups on the remaining Kosovo Serb enclaves in March 2004.[15] The fighting resulted in 19 dead and 900 injured, while 300 houses and churches were burned and 3,500 Serbs were internally displaced. However, even more significantly, the events came to show that KFOR and UNMIK did not control the situation and were unable to enforce law and order in Kosovo.

As a result, the West abandoned its insistence on standards and in early 2006 commenced the international negotiations on the final status of the province. The UN-backed talks, led by UN Special Envoy Martti Ahtisaari, began in February 2006. Whilst some progress was made on technical matters, throughout the talks both Serbs and Kosovo Albanians remained diametrically opposed on the question of the status itself. In February 2007, Ahtisaari, acting more in the role of arbiter than mediator, delivered a draft status settlement proposal to leaders in Belgrade and Pristina, which was the basis for a draft UN Security Council Resolution which proposed 'supervised independence' for the province. Ahtisaari clearly copied the protectorate model of Bosnia and Herzegovina when calling for the establishment of an International Steering Group (ISG) comprising key international stakeholders who were to appoint an International Civilian Representative (ICR) and seek UN Security Council endorsement of the appointment. The ICR and the EU Special Representative (EUSR), appointed by the Council of the European Union, were to be the same person. The ICR was entrusted to exercise certain powers to ensure and supervise the full implementation of this settlement, including the power to take measures, as necessary, to prevent and remedy breaches of this settlement. The mandate of the ICR was envisaged to continue until the ISG determined that Kosovo had implemented the terms of the settlement. Finally, the ISG was to eventually provide direction on the ultimate phasing-out of the ICR.

A draft resolution, backed by the US, UK and other European members of the Security Council was presented and rewritten in an attempt to accommodate Russia, which was concerned that such a resolution would undermine the principle of state sovereignty. Russia, one of five permanent members of the Security Council, insisted that it would not support a resolution that was not the product of an agreement between Belgrade and Kosovo Albanians. After weeks of discussions at the UN, the US, UK and other European members of the Security Council formally 'discarded' a draft resolution backing Ahtisaari's proposal on 20 July 2007.

In August 2007, a 'Troika' consisting of negotiators from the EU, US and Russia launched a new effort to reach a status outcome acceptable to both Belgrade and Pristina. The attempt expectedly failed and led to unilateral proclamation of independence by the Assembly of Kosovo on 17 February 2008. At the time of writing in autumn 2009, 62 mainly Western and West-allied countries have recognized the independence of the Republic of Kosovo. Yet Serbia continues to claim sovereignty over Kosovo in accordance with the existing UNSC Resolution 1244. Recently, the UN General Assembly has given support for the Serbian initiative to seek an advisory opinion by the International Court of Justice on the recognition of Kosovo. Furthermore, Belgrade has given its full political and economic support to the three Serb-dominated municipalities in Northern Kosovo. The municipalities refused to acknowledge the unilaterally proclaimed independence of the province and in 2009 continue to apply the laws of Serbia. Internationally, China and Russia continue to threaten the use of their veto powers in the UN Security Council, while even in the General Assembly there is little support for the independence, thus leaving Kosovo in something of an international legal limbo.

The European Union Rule of Law Mission in Kosovo (EULEX) was to start its deployment in February 2008, initially with the idea of supporting the implementation of the Ahtisaari plan. It is the largest civilian mission ever launched under the European Security and Defence Policy (ESDP), and the central aim is to assist and support the Kosovo authorities in the rule of law area, specifically in the police, judiciary and customs areas. It is a technical mission made up of some two thousand judges, prosecutors and riot police that will monitor, mentor and advise whilst retaining limited executive powers. However, due to the lack of a new UN resolution, it was considered illegal by Serbia and Russia. Eventually, after many turns, in December 2009 EULEX adopted status-neutral mission, that is, it accepted that it was no longer implementing the Kosovo independence or Ahtisaari plan, and recognized UNSC 1244 and their work under the framework of the UNMIK which was initially supposed to be phased out (Jeremić 2008). In other words, EULEX de facto accepted the legal status of Kosovo as prior to the proclamation of independence, much to Albanian disapproval (Jeremić 2008). While this type of compromise provided EULEX with Serbian support and access to Serb-dominated areas in the north, it also resulted in the attacks on EULEX staff by Kosovo Albanians (Phillips 2009).

Focus on Economic Development

One of the main challenges facing the international community since its assumption of responsibility over Kosovo in 1999 has been the development of an overarching strategy for the sustainable economic development of Kosovo. Growth rates in Kosovo remain moderate (13 per cent in 2001, 2 per cent in 2004, –1 per cent in 2005, 3.1 per cent in 2006, 3.5 per cent in 2007, and 5.4 per cent in 2008 (Reuters 2008)), and Kosovo's economy is still far from being sustainable. This is particularly reflected in an extremely high trade deficit, in which imports (1.2 billion euros in 2005 and 1.3 billion in 2006) outnumber exports (0.005 billion euros in 2005 and 0.008 billion in 2006) by a factor of ten. Growth has been significantly driven by foreign aid inflows and remittances from abroad.[16] The GDP per capita is estimated at 1,100 euros (Reuters 2008), and unemployment remains pervasive at around 45 per cent of the labour force (European Commission 2010).

Expert analyses conclude that Kosovo does not have particular competitive comparative advantages (Wittkowsky 2003). It is rich primarily in labour force and minerals, particularly lignite. Labour, however, is relatively expensive given that the international presence and introduction of the euro have pushed the costs of living and wages upwards. Furthermore, labour skills only partly meet the needs of modern Western enterprises (Wittkowsky 2003). In addition, the infrastructure is outdated and insufficient; for example, Kosovo suffers from frequent power outages as it does not produce enough electricity and the power grid is poorly equipped to deal with the daily demands of the population and industry.

Moreover, the situation of the fresh water supply is highly problematic. The issues are numerous; many fresh water sources are contaminated by industry and are considered a serious health risk to the population. Furthermore, water supplies dropped drastically due to drier winters in recent years,[17] while much of the water infrastructure is in bad condition. It has also been observed that water shortages in urban areas are often connected to a lack of electricity (UNMIK 2008).

International experts have suggested that Kosovo's deposits of minerals and lignite could be the foundation of a resource-based industry (i.e., ore concentration and energy production for export), especially since Kosovo possesses the second-largest deposits of lignite in Europe and the fifth-largest in the world. However, the problem is that this type of industry is capital intensive – that is, it needs external investments – while having only limited linkages with the rest of the economy, thus impacting unemployment in a very limited way (Wittkowsky 2003). However, there are numerous other issues that raise questions about the sustainability of such strategies.

Lignite as a Bad Example

At 14,700 megatonnes, Kosovo has the world's fifth-largest proven reserves of lignite, one of the lowest-quality coals. The lignite is distributed across the Kosovo, Dukagjin and Drenica basins, although mining has so far been restricted to the Kosovo basin (World Bank 2008). Lignite reserves are found in two main basins and are currently being mined in Bardh and Mirash opencast mines covering some 9 km^2. The annual lignite production is (as of 2009) around 7 million tonnes. Bardh and Mirash mines supply the thermal power plant 'Kosovo B', and Mirash alone supplies power plant 'Kosovo A'. Lignite is excavated by bucket-wheel excavators and transported by two belt conveyor lines (with a transport capacity per belt of 1,400 tonnes per hour or 33,000 tonnes per day) to the separation plants. The lignite is deposited close to the power plants, in open yards.

The main domestic and independent sources of power are the power plants Kosovo A and B. Both are lignite-fired power plants and have a capacity to produce 800 megawatt hours and 2 times 290 megawatt hours, respectively (World Bank 2008, 100–4). The power plants and the disposal sites are located in the municipality of Obilić some 3 km from the capitol city of Pristina. Kosovo A has five units that were built in two phases (from 1962 to 1964 and from 1970 to 1975). Kosovo B has two units built between 1983 and 1984. It is important to note that the two power plants differ in terms of environmental impact given their differences in age and technology. Namely, the Western-designed Kosovo B is 15 years old and is considered cleaner than the older, Russian-designed Kosovo A, which has one or two units (out of five) operating intermittently and at reduced capacity (REC Field office in Kosovo and Sida 2000).

One big problem is that Kosovo A and B (both thermal power plants) suffer mainly from a lack of maintenance and are not continuously working; for example unit A1 is rarely put into operation; unit A2 has been out of service for a long time because of the failure of the main transformer; unit A3 is presently working up to 125 megawatts because of damages in the boiler that do not allow pressure to reach the optimum level; unit A4 was repaired and is capable of producing 125 megawatts; and unit A5 is no longer in operation because part of its machinery has been used to repair units A2 and A3. During 2006 and 2007 the emergency repair of boilers and capital overhauls of units A3 and A4 was carried out. Works are still ongoing in 2009 with unit A5; they were started in 2007 and were to be completed in 2008. Commercial operation resumed at the beginning of April 2008. Capital overhauls have also been carried out in both units of Kosovo B during 2007. The power generation efficiency is estimated at between 16 and 25 per cent at Kosovo A and at 30 per cent at Kosovo B (World Bank 2008). As a result, most of the country, and particularly Pristina, does not always have enough electricity to supply its growing population and outages are regular. In order to deal with the energy problem, the international community has supported the project to build a larger 2,100 megawatt lignite-fired power plant, 'Kosovo C', which is expected to be completed in 2012 (World Bank 2008).

The plan to continue with the use of lignite-powered thermal power plants has a number of environmental and political shortcomings that ought to be taken into consideration.[18] Uncontrolled gas emissions from power plants consist of a high level of carbon dioxide and dust (Krasniqi 2009). Lignite is transported by open belt conveyer from the mines to the separation plant and is then distributed by internal belt conveyer systems which produce a substantial amount of dust, affecting populated areas in the vicinity of the mine. According to the Wold Bank assessment, a substantial amount of bottom ash and fly ash are produced during the combustion process. Bottom ash and fly ash from Kosovo A (units 1 and 2) are transported to the disposal sites as slurry without re-circulation of the water, leading to water pollution. Fly ash from other units is dry-transported by air to a temporary storage facility at the plants, where it is mixed with water and transported by belt conveyers to the disposal site close to the power plants. Kosovo A has five stacks 100 m high, while Kosovo B has only one stack 182 m high. Dust capture is provided by electrostatic precipitators in all units. There is neither desulphurization nor denitrification in Kosovo A or Kosovo B. The power plants are not provided with wastewater treatment plants. The water necessary for the plant to prepare processed water is taken from the Llapi River flowing near the power plant; when the river flow rate is too low (particularly during summer seasons) water is taken from the Iber-Lepenc canal. The solid residuals from the water treatment are disposed together with the ashes. The installations are badly maintained. At the Kosovo A site, there is a drying plant in which a minor part of lignite is transported and treated to be sold to industrial customers; the drying plant is working at 1 to 2 per cent of its installed capacity.

It has been noted that the heavy industry of Kosovo traditionally paid no attention to its environmental impact. Industry was energy intensive, not very efficient and characterized by air, water and soil contamination because of 'dirty' production (i.e., no filters, untreated waste, leakages, etc.). For example, the total area covered by industrial waste dumps and/or transformed due to opencast mining extends to over 10,000 hectares. So far, no rehabilitation or re-vegetation of the waste dumps has been carried out (REC Field office in Kosovo and Sida 2000). According to the World Bank's recent study, residents of the surrounding settlements of Dardhishte, Hade, Palaj and Grabovac in Poshtem are particularly concerned about health issues that they associate with the mines and power plants. Respiratory diseases are prevalent health complaints in these communities. During project community consultations undertaken by the World Bank, residents have complained about the poor air quality and effects of pollution. During the winter, the smoke combined with the micro-climate conditions generates a dense fog, which causes visibility problems (World Bank 2008).

The Five main health issues affecting communities are respiratory diseases, heart and lung disease, cancer, mental health problems and diabetes. Respiratory diseases are the most prevalent health issue in Hade, Palaj and Grabovac, all of which are in close proximity to the existing Kosovo A and B sites.[19] Cancer was cited as being the most common cause of death for residents of Dardhishte and Sibovac. Twenty-six per cent of all respondents stated that they or members of their household had experienced serious health problems in the last five years (World Bank 2008, 210–30).

Another significant issue to be considered is that the area of the planned new mining field is mainly inhabited by large families who work in agricultural enterprises or independently as subsistence farmers.[20] The production and sale of agricultural products is cited as an important source of income support by local residents. The new mine will acquire approximately 13 per cent of the territory of the municipality of Obilić. This area, planned for mining development, is largely composed of fertile land, while the remaining parts are settlements are roads or forests. Thus, a number of villages in the area will have to resettle prior to the mining in connection with Kosovo C.

According to existing surveys, respondents who saw the possible need to move away from the area due to the project as a problem, were most numerous in Hamidi (43 per cent) and Obilić (39 per cent), and least numerous in Dardhishte (16 per cent). Also, Palaj/Crkvena Vodica and Hade had the greatest number of respondents who said that the introduction of significant limitations on the construction of new or reconstruction of old buildings related to the building of Kosovo C would be a problem (54 and 49 per cent, respectively) (World Bank 2008, 215). However, focus groups, workshops and surveys indicate that most respondents from the villages experience negative impacts from the current power plant on their lives. According to the World Bank, the explicit request coming from the majority of focus group respondents in two settlements, Hade and the Serb community living in Crkvena Vodica, was immediate relocation of all households living in these two villages. Their request comes as a result of current pollution levels, extensive noise coming from current activities at the power plant and insecurity about the future progress of the new mine (World Bank 2008). Yet, as the plans are being made for future resettlements, the authorities will need to find ways to secure alternative sources of income for the displaced population, a very difficult task in a country with persisting unemployment figures of around 40 per cent.

Another complicating issue concerns the use of water as a cooling medium for the turbines in the power plants. As the World Bank has noted, there is the potential for conflicting demands from various water users, i.e., one needs to asses the growing needs for fresh water vis-à-vis the industrial needs. This is an issue of urgency as water stress already occurs, demonstrated by the frequent shortages in summer in the potable water supply to Pristina and other municipalities supplied by the Pristina Water Supply Company (World Bank 2008, 220). In addition, some 30 per cent of water for Obilić and Pristina is supplied from the artificial lake of Gazivoda which is situated in Serb-controlled Northern Kosovo. The Gazivoda's water is used both for drinking and as a coolant in the Kosovo B power station. During the proclamation of Kosovo's independence, Albanian politicians called upon NATO to assume control over Gazivoda as Serb authorities in Northern Kosovo threatened to cut of water supply in response to the Kosovo Albanian proclamation of independence (Quetteville 2007). According to UNMIK officials, the Gazivoda complex is critically important for Kosovo, but the people running the installation are all Serbs from the local area. Yet, without Gazivoda it is questionable whether Kosovo could survive – not just in terms of drinking water, but also in terms of electricity. Nevertheless, all suggestions to put KFOR troops around Gazivoda were strongly rejected by Russia (Quetteville 2007). And while the Serb authorities, under great diplomatic pressure, restrained themselves from cutting off the supply in 2008, the political issue remains unresolved in autumn 2009.

The Kosovo Serb authorities in Northern Kosovo refuse to recognize the authorities of the self-proclaimed Republic of Kosovo and continue to operate according to the laws of Republic of Serbia. In that vein, they do not recognize the Kosovo Energy Company (KEK) and refuse to pay electricity bills to it. In an attempt to rebuff the challenge from the Serb provinces, the KEK decided to cut off all electricity to Northern Kosovo on 17 October 2009. This was done despite the calls from UNMIK for them to restrain themselves from irresponsible behaviour (Beta/B92 News 2009). In a response, the authorities of the Republic of Serbia connected Northern Kosovo to its grid in central Serbia. Also, the Kosovo Serbs continue to rely heavily on the electricity supply from the hydro power plant on Gazivoda. Also, it has been reported that from November 2009 all citizens of Northern Kosovo will be paying electricity bills to Elektroprivreda Srbije (EPS) (Beta/B92 News 2009). According to Kosovo Serb representatives, the issue of the power supply to the north of Kosovo has been politicized, and that the KEK had given an ultimatum to Kosovo Serbs in an attempt to integrate the north into Kosovo's institutions (Beta/B92 News 2009). As the situation stands at the time of writing, KEK employees attempted a takeover of the main transformer station in the village of Valač, but failed as local Serbs put up resistance. The Serb authorities have also threatened to consider countermeasures, and the situation remains tense and unresolved (Beta/B92 News 2009).

Concluding Remarks

This chapter investigates whether contemporary liberal peacebuilding projects have the capacity to address and provide environmental security to the same extent that they offer societal security. There is a theoretical circle describing a dilemma between environmental and societal insecurity, based on their reciprocal negative effects on each other. Thus, attempting to address the security dilemma can cause a new security problem on the other side of the circle. Environmental and societal security need to be addressed simultaneously to reduce the danger of recurring conflicts. This seems best possible by emphasizing sustainable development through the actors involved in the peacebuilding project. The case study of Kosovo and the present peacebuilding projects clearly demonstrate how environmental and societal security issues intertwine in an international attempt to secure durable peace in the province.

One of the key problems for sustainable peacebuilding is the lack of economic alternatives in Kosovo. This leads international and local actors into the dilemma of abandoning environmental issues and preferring options like opencast lignite mines and thermal power plants. Yet, these have a negative impact on the environment, fresh water supply and health of the local population. Furthermore, they go against international efforts to cut carbon emissions in an effort to curb global warming.

Another major problem is that the technology chosen for the economic and energy development of Kosovo depends on the supply of water, which is generally scarce in the region. This increases competition as other demands, like the supply of drinking water, have to be addressed as well. This is particularly problematic as it ties in the unresolved political and legal status of the province. Much of the water supply for both the electric plants and human consumption comes from the Serb-controlled Northern Kosovo. Kosovo Serbs feel threatened by both external and Kosovo Albanian attempts to impose a new Kosovo Albanian state on them, while Kosovo Albanians feel threatened by the prospect that Kosovo Serbs could threaten the water supply for the rest of Kosovo, affecting the availability of fresh water and electricity.

In this regard, the case illustrates how the interplay of the environmental and security dilemmas can lead to new tensions in Kosovo, because the exiting liberal peacebuilding frameworks are unable to address both environmental and societal issues simultaneously. It remains, however, questionable whether and how the energy problems of Kosovo could be solved in a sustainable manner. The easiest way, lignite mining and thermal power plants, has to be questioned as a feasible long-term solution for bringing a sustainable peace. Perhaps a job-creating, longer-term, cleaner energy solution would have to rely on alternative sources. Taking global environmental concern and the regional intentions of the European member states into consideration, such a focus would be more appropriate as a durable solution, and could perhaps provide a more sustainable alternative for building peace in the region.

Notes

1 It is necessary to distinguish between state-building and nation-building: while the first is focusing on the reconstruction of institutions, the latter is driven by the creation or establishment of a common identity. Both processes might follow one another or happen simultaneously, or be in conflict with one another. See Kostić (2007) and Swain and Krampe (2011).
2 Considering the urgency of economic and social problems faced by post-conflict societies, the type of economic policies which are frequently promoted include (a) privatization of the industrial sector, (b) creation of conditions for external investments and (c) urbanization.
3 In contemporary post-conflict settings international and regional organizations and actors; national and local governmental and civil society organizations; and international and local businesses, to just mention a few, are all playing a role in determining the future of the effected societies, actors and institutions.
4 For an comprehensive overview of critical reflections regarding of the liberal peacebuilding model, see Chandler (2009).
5 Both Paris (2004) and Doyle (2002) tend to define durable peace in terms of a peace that lasts long after the departure of external administrators.
6 Sustainable development can be defined as 'development that meets the needs of the present without compromising the ability of future generations to meet their own needs' (World Commission on Environment and Development 1987).
7 One of the strongest migration flows is from rural to urban areas. While in 1950 about 29 per cent of the world's population was living in cities, it was projected that in 2010 for the first time, more than half of the world's population will live in urban areas (3,494,607,000, that is, 50.6 per cent), see UN DESA - Population Division (2009).
8 The war was fought by Serbia, Bulgaria, Montenegro and Greece against Albania which was allied with the Ottoman Empire (Jansen 2008).
9 While in the republics Slovenia, Croatia, Serbia, Bosnia and Herzegovina, Macedonia, and Montenegro were defined as the constituent Yugoslav nations, the provinces Vojvodina and Kosovo had demographic majorities which were made up of the national minorities, Hungarians and Albanians, i.e., the groups whose motherlands were outside Yugoslavia. Thus, Vojvodina and Kosovo were defined as provinces which although part of the Yugoslav federation were formally under the SR Serbia.
10 The declaration of independence of Kosovo is a continuation of the separation of many Yugoslavian Republics, but compared to Bosnia and Croatia, which received international attention and recognition, the situation in Kosovo was mainly unrecognized. See Jansen (2008).
11 The Federal Republic of Yugoslavia consisted of Serbia and Montenegro.
12 In other words, as KFOR failed in its task to guarantee the security of Kosovo Serbs, most of its population left Kosovo.

13 There are still no exact numbers about battle-related death. For detailed information about battle-related death during the Kosovo War, see Uppsala Conflict Data Program (2010).
14 For more, see UNSC (1999).
15 The alleged pretext was the drowning of an Albanian boy who was supposedly chased into the River Ibar by a Serbian mob.
16 Remittances from Kosovo Albanians living abroad account for an estimated 13 per cent of GDP, and foreign assistance for around 34 per cent of GDP; see European Commission (2010).
17 About 80 per cent of all Kosovo municipalities have suffered from water shortages in the last five years, in 70 per cent of which, the situation has became more severe in recent years; see UNMIK (2008).
18 For the broader analysis, see World Bank (2008).
19 However, one should note that 38 per cent of all respondents are smokers.
20 Approximately 60 per cent of the population living in the region are farmers (World Bank 2008).

References

Adams, W. M. 2006. 'The Future of Sustainability: Re-thinking Environment and Development in the Twenty-First Century'. Report of the IUCN Renowned Thinkers Meeting, 29–31 January 2006. IUCN, The World Conservation Union.

Atwood, J. Brian. 1994. 'Nation-Building and Crisis Prevention in the Post-Cold War World'. *The Brown Journal of World Affairs* 2(1): 11–18.

Bakic-Hayden, M. 2004. 'National Memory as Narrative Memory: The Case of Kosovo'. In Maria Todorova (ed.), *National Memory in Southeastern Europe*. London: Hurst & Co.

Bar-Tal, D. 2000. *Shared Beliefs in a Society, Social Psycological Analysis*. Thousand Oaks, London and New Delhi: Sage.

Barnett, Jon and W. Neil Adger. 2007. 'Climate Change, Human Security and Violent Conflict. *Political Geography* 26(6): 639–55.

Beck, U. 1987. *Risikogesellschaft* [Risk Society]. Frankfurt am Main: Suhrkamp.

———. 2007. *Weltrisikogesellschaft: Auf der Suche nach der verlorenen Sicherheit* [World Risk Society: Searching for the Lost Security]. Frankfurt am Main: Suhrkamp.

Beta/B92 News. 2009. 'Belgrade Restores Power to Northern Kosovo'. *Beta/B92 News*, 20 October.

Brown, O., A. Hammill and R. McLeman. 2007. 'Climate Change as the New Security Threat: Implications for Africa'. *International Affairs* 83(6): 1141–54.

Chandler, David. 2006. *Empire in Denial: The Politics of State-Building*. London: Pluto Press.

———. 2009. What do we do when we critique liberalism? The uncritical critique of 'liberal peace'. Paper presented at the Millennium Conference: After Liberalism, London School of Economics, 17–18 October.

Chesterman, S. 2005. *You, the People: The United Nations, Transitional Administration, and State-building*. New York: Oxford University Press.

Conca, Ken. 2006. Environmental peacebuilding in war-torn societies: Some lessons from the UN Environmental Programme's experience with post-conflict environmental assessment. Paper presented at the 47th Annual Convention of the International Studies Assosication, San Diego, 22–5 March.

Conca, Ken and Geoffrey D. Dabelko (eds). 2002. *Environmental Peacemaking*. Washington, Baltimore and London: Woodrow Wilson Center Press and The Johns Hopkins University Press.

Detraz, Nicole and Michele M. Betsill. 2009. 'Climate Change and Environmental Security: For Whom the Discourse Shifts'. *International Studies Perspectives* 10(3): 303–20.

Deutsch, K. 1966. *Nationalism and Social Communication: Inquiry into the Foundations of Nationality*. Cambridge, MA: MIT Press.

Doyle, Michael W. 2002. 'Strategy and Transnational Authority'. In S. Stedman, D. Rothchild and E. Cousens (eds), *Ending Civil Wars: The Implementation of Peace Agreements*. Boulder, CO: Lynne Rienner.

European Commission. 2010. 'International Economic Issues'. Brussels: Economic and Financial Affairs.

Gellner, Ernest. 1983. *Nations and Nationalism*. Oxford: Blackwell.

Gleditsch, Nils Petter. 1998. 'Armed Conflict and the Environment: A Critique of the Literature'. *Journal of Peace Research* 35(3): 381–400.

Graeger, Nina. 1996. 'Environmental Security?' *Journal of Peace Research* 33(1): 109–16.

Harbom, Lotta and Peter Wallensteen. 2005. 'Armed Conflict and Its International Dimensions, 1946–2004'. *Journal of Peace Research* 42(5): 623.

Hobsbawm, E. J. 1990. *Nations and Nationalism since 1780*. Cambridge: Cambridge University Press.

Homer-Dixon, T. F. and J. Blitt. 1998. *Ecoviolence: Links Among Environment, Population and Security*. Rowman & Littlefield.

Hroch, M. 1993. 'From National Movement to the Fully-formed Nation: The Nation-Building Process in Europe. *New Left Review* 198: 3–20.

Jahn, Beate. 2007a. 'The Tragedy of Liberal Diplomacy: Democratisation, Intervention, Statebuilding (Part I)'. *Journal of Intervention and Statebuilding* 1(1): 87–106.

———. 2007b. 'The Tragedy of Liberal Diplomacy: Democratisation, Intervention, Statebuilding (Part II)'. *Journal of Intervention and Statebuilding* 1(2): 211–29.

Jansen, G. R. 2008. *Albanians and Serbs in Kosovo: An Abbreviated History: An Opening for the Islamic Jihad in Europe*. Online: http://lamar.colostate.edu/~grjan/kosovohistory.html (accessed 1 December 2008).

Jeremić, Vuk. 2008. 'EULEX Acceptable, with Conditions'. *Tanjug*, 2 November.

Kaldor, M. 2006. *New and Old Wars: Organized Violence in a Global Era*. Polity Press.

Kaufman, J. E. 2002. *NATO and the Former Yugoslavia: Crisis, Conflict, and the Atlantic Alliance*. Lanham: Rowman & Littlefield.

Kostić, R. 2007. *Ambivalent Peace: External Peacebuilding, Threatened Identity and Reconciliation in Bosnia and Herzegovina*. Uppsala: Department of Peace and Conflict Research, Uppsala University.

———. 2008. 'Nation-building as an Instrument of Peace? Exploring Local Attitudes Towards International Nation-building and Reconciliation in Bosnia and Herzegovina'. *Civil Wars* 10(4): 386–414.

Krasniqi, Ibrahim. 2009. 'Modern Technologies in New Lignite Power-plant in Kosovo and their Impact on Energy and Environmental Security in Energy and Environment: Challenges to Security'. In Stephen Stec and Barry Besnik (eds), *Energy and Environmental Challanges to Security*. Springer.

Lee, James R. 2009. *Climate Change and Armed Conflict: Hot and Cold Wars*. New York: Routledge.

MacGinty, Roger. 2006. *No War, No Peace: The Rejuvenation of Stalled Peace Processes and Peace Accords*. Basingstoke: Palgrave Macmillan.

Magnusson, Kjell. 1999. 'Rambouilletavtalet. Texten, förhandlingarna, bakgrunden' [The Rambouillet Accords. Text, Negotiations, Background]. Uppsala.

Mandelbaum, M. 2002. *The Ideas that Conquered the World: Peace, Democracy and Free Markets in the Twenty-first Century*. New York: Public Affairs.

Matthew, Richard, Oli Brown and David Jensen. 2008. *From Conflict to Peacebuilding: The Role of Natural Resources and the Environment*. Nairobi: United Nations Environment Programme.

Nordas, Ragnhild and Nils Petter Gleditsch. 2007. 'Climate Change and Conflict'. *Political Geography* 26(6): 627–38.

O'Neill, W. G. 2002. *Kosovo: An Unfinished Peace*. Boulder, CO: Lynne Rienner.

Ohlsson, Leif. 2000. 'Livelihood Conflicts. Linking Poverty and Environment as Causes of Conflict'. Environmental Policy Unit. Stockholm: Sida.

Ott, Konrad. 2003. 'The Case for Strong Sustainability'. In Konrad Ott and P. Thapa (eds), *Greifswald's Environmental Ethics*, 59–64. Greifswald: Steinbecker Verlag Ulrich Rose.

Paris, Roland. 2004. *At War's End: Building Peace after Civil Conflict*. New York: Cambridge University Press.

Percival, Val and Thomas Homer-Dixon. 1998. 'Environmental Scarcity and Violent Conflict: The Case of South Africa'. *Journal of Peace Research* 35(3): 279–98.

Phillips, Leigh. 2009. 'Violent Protests against EU Mission in Kosovo'. *EU Observer*, 26 August.

Quetteville, Harry de. 2007. 'UN Cites Serb Threat to Kosovo's Energy'. *Daily Telegraph*, 18 December.

Raleigh, Clionadh and Henrik Urdal. 2007. 'Climate Change, Environmental Degradation and Armed Conflict'. *Political Geography* 26(6): 674–94.

REC Field office in Kosovo and Sida. 2000. 'Strategic Environmental Analysis of Kosovo'. Pristina.

Reuters. 2008. *Main Kosovo Indicators* Online: www.reuters.com

Richmond, Oliver P. 2007. 'The Problem of Peace: Understanding the "Liberal Peace"'. *Conflict, Security, Development* 6(3): 291–314.

Rivkin, A. 1969. *Nation-Building in Africa: Problems and Prospects*. New Jersey: Rutgers University Press.

Roe, P. 1999. 'The Intrastate Security Dilemma: Ethnic Conflict as a "Tragedy"?' *Journal of Peace Research* 36(2): 183–202.

_____. 2005. *Ethnic Violence and the Societal Security Dilemma*. New York: Routledge.

Swain, Ashok. 1993. *Environment and Conflict: Analysing the Developing World*. Uppsala: Department of Peace and Conflict Research, Uppsala University.

_____. 1996. 'Environmental Migration and Conflict Dynamics: Focus on Developing Regions'. *Third World Quarterly* 17(5): 959–73.

_____. 1997. 'Environmental Security: Cleaning the Concept'. *Peace and Security* 29: 31–8.

Swain, Ashok and Florian Krampe. 2011. 'Stability and Sustainability in Peace Building Systems and Warfare Ecology'. In G. E. Machlis, T. Hanson, Z. Špirić and J. E. McKendry (eds), *Warfare Ecology: Synthesis, Priorities and Policy Implications for Peace and Security*. NATO Science for Peace and Security. Springer.

Tanjug. 2008. 'Thaci Wants Unconditional EULEX Deployment'. Tanjug, 4 November.

Trombetta, M. J. 2008. 'Environmental Security and Climate Change: Analysing the Discourse'. *Cambridge Review of International Affairs* 21(4): 585–602.

Ullman, Richard H. 1983. 'Redefining Security'. *International Security* 8(1): 129–53.

UN DESA Population Division. 2009. *World Population Prospects: The 2006 Revision and World Urbanization Prospects: The 2007 Revision*. Online: http://esa.un.org/unup UN General Assembly. 2005. *2005 World Summit Outcome (A/60/L.1)*. New York: United Nations.

UN Peacebuilding Commission. 2008. 'Synthesis Report and Summary of Discussions: Key Insights, Principles, Good Practices and Emerging Lessons in Peacebuilding'. New York.

UNSC. 1999. United Nations Security Council Resolution 1244. Adopted by the Security Council at its 4011th meeting, 10 June 1999. New York.

UNMIK. 2008. 'Water Supply Issue in Kosovo'. Pristina: United Nations Interim Administration Mission in Kosovo.

Uppsala Conflict Data Program. 2010. *UCDP Database*. Online: www.ucdp.uu.se/database (accessed 15 November 2010).

Wæver, Ole. 1993. *Identity, Migration, and the New Security Agenda in Europe*. New York: St. Martin's Press.

Wallensteen, Peter and Ashok Swain. 1997. 'Environment, Conflict and Cooperation'. In vol. 2 of D. Brune, D.V. Chapman, M. D. Gwynne and J. M. Pacyna (eds), *The Global Environment. Science, Technology and Management*, 691–704. Weinheim: VCH Verlagsgemeinschaft mbH.

Wittkowsky, Andreas. 2003. 'Next Steps for Kosovo's Medium-Term Economic Development'. United Nations Interim Administration Mission in Kosovo.

World Bank. 2008. 'Strategic Environmental and Energy Assessment: Kosovo C.'. World Bank.

World Commission on Environment and Development. 1987. 'Report of the World Commission on Environment and Development. Our Common Future'. A/43/427. New York: UN General Assembly.

Chapter 4

THE RISING CHINA AND MAINTAINING THE INTERNATIONAL ORDER: SOME REFLECTIONS[1]

Zou Keyuan

Introduction

With the rise of China, people around the world are wondering whether this rising power would change the existing international order, including the legal order. Economically, China is now one of the most significant trading countries, and its economy threatens to overtake the largest economy in the world (that of the US) in the not too distant future. Most importantly, its consistent two-digit growth rate in the last three decades has also made the Chinese economy the fastest-growing economy in the world. Since its accession to the World Trade Organization (WTO), its GDP has grown more than 10 per cent annually.[2] China has also been one of the largest recipients of foreign direct investment (FDI) inflow for many years,[3] and is certainly going to stay that way for many years to come. Demographically, China is the largest country in the world with a total population of over 1.3 billion. Politically, China is one of the five permanent members of the United Nations Security Council. It is common perception that the trend of China's ascendancy will continue well into the foreseeable future. The world political landscape will inevitably change in response to the rise of China, and so will the global order. Not surprisingly, it has been predicted that: 'Asia will alter the rules of the globalizing process' and 'Asian giants may use the power of their markets to set industry standards, rather than adopting those promoted by Western nations or international standards bodies' (National Intelligence Council 2004, 28). While these comments are often made in the context of the economic ascendancy of Asian nations in the globalized world, Asian influences over the international order will probably exceed those that Asian nations have made in international economic institutions such as the WTO. Indeed, both China and India have realized their importance and indispensability in the development of the future international order, as they have stated clearly that 'they are two major powers in the formulation of the multi-polar international order and their simultaneous developments will exert an active influence over the future international system' (Sino-Indian 2006).

The current international order is a result of the order reconstructed after World War II with the establishment of the United Nations (UN) and its associated specialized intergovernmental organizations. The UN was established in 1946 with the fundamental purpose of maintaining world peace and security, and of promoting the development of friendly relations and cooperation among nations. The UN also plays an active role in international law-making. The Sixth Committee of the UN General Assembly is the primary forum for the consideration of legal questions in the General Assembly where every UN member can have representation. The International Law Commission, established in 1948, is a special organ within the UN with the mandate of progressive development and codification of international law, and has so far adopted a number of important international conventions including the four Geneva Law of the Sea Conventions,[4] the 1997 Convention on the Law of Non-navigational Uses of International Watercourses, and the 1963 Vienna Convention on Diplomatic Relations, to name a few. Furthermore, the UN sponsors diplomatic conferences to make international treaties. For example, the Third United Nations Conference on the Law of the Sea (1973–82) adopted the United Nations Convention on the Law of the Sea (LOS Convention), which has been regarded as a 'constitution for the oceans' (Koh 1983, xxviii).

As of November 2009, there were 192 members of the UN including China. Being a UN member, China is bound by the Charter of the United Nations, including its legal principles, and must carry out its corresponding obligations.[5]

The UN Charter set out seven fundamental principles guiding international relations including (1) the principle of the sovereign equality of all its members; (2) the commitment of all members to fulfil in good faith the obligations assumed by them in accordance with the charter; (3) the settlement of international disputes by peaceful means; (4) refraining in international relations from the threat or use of force against the territorial integrity or political independence of any state, or in any other manner inconsistent with the purposes of the UN; (5) giving the UN every assistance in any action it takes in accordance with the charter; (6) ensuring that non-UN members act in accordance with the UN principles so far as may be necessary for the maintenance of international peace and security; and (7) non-intervention in matters which are essentially within the domestic jurisdiction of any state (UN Charter 1945, art. 2).

These principles, except for principles five and six which are specifically designed for the United Nations itself, are basic principles of international law. For UN members, these principles are regarded as superior to others, as the UN Charter clearly provides that 'in the event of a conflict between the obligations of the Members of the United Nations under the present Charter and their obligations under any other international agreement, their obligations under the present Charter shall prevail' (UN Charter 1945, art. 103). This means that in the event that there is such a conflict between UN obligations and obligations under any bilateral and/or multilateral agreement signed by China, China should fulfil the UN obligations first.

China's Reform and Integration into the World Community

The People's Republic of China (PRC) was founded in 1949 and celebrated its 60th anniversary on 1 October 2009. For the last six decades, China has experienced many great events. Despite some man-made disasters such as the Cultural Revolution (1966–76), China turned over a new leaf after 1978 when it began its economic reform and open door policy. With the fast pace of its economic development, China has tried very hard to integrate itself into the world community. During the 1980s China shifted from its previous ideologically focused foreign policy to a more pragmatic one. It turned its attention to national interests by creating a peaceful environment for its economic development. After Deng Xiaoping's trip to South China in 1992, China began to shift its centrally planned economy to a market economy. As a result, the country became more open to the outside world.

A most significant development in China's integration into the world was its decision to join the WTO. China applied for the restoration of its membership in GATT (the General Agreement on Tariffs and Trade) as early as 1986, but it was only on 31 December 2001 that China became a formal member of the WTO. By entering into the organization, China was obliged to meet the legal requirements set forth by the WTO and implement the legal principles such as transparency and accountability. Internally, it needed to bring its relevant laws and regulations in line with those of the WTO, particularly those governing economic activities such as foreign investment, foreign trade, and banking. Externally, China signed more international treaties to further open itself to the outside world. According to one Chinese source in 2005, China was a party to 273 multilateral international treaties, out of which 239 became applicable to China only after 1979 (Xue 2005, 136).

In addition to joining the UN and its specialized agencies such as the International Maritime Organization and the International Labour Organization, China has become a member of other international intergovernmental organizations. With the arrival of the 1990s, China's involvement in international affairs became even more active. While still sticking to the Five Principles of Peaceful Co-existence – i.e., mutual respect for sovereignty and territorial integrity, non-aggression, non-interference in internal affairs, equality and mutual benefit, and peaceful co-existence[6] – China began to carry out a foreign policy with a global outlook. As China claims, the Five Principles constituted the basis for China to have established and developed diplomatic relations with 165 countries; carry out trade, economic, scientific, technological and cultural exchanges and cooperation with over 200 countries and regions; resolve the boundary issues with neighbours; and maintain peace and stability in its surrounding areas (Wen 2004). During the 11th Meeting of Diplomatic Envoys held from 17 to 20 July 2009, President Hu Jintao made an important speech indicating the direction of China's new foreign policy. While emphasizing the theme of peace and development and the overall strategy of China's diplomacy,[7] Hu for the first time put forward 'area-specific diplomacy' concerning global issues such as the financial crisis, energy security and climate change in order to increase China's say in world affairs (Chen 2009).

Acting as an Emerging Global Power

It is generally recognized that China has increased its influence in decision-making for world affairs and may play a greater role in future.

Maintaining International Peace and Security

Peace and security is a top priority of the UN agenda, particularly for its Security Council which has the mandate of maintaining world peace and security.

Fighting against Terrorism and Other International Crimes

After the 9/11 terrorist attacks, terrorism has become a global threat. As the UN Security Council declared, any acts of terrorism 'constitute a threat to international peace and security', and called all UN members to fight against it (UNSC 2001). China is also threatened by terrorism, and as a permanent member of the UN Security Council, it is obliged to support the implementation of such a mandate. China expressed its position at the UN forum as follows:

> Terrorism is the common enemy of humankind. All forms of terrorism,
> no matter when or where they occur and whatever their motivation,

should be combated with determination. The international fight against terrorism should be consistent with the principles and purposes of the Charter of the United Nations and underlying norms and principles of international law. It should address both the symptoms and root causes of the phenomenon while avoiding the use of double standards.[8]

In response to the call from the UN to combat terrorism, China has joined the international treaties on terrorism sponsored by the UN, including: the 1973 Convention on the Prevention and Punishment of Crimes against Internationally Protected Persons, including Diplomatic Agents (5 August 1987); the 1979 International Convention against the Taking of Hostages (26 January 1993); the 1988 Convention for the Suppression on Unlawful Acts Against the Safety of Maritime Navigation (1 March 1992); the 1997 International Convention for the Suppression of Terrorist Bombings (13 November 2001); and the 1999 International Convention for the Suppression of the Financing of Terrorism (20 April 2002). China also signed the 2005 International Convention for the Suppression of Acts of Nuclear Terrorism on 14 September 2005, but has not yet ratified it.

In order to fight against terrorism within the country and in its surrounding areas, China initiated and together with Russia and other Central Asian countries established the Shanghai Cooperation Organization (SCO) on 15 June 2001. At the same time the Shanghai Convention against Terrorism, Separatism and Extremism was adopted by the SCO member states. They pledged to exert every effort to maintain regional security and cooperate closely to fight against terrorism (Shanghai 2001). In 2002, the SCO members signed the Agreement on Establishing an Anti-Terrorist Regional Office. The SCO also cooperates with other countries for its anti-terrorism purpose; for example, SCO members together with Afghanistan adopted a Plan of Action to Combat Terrorism, Drugs Smuggling and Organized Crimes in 2009 (China MFA 2009d). Apart from joining in multilateral and regional arrangements against terrorism, China has also since 2002 signed bilateral cooperative agreements on the fight against terrorism with its neighbouring countries including Kazakhstan, Kyrgyzstan, Pakistan, Turkmenistan, Tajikistan and Uzbekistan.

Concerned with the potential threat of the acquisition of nuclear weapons by terrorists, China expressed its position that: 'Nuclear terrorism is a severe challenge faced by the international community. China always firmly opposes terrorism of any forms [sic], including nuclear terrorism, and upholds the purpose and objective of the Global Initiative to Combat Nuclear Terrorism' (China MFA 2009b).[9] As one of the initial partners of the Global Initiative, China has taken part in all its meetings and activities, and has taken effective measures to realize its objectives. In December 2007, for example, China and the US held a workshop on radiation emergency response in Beijing under the framework of the initiative (China MFA 2009b).

Another international crime related to terrorism is piracy. Although piracy can be traced back to the early days of human civilization, it has been revived since the 1990s and become an international concern. Piratical incidents occur in the South China Sea as well as in the Malacca Straits, threatening the safety of navigation and seafarers' property and lives. Since most of its imported oil is transported from Middle East to Chinese ports through the Malacca Straits and the South China Sea, China regards the sea routes located in these sea areas as critical to its energy security as well as its maritime security. For the purpose of maintaining maritime security in the region, China has cooperated closely with other countries to combat piracy at sea.

International law has established an obligation on states to cooperate in the suppression of piracy and grants states certain rights to seize pirate ships and criminals. According to the LOS Convention, all the countries have the obligation to 'cooperate to the fullest possible extent in the repression of piracy on the high seas or in any other place outside the jurisdiction of any State' (LOS Convention 1982, art. 100), and 'every State may seize a pirate ship or aircraft, or a ship or aircraft taken by piracy and under the control of pirates, and arrest the persons and seize the property on board' (LOS Convention 1982, article 105). China, as a signatory to the LOS Convention, is obliged to cooperate with other countries in the fight against piracy and exercise its law enforcement. While there is no 'crime of piracy' in the Chinese legal system, Chinese courts have tried several piracy cases in accordance with its criminal law.[10]

For regional maritime security, China and another 15 Asian countries – including 10 member states of the Association of Southeast Asian Nations (ASEAN), Bangladesh, India, Japan, Sri Lanka and South Korea – signed the Regional Cooperation Agreement on Combating Piracy and Armed Robbery against Ships in Asia (ReCAAP) in 2004. The agreement obliges contracting states to (a) prevent and suppress piracy and armed robbery against ships; (b) arrest pirates or persons who have committed armed robbery against ships; (c) seize ships or aircraft used for committing piracy or armed robbery against ships; and (d) rescue victim ships and victims of piracy or armed robbery against ships (ReCAAP 2007, art. 3). For cooperation purposes, the contracting parties should endeavour to render mutual legal assistance as well as extradition for piracy suppression and punishment. The agreement entered into force in September 2006 and the Information Sharing Centre (ReCAAP ISC) was accordingly established in Singapore.[11]

In June 2008 the UN Security Council passed a resolution on combating acts of piracy and armed robbery off Somalia's coast (UNSC 2008). When the Security Council expressed its grave concern about piracy and armed robbery against vessels in the waters off the coast of Somalia, it stated that such piratical incidents exacerbated the situation in Somalia 'which continues to constitute a threat to international peace and security in the region' (UNSC 2008). Therefore, the Security Council decided to act under Chapter VII of the Charter of the United Nations. It urges 'states whose naval vessels and military aircraft operate on the high seas and airspace off the coast of Somalia to be vigilant to acts of piracy and armed robbery' and

> to cooperate with each other, with the IMO [International Maritime Organization] and, as appropriate, with the relevant regional organizations in connection with, and share information about, acts of piracy and armed robbery in the territorial waters and on the high seas off the coast of Somalia, and to render assistance to vessels threatened by or under attack by pirates or armed robbers, in accordance with relevant international law. (UNSC 2008)

More significantly, the Security Council decided that

> for a period of six months from the date of this resolution, States cooperating with the TFG [Transitional Federal Government of Somalia] in the fight against piracy and armed robbery at sea off the coast of Somalia, for which advance notification has been provided by the TFG to the Secretary General, may: (a) enter the territorial waters of Somalia for the purpose of repressing acts of piracy and armed robbery at sea, in a manner consistent with such action permitted on the high seas with respect to piracy under relevant international law; and (b) use, within the territorial waters of Somalia, in a manner consistent with action permitted on the high seas with respect to piracy under relevant international law, all necessary means to repress acts of piracy and armed robbery. (UNSC 2008)

It is the first time that the UN Security Council had placed the issue of sea piracy on its agenda and treated it as a matter threatening international peace and security. According to the UN Charter, UN member states are obliged to implement UNSC resolutions as it is stipulated that UN members agree to accept and carry out the decisions of the Security Council in accordance with the charter (UN Charter 1945, art. 25). China, for the first time ever, sent warships to the areas around Somalia contributing to the international efforts to crack down on Somali piracy. The first Chinese naval fleet consisting of two destroyers and a large supply vessel completed its first escort mission on 6 January 2009 for four Chinese merchant ships (China Daily 2009). As expressed by the Foreign Ministry spokesman on 20 December 2008, the task of the Chinese navy is to protect Chinese ships and crew on board as well as ships carrying humanitarian relief materials provided by international organizations including the World Food Programme, in strict compliance with the UN Security Council resolutions and international law (Zhu 2009, 511). According to a circular issued by the Ministry of Transport, Chinese merchant vessels including those from Hong Kong, Macao and Taiwan can apply for naval escort when entering the Gulf of Aden and the Somali maritime vicinity through the Chinese Association of Shipowners (Circular 2008).

While China has sent its naval forces to the Somali waters to escort merchant vessels sailing into that area in order to prevent potential attacks by Somali pirates, China is dubious of another scheme for maritime security initiated by the United States – the Proliferation Security Initiative (PSI).

The PSI is an effort to consider possible collective measures among the participating countries, in accordance with national legal authorities and relevant international laws and frameworks, in order to prevent the proliferation of weapons of mass destruction (WMDs), missiles and related materials that pose threats to the peace and stability of the international community. It was first put forward by then American president George W. Bush on 31 May 2003 during a speech in Krakow, Poland (Bush 2003). The PSI is administered by the 'core group' countries, which consisted of eleven countries – Japan, US, UK, Italy, the Netherlands, Australia, France, Germany, Spain, Poland and Portugal – which were later joined by four others – Canada, Singapore, Russia and Norway.

China's feeling towards PSI is complex. As the spokesperson of the Chinese Foreign Ministry expressed in 2005, China agreed with the objective of PSI, but doubted whether the PSI by taking coercive interception at sea would go beyond the reign of international law (China MFA 2004). China's position on PSI is clearly summarized on its Foreign Ministry website as follows:

China understands the concern of PSI participants over the proliferation of WMD [sic] and their means of delivery and shares the non-proliferation goal of the PSI. China supports the cooperation among the PSI participants within the framework of international law. However, the international community including China remains concerned about the possibility that the interdiction activities taken by PSI participants might go beyond the international law. (China MFA 2009e)

While China has concerns about PSI, it does not close its door to PSI, stating that 'we would like to exchange views with relevant countries on this point' (China MFA 2004). On the other hand, given the right reasons, China might support military interdiction or naval inspection in the future. China's naval presence in the Somali waters is at least indirect evidence to support the objectives of PSI.

Apart from its efforts and commitments to international obligations to combat terrorism and piracy, China has become involved in other endeavours initiated by the UN. China has become a party to other international treaties against crimes of international concern including the 2000 UN Convention against Transnational Organised Crimes (2001) and the 2003 UN Convention against Corruption (2006).

Humanitarian Intervention

As China firmly sticks to its Five Principles of Peaceful Coexistence, it has pledged not to intervene in the internal affairs of any other countries and opposes such intervention by other big powers.

After the Chinese embassy bombing incident happened in Belgrade in May 1999, China sharply criticized the Western approach to humanitarian intervention. To China, 'international intervention does not have a legitimate political basis and violates the Charter of the United Nations and international law'; it is designed to 'promote the interests of an intervening state rather than those of the people of the target state', and thus it 'causes more harm than good' (Jia 2003, 22–3). Some Chinese legal scholars even blame the US for causing a crisis in international humanitarian law by its invasion of Iraq and its maltreatment of Iraqi prisoners of war, as the fact that the US does not bear any liability in international law puts international humanitarian law in a dilemma (Mu and Wang 2005, 61–3). However, in recent years there has been some subtle change in China's position regarding sovereignty and humanitarian intervention. Intervention may be considered acceptable 'under exceptional circumstances, such as when a national government practices racist policies, kills its people en masse, or collapses only to leave slaughtered people in its wake' (Jia 2003, 31). Furthermore, China supports international intervention sponsored and/or authorized by the UN and has sent troops to join UN Peacekeeping Forces in recent years.

China's White Paper on National Defence in 2008 recorded China's involvement in UN peacekeeping activities:

Since 1990 the PLA [People's Liberation Army] has sent 11,063 military personnel/time to participate in 18 UN peacekeeping operations.

Eight lost their lives on duty. As of the end of November 2008, China had 1,949 military peacekeeping personnel serving in nine UN mission areas and the UN Department of Peacekeeping Operations. Among them, there were 88 military observers and staff officers; 175 engineering troops and 43 medical personnel for the United Nations Organization Mission in the Democratic Republic of the Congo (UNMONUC); 275 engineering troops, 240 transportation troops and 43 medical personnel for the United Nations Mission in Liberia (UNMIL); 275 engineering troops, 100 transportation troops and 60 medical personnel for the United Nations Mission in the Sudan (UNMIS); 275 engineering troops and 60 medical personnel for the United Nations Interim Force in Lebanon (UNIFIL); and 315 engineering troops for the African Union/United Nations Hybrid Operation in Darfur (UNAMID). Since 2000, China has sent 1,379 peacekeeping policemen/time to seven mission areas. At present, 208 Chinese peacekeeping policemen are in Liberia, Kosovo, Haiti, Sudan and East Timor for peacekeeping operations. (White Paper 2009)

It is clear that China now does not totally oppose third party intervention and supports such intervention under the authorization of the UN. Sending warships to the Somali waters can also be seen as an intervention for the purpose of maintaining peace and security in that region.

A related issue is the newly emerged concept of the 'responsibility to protect'. It is argued that: 'State sovereignty implies responsibility, and the primary responsibility for the protection of its people lies with the state itself. Where a population is suffering serious harm, as a result of internal war, insurgency, repression or state failure, and the state in question is unwilling or unable to halt or avert it, the principle of non-intervention yields to the international responsibility to protect' (ICISS 2001, xi). China has reservations about this concept. In the discussion on the issue of Protection of Persons in the Event of Disasters at the 6th Committee of the 63rd Session of the UN General Assembly on 3 November 2008, the Chinese delegation considered it unhelpful to introduce this concept into the area of disaster relief since there were controversies as to its connotation and applicability (Chinese Mission 2008c). According to a Chinese legal scholar and senior diplomat, the concept may suggest that: 'Any state could step in and take action against another state when the situation, in its opinion, constitutes a violation of human rights in the territory of the latter state. Obviously, this would be even more intrusive than the traditional theory of humanitarian intervention' and 'any unduly broad and unlimited claim for responsibility to protect may only result in undesired intervention' (Xue 2007, 90).

International Disarmament

Regarding arms control and disarmament, in particular nuclear disarmament, China has so far taken several steps both internally and externally. As a nuclear-weapon state, China acceded to the Treaty on the Non-Proliferation of Nuclear Weapons (NPT) in 1992. It declared a moratorium on nuclear weapon test explosions on 30 July 1996 and signed the Comprehensive Nuclear-Test-Ban Treaty (CTBT) on 24 September 1996. China has called for all nuclear-weapon states to take the following measures to further promote the nuclear disarmament process:

– An international legal instrument on the complete prohibition and thorough destruction of nuclear weapons should be concluded at an early date.
– Nuclear disarmament should be a just and reasonable process of gradual reduction toward a downward balance. The two countries possessing the largest nuclear arsenals bear special and primary responsibilities for nuclear disarmament. They should earnestly comply with the treaties already concluded on reduction of nuclear weapons and further reduce their nuclear arsenals in a verifiable and irreversible manner so as to create conditions for achieving the ultimate goal of complete and thorough nuclear disarmament.
– Before the goal of complete prohibition and thorough destruction of nuclear weapons is achieved, nuclear-weapon states should commit themselves to no first use of nuclear weapons and undertake unconditionally not to use or threaten to use nuclear weapons against non-nuclear-weapon states or nuclear-weapon-free zones.
– Nuclear-weapon states should abandon the policies of nuclear deterrence based on the first use of nuclear weapons and reduce the role of nuclear weapons in their national security.
– Nuclear disarmament measures, including intermediate measures, should follow the guidelines of maintaining global strategic balance and stability and undiminished security for all. (China MFA 2009c)

In order to prevent the proliferation of nuclear and biological/chemical armaments, China took an internal step to enact a series of laws and regulations including the Regulations on Control of Nuclear Export (1997), the Regulations on Export Control of Nuclear Dual-Use Items and Related Technologies (1998), the Regulations on Export Control of Dual-Use Biological Agents and Related Equipment and Technologies (2002), the Regulations on the Administration of Controlled Chemicals (1995), the Measures on Export Control of Certain Chemicals and Related Equipment and Technologies

(2002), the Regulations on Export Control of Missiles and Missile-related Items and Technologies (2002), and the Regulations on the Administration of Arms Export (1997). China amended the Regulations on the Control of Nuclear Exports in November 2006, the Regulations on the Control of Dual-use Nuclear Items and Related Technologies Exports in January 2007 and its Control List in July 2007. The Chinese government updated the 'Catalogue of Dual-use Items and Technologies Subject to Import and Export License' in December 2008.

Externally, China has held regular arms control and non-proliferation consultations with a dozen countries and the EU, and non-proliferation dialogues with NATO. China has joined the Zangger Committee and the Nuclear Suppliers Group (NSG) and keeps in contact and exchanges with the Missile Technology Control Regime (MTCR), the Wassenaar Arrangement and the Australia Group (China MFA 2009a).

Additionally, China acceded to the 1972 Convention on the Prohibition of the Development, Production and Stockpiling of Bacteriological (Biological) and Toxin Weapons and on Their Destruction (BWC) in 1984 and ratified the 1993 Convention on the Prohibition of the Development, Production, Stockpiling and Use of Chemical Weapons and on Their Destruction (CWC) in 1997.

Promoting a New Legal Order for Environment and Economy

International Climate Change Regime

China is the country with the highest level of emissions having surpassed the US. The Netherlands Environmental Assessment Agency (MNP) found that 'China topped the list of CO_2 emitting countries, surpassing the USA by an estimated 8%' in 2006 (Chinese CO_2 2007). For that reason, China is very important as a key player in the establishment and implementation of the new global climate change regime. However, as a developing country, China has no compulsory duty to reduce greenhouse gas emissions under the existing international climate change regime, though domestically China has made a series of reduction efforts.

In June 2007 China published a long – and perhaps most significant – document, the 'National Climate Change Programme' (NDRC 2007). Following it, China established the Leading Work Group on Climate Change Adaptation, Energy Saving and Emission Reduction with Premier Wen Jiabao as head. The group held its first meeting on 9 July 2007 in Beijing, requesting its member units to strictly implement the Programme (Action Plan) and the Work Programme on Comprehensive Energy Saving and

Emission Reduction; it also deliberated over documents on the departmental division of labour in the implementation of the two programmes (*People's Daily* 2007a, 1). On 29 October 2008, China released its first white paper on climate change – 'China's Policies and Actions for Addressing Climate Change'. In this document, China pledged to strive 'to control and mitigate the emission of greenhouse gases and continuously enhance the capability of adapting itself to climate change' as 'a responsible developing country' (Chinese Mission 2008b).

In response to international pressure China emphasizes the principle of 'common but differentiated responsibilities', as recently expounded by the Chinese Foreign Minister Yang, that the basic principles embodied in the United Nations Framework Convention on Climate Change (UNFCCC) and Kyoto Protocol – including the 'common but differentiated responsibilities' – constitute the basis for climate change cooperation in the world community. As he said, global climate change is caused mainly by long-term historical emissions as well as the current high per capita emissions of the developed countries. Thus, after 2012 the developed countries should continue to bear the emission reduction obligation and to strengthen technology transfer to developing countries. Historic greenhouse gas emissions from developing countries are small, and their current emissions belong to survival and development emissions; thus the means and methods for them to adapt to global climate change is to draw up and implement sustainable development strategies as well as participating in Clean Development Mechanism (CDM) cooperation.[12] In Hu Jintao's speech to the UN Summit on Climate Change in September 2009, he promised that China would fight for a significant cut in carbon emissions including the following measures: (a) to intensify efforts to conserve energy and improve energy efficiency through a cut of carbon dioxide emissions per unit of GDP from the 2005 level by a notable margin by 2020; (b) to develop renewable energy and nuclear energy by increasing the share of non-fossil fuels in primary energy consumption to around 15 per cent by 2020; (c) to increase forest carbon sinks through the increase from the 2005 levels of forest coverage by 40 million hectares and forest stock volume by 1.3 billion cubic meters by 2020; and (d) to develop green economy, low-carbon economy and circular economy, and enhance research, development and dissemination of climate-friendly technologies (Hu Jintao 2009).

As we know, the limits set forth in the Kyoto Protocol will expire in 2012. For that reason, the world community needs to negotiate and formulate a new deal for the emission reduction scheme. It is unknown whether China would accept a compulsory duty of reduction under the post-Kyoto regime which is currently to be negotiated among the world community members. China has realized that there are difficulties for developing countries in the climate negotiations since they 'lack the necessary technical capacity and human resources to back up their negotiations' (Xue 2007, 88).

Nevertheless, China has already begun its cooperation with other countries in this respect. China and the EU issued the Joint Declaration on Climate Change which established the bilateral Partnership on Climate Change at the EU-China Summit in Beijing on 5 September 2005. In March 2006, China and the EU held their first Bilateral Consultation on Climate Change under the framework of the China-EU Partnership on Climate Change, extensively exchanging views on their respective climate policies and international negotiation. On the second consultation held in Beijing in October 2006, the two sides adopted the China-EU Partnership on Climate Change Rolling Work Plan which became the basis for the Sino-European cooperation (China MFA, 2006b). According to the Work Plan, the China-EU Partnership is 'to provide a mechanism for the EU and China to take a strategic view of shared climate change objectives, and to take an overview of, give direction to and develop bilateral cooperation activities that contribute to these objectives' (China MFA, 2006b).

In October 2009 China and India signed the Agreement on Cooperation in Response to Climate Change to officially establish partnership in response to climate change. Based on the agreement, a bilateral working group is to be established to hold annual meetings and to exchange views and information on issues relating to international climate negotiations and domestic policies and measures. Clearly the big developing countries like China and India have received tremendous pressure from the international community requesting them to bear more responsibility in finding a more effective way to combat climate change. This agreement to some extent can be regarded as an alliance agreement to take a concerted step in response to international pressures.

Towards a New International Economic Order

The current international economic order is characterized by the post–World War II arrangements at Bretton Woods with the establishment of the institutions such as the World Bank, the International Monetary Fund (IMF) and the GATT (later the WTO). China joined the WTO in 2001 and agreed to open its domestic market and revise its relevant domestic laws in compliance with WTO norms and rules. China is also a member state of the World Bank and the IMF.

However, China still advocates the establishment of a new international economic order. During the UN Millennium Summit held in September 2000, then Chinese president Jiang Zemin made an important speech expounding China's position to establish a just and reasonable international political and economic order. China is concerned with the serious imbalance in economic development between North and South. China's status as a market economy is not yet recognized by the US and EU, and China's voting rights in the IMF are only 3.72 per cent, behind Canada, France, Germany, Italy, Japan, UK, and far behind the US which holds 16.83 per cent, a de facto decisive veto power in the decision-making of the organization. With the increase of its economic power, China began to complain about the voting rights in such international financial organizations as the IMF. In its Position Paper at the 63rd Session of the United Nations General Assembly in 2008, China called for an international financial reform which

> should focus on reflecting the changes in the world economic pattern, increasing the say and representation of developing countries, reducing their risks in participating in economic globalization and shaping an institutional framework that is conducive to sound and sustainable development of the world economy. (Chinese Mission 2008a)

During the G20 Summit held in September 2009, China expressed several of its concerns about how to monitor speculative trans-border transfer of assets; to increase the voice of developing countries in the IMF and other international organizations; and to enhance the role of special drawing rights in the IMF so as to decrease world dependence on the US dollar. It is reasonably assumed that 'if a new Bretton Woods conference were held today, it is clear that delegates would design a different IMF, because both attitudes and circumstances are fundamentally different that they were at the end of World War II' (Dodge and Murray 2006, 364).

The focal shift from G8 to G20 in managing world economic affairs is a remarkable change in the North–South relations. It reflects the fact that developing countries, particularly the big ones, can now play an indispensable role in world economic management. The world economic organizations have agreed to increase voting rights of the developing countries to above 5 per cent in the IMF and 3 per cent in the World Bank (*People's Daily* 2009b, 3), though the increase is not big enough. On the other hand, it is to be noted that the international regime for economic and financial arrangements still remains in the hands of the Western countries led by the US, and the existing international economic order will not be fundamentally changed in the foreseeable future.

The other pillar in China's advocacy for the establishment of a new international economic order is South–South cooperation as a key element in China's foreign policy. During the Third UN Conference on the Law of the Sea (1973–82), China usually sided with the G77 regarding the establishment of a new maritime order, now enshrined in the 1982 LOS Convention.

In recent years with the increase of its economic power, China has also increased its financial aid to developing countries. In September 2009, China adopted six important measures to assist developing countries in agriculture, food aid, education and training, health, sanitation, energy, debt relief and zero tariffs. According to these measures, China will increase agricultural technical model centres to 30 and experts and technicians to 2,000; contribute $30 million to the Food and Agriculture Organization (FAO) to set up a trust fund to enhance the agricultural productivity of developing countries; export grain to developing countries suffering from food shortage; increase scholarships to 10,000 to students from developing countries studying in China and train 1,500 principals and teachers from Africa; remit due debts owed by the least developed countries and give them a zero-tariff treatment for 95 per cent of their products exported to China; and help to develop and utilize clean energy by building 100 clean energy projects in developing countries in the next five years (*People's Daily* 2009a, 3).

Approaches to International Dispute Settlement

The peaceful settlement of international disputes is a well-established and universally accepted principle of international law. The Charter of the United Nations requires UN member states to solve their disputes in a peaceful manner through 'negotiation, enquiry, mediation, conciliation, arbitration, judicial settlement, resort to regional agencies or arrangements, or other peaceful means of their own choice' (UN Charter 1945, art. 33).

China always prefers bilateral negotiations for dispute settlement between states. In the international arena, China has advocated negotiation as the most practical means of dispute resolution. In practice, China has resolved a number of bilateral disputes (over borders, nationality, etc.) with other countries by negotiation and consultation. The hand-over of Hong Kong and Macao was a result of negotiations between China and the UK and Portugal, respectively. The 'one country, two systems' model for the settlement of international disputes can be regarded as a Chinese contribution to international law.

As for judicial means, however, China's attitude is very reserved. So far there has been no dispute between China and another state submitted to the International Court of Justice (ICJ) or other international tribunals. During the Sino-India border conflict in 1962, China refused India's proposal to submit the border dispute to arbitration by stating that

the Sino-India border dispute is an important matter concerning the sovereignty of the two countries, and the vast size of more than 100,000 square kilometres of territories. It is self-evident that it can only be resolved through direct bilateral negotiations. It is never possible to seek a settlement from any form of international arbitration. (Gao 1995, 611–12)

However, after the 1980s, China changed its policy towards international arbitration by consenting to arbitration in treaties China concluded and acceded to, but confined it only to economic, trade, scientific, transport, environment and health areas.

In recent years there are signs to show that China is more and more comfortable with arbitration mechanisms. This can be reflected in the conclusion of the 'Agreement on Dispute Settlement Mechanism of the Framework Agreement on Comprehensive Economic Co-Operation Between the Association of Southeast Asian Nations and the People's Republic of China' on 29 November 2004 (Agreement 2004). It came into force on 1 January 2005 and designates three means of dispute settlement in international law as its working mechanisms including consultation, conciliation or mediation, and arbitration. If the consultations could not solve the dispute within the prescribed time limit, the complaining party may make a written request to the party complained against to appoint an arbitral tribunal. The signing of this agreement is hailed as having 'far-reaching significance' even beyond the China–ASEAN relations as it is 'a sign of the changing attitude of the Chinese government towards international dispute settlement methods', and it is the first time that China 'had signed such a special and detailed agreement with other states or international organizations' (Zeng 2006, 54–5). China also uses the dispute settlement mechanism of the WTO; from 2002 to 2009 China submitted six complaints to and responded to 17 cases before the WTO Dispute Settlement Body.[13]

Some international conventions require the contracting states to accept compulsory judicial dispute settlement procedures. For instance, the LOS Convention obliges its states parties to select at least one of the compulsory procedures: special arbitration, arbitration, ICJ and the International Tribunal for the Law of the Sea (ITLOS). Upon the ratification of the convention, China did not state which mechanism it had accepted. Under such circumstances, China was deemed to have accepted the mechanism of arbitration.[14] On 7 September 2006, China made a declaration under Article 298 of the LOS Convention to exclude certain disputes with other countries (such as those concerning maritime delimitation, territorial disputes or military use of the ocean) from the jurisdiction of an international judiciary or arbitration (China MFA 2006a).

Meanwhile, China's attitude towards the role of international courts in dispute settlement is even more passive. China has usually made a reservation about the clause of judicial settlement by the ICJ in the treaties to which China is a party. On 5 September 1972, China declared that it did not recognize the statement of the former Chinese government on Acceptance of the Compulsory Jurisdiction of the International Court of Justice. In fact, China refused to settle any dispute with other countries through the ICJ (Gao 1995, 612). On the other hand, as a UN Security Council member, China has nominated judges of Chinese nationality to the ICJ as well as to other international courts. Due to the fact that the judges are usually from the West, China is doubtful about the impartiality and justice the international judiciary can maintain.

It is true that once the countries concerned submit their dispute to the international court for settlement, the judicial proceedings are beyond their control and they cannot be sure whether the final judicial ruling will be favourable or unfavourable for them. Since China lacks high quality judicial personnel, it is difficult for China to assess a possible judicial result before its submission. The simplest way is to reject the jurisdiction of the ICJ or international tribunals. While China's passive attitude is understandable since China only began its judicial reform in the 1990s and has attempted very earnestly to professionalize its judicial team, such blunt rejection could bring harm to China's improved image of being a responsible big country as it has claimed.

Conclusion

China's influence in world affairs is evident. Take Hu Jintao's recent trip to the United States in September 2009 as an example, it was the first time that a Chinese leader participated in so many summit meetings and it was also the first time that a Chinese head of state attended the meetings of the UN General Assembly for last 60 years. China's increased role can also be seen from its contributions to the UN membership fees, which increased from less than 1 per cent in 2000 to about 3.2 per cent in 2010 (see Table 4.1).

Although the rising China is no doubt playing a more active and on some occasions a more critical role in international affairs, it is not yet a global power which can direct the course of change in the international order. It is sure that China is a maintainer and supporter of the existing international legal order, rather than a challenger – and much less an overthrower – of the current order. This can be seen from Chinese statements made at the UN forum, that the authority of the UN Charter must be maintained and that 'defending the authority of the Charter is essential for maintaining the rule of law at the international level' (Duan 2007, 187). It is commonly perceived that China is generally satisfied with its current position in the existing international system. In this context, G. John Ikenberry (2008, 23–37) is correct that China 'is increasingly working within, rather than outside of, the Western order', though his term 'Western order' is problematic since the current international order is obviously not purely Western.

Working within the current international order does not mean that China is contented with the international system in all aspects. Since its rise as an economic power, China has demanded a bigger say in international financial and banking affairs as discussed above, and has even attempted to call for the establishment of a new international economic order. However, as is evident from Chinese history, China's foreign policy is subject to changes and adjustments from time to time. If it is accommodated satisfactorily in the current international economic order, it is very likely that China will drop its call for a new order and live within the existing one.

While China demands a bigger and more vigorous say, it should consider whether it is ready to assume more responsibilities in world affairs. It has rightly been pointed out that

> power comes with responsibility. China's rising status in the international community provides it with greater influence and benefits; at the same time, it demands greater responsibility, including demonstration that it complies with international rules and practices that, in turn, may impose constraints and costs. (Yuan 2008, 66)

China faces a real challenge in assuming its global responsibilities. There may be several benchmarks against which to observe China's readiness in this regard.

Firstly, in the area of international human rights, it remains to be seen whether China ratifies the 1966 UN Covenant on Political and Civil Rights. China signed this international treaty in 1998, but there has been a delay of more than a decade in its ratification. The application of this covenant to China will surely bring about a big improvement of China's human rights record.

Secondly, in the area of the global environmental regime, it remains to be seen whether China will make concessions in the climate negotiations and accept some mandatory emission reduction targets. As the largest carbon emission country in the world now, China's position is critical to the formulation of the post-Kyoto regime for climate change.

Thirdly, in the area of international criminal justice, it remains to be seen whether China will ratify the 1998 Rome Statute of the International Criminal Court and participate in the activities of that court. Although China attended the negotiations and adoption of the Rome Statute, it maintains

Table 4.1. China's contributing payments to the
United Nations

Year	Percentage
2000	0.995
2001–2003	1.54
2004–2006	2.053
2007–2009	2.667
2010–2012	3.189

Source: Prepared by the author, based on Liu (2009).

reservations on the statute and has only sent observers to the meetings of the court, which was established in 2002. A related issue is whether China will change its attitude towards the ICJ. If China can use this most authoritative international judicial organ in the near future, such a positive change would be just the right response to the call from the UN to realize rule of law at both international and national levels.

Chinese president Hu Jintao put forward the idea of constructing 'a harmonious world' at the Asian-African Summit in Jakarta in April 2005 and reiterated it at the UN headquarters in September later that year. There is no doubt that a harmonious world needs a well-articulated order. It is an imperative task for China to promote and develop the international order so as to build the idealistic, harmonious world it has advocated. In this respect, China's contributions are indispensable and will benefit both the world community and its continuing rise.

Notes

1 This study is based on the author's keynote speech at the 2009 Conference of the Swedish Network of Peace, Conflict and Development Research: 'The Development and Security Nexus'. Hosted by the Center for Pacific Asia Studies (CPAS), Department of Oriental Languages, Stockholm University, Stockholm, Sweden on 6–7 November 2009.

2 More precisely, 9.1 per cent, 10 per cent, 10.1 per cent, 10.4 per cent, 11.6 per cent, 13 per cent and 9 per cent in the successive years from 2002 to 2008. See Invest in China (2007) and NBSC (2009).

3 See annual World Investment Reports published by the World Bank, e.g., 'United Nations Conference on Trade and Development', *World Investment Report 2008*, online: https://www.wbginvestmentclimate.org/toolkits/investment-generation-toolkit/upload/wir2008overview.pdf (accessed 19 October 2011).

4 These include the Convention on the High Seas, the Convention on the Continental Shelf, the Convention on Fishing and Conservation of the Living Resources of the High Seas, and the Convention on the Territorial Sea and the Contiguous Zone, all

adopted on 29 April 1958. However, a new and more comprehensive convention was adopted in 1982, and that is the UN Convention on the Law of the Sea. Though the four Geneva Conventions on the Law of the Sea are not obsolete, the 1982 Convention should prevail, as between States Parties, over the Geneva Conventions.

5 As Article 4 of the UN Charter provides, UN membership is open to those nations which accept the obligations contained in the Charter and are able and willing to carry out these obligations.

6 These principles first appeared in the Agreement on Trade and Intercourse between the Tibet Region of China and India signed by China and India on 29 April 1954. Text is available in United Nations Treaty Series (1958) 299:59.

7 Four strategies of China's diplomacy, which were set forth at the 10th Meeting of Diplomatic Envoys in 2004, include: big powers are key, surrounding areas are a priority, developing countries are a base and multilateralism is an important forum.

8 S/PV.5053 (8 October 2004), p. 8; compiled in Chen (2005, 287–8).

9 This initiative was formulated in 2006.

10 For details, see Zou (2009, 341–44).

11 For details, see the ReCAAP (2007).

12 See *People's Daily* (2007b, 3). For reference on the principle of 'common but differentiated responsibilities', see Halvorssen (2007, 247–65).

13 For details, see WTO (2009).

14 Article 287 (3) of the LOS Convention provides that: 'A State Party, which is a party to a dispute not covered by a declaration in force, shall be deemed to have accepted arbitration in accordance with Annex VII'.

References

ASEAN. 2004. 'Agreement on Dispute Settlement Mechanism of the Framework Agreement on Comprehensive Economic Co-Operation Between the Association of Southeast Asian Nations and the People's Republic of China'. 29 November 2004. Association of Southeast Asian Nations. Online: http://www.aseansec.org/16636.htm (accessed 21 April 2008).

China Daily. 2009. 'Navy Escorts 4 Vessels Off Somalia on Day One'. 7 January 2009. China Daily. Online: http://www.chinadaily.com.cn/china/2009-01/07/content_7373037.htm (accessed 20 January 2009).

Chen Qiang. 2005. 'Chinese Practice in Public International Law: 2004 (I)'. *Chinese Journal of International Law* 4(1): 285–96.

Chen Xiangyang. 2009. 'Direction of China's Grand Diplomacy in the New Time'. 28 July 2009. *Outlook News Weekly*. Online: http://www.zaobao.com.sg/wencui/2009/07/liaowang090728g.shtml (accessed 28 July 2009).

China MFA. 2004. Foreign Ministry Spokesperson Zhang Qiyue's press conference on 4 November 2004. Ministry of Foreign Affairs, the People's Republic of China. Online: http://www.fmprc.gov.cn/eng/xwfw/s2510/t169072.htm (accessed 29 October 2005).

_____. 2006a. 'China's Declaration in Accordance with Article 298 of the United Nations Convention on the Law of the Sea'. 7 September 2006. Ministry of Foreign Affairs, the People's Republic of China. Online: http://www.fmprc.gov.cn/chn/wjb/zzjg/tyfls/wjzdtyflgz/zgzhyflydgz/t270754.htm (accessed 6 February 2007).

_____. 2006b. 'China-EU Partnership on Climate Change Rolling Work Plan'. 16 October 2006. Ministry of Foreign Affairs, the People's Republic of China.

Online: http://www.fmprc.gov.cn/eng/wjb/zzjg/tyfls/tfsxw/t283051.htm (accessed 25 July 2007).

_____. 2009a. 'China and Multilateral Export Control Mechanisms'. 10 August 2009. Ministry of Foreign Affairs, the People's Republic of China. Online: http://www.fmprc. gov.cn/eng/wjb/zzjg/jks/kjlc/fkswt/t410728.htm (accessed 19 October 2009).

_____. 2009b. 'Global Initiative to Combat Nuclear Terrorism'. 10 August 2009. Ministry of Foreign Affairs, the People's Republic of China. Online: http://www.fmprc.gov.cn/ eng/wjb/zzjg/jks/kjlc/hwt/t410731.htm (accessed 19 October 2009).

_____. 2009c. 'Nuclear Disarmament'. 10 August 2009. Ministry of Foreign Affairs, the People's Republic of China. Online: http://www.fmprc.gov.cn/eng/wjb/zzjg/jks/ kjlc/hwt/t410746.htm (accessed 26 October 2009).

_____. 2009d. 'Plan of Action to Combat Terrorism, Drugs Smuggling and Organized Crimes in 2009'. Ministry of Foreign Affairs, the People's Republic of China. Online: http://www.fmprc.gov.cn/chn/pds/ziliao/1179/t554797.htm (accessed 20 October 2009).

_____. 2009e. 'The Proliferation Security Initiative'. 10 August 2009. Ministry of Foreign Affairs, the People's Republic of China. Online: http://www.fmprc.gov.cn/eng/wjb/ zzjg/jks/kjlc/fkswt/t410725.htm (accessed 19 October 2009).

Chinese CO2. 2007. Chinese CO2 emissions in perspective: intercomparison of CO2 emissions of countries and burden sharing of emission reductions'. (Press release, 22 June 2007). Climate Change Info Mailing List. (No longer available online).

Chinese Mission. 2008a. 'Position Paper of the People's Republic of China at The 63rd Session of the United Nations General Assembly'. 16 September. Permanent Mission of the People's Republic of China to the UN. Online: http://www.china-un.org/eng/ ldhy/63rd_unga/t512988.htm (accessed 10 January 2011).

_____. 2008b. 'China's Policies and Actions for Addressing Climate Change'. Information Office of the State Council. October 2008. Permanent Mission of the People's Republic of China to the UN. Online: http://www.china-un.org/eng/hyyfy/ t521513.htm (accessed 29 October 2009).

_____. 2008c. 'Statement by H.E. Ambassador Liu Zhenmin, Deputy Permanent Representative of China to the UN, at the Sixth Committee of the 63rd Session of the UN General Assembly, on Item 75: Report of the International Law Commission on the Work of its 60th Session – Part Three'. 3 November 2008. Permanent Mission of the People's Republic of China to the UN. Online: http://www.china-un.org/eng/ hyyfy/t520980.htm (accessed 29 October 2009).

Circular. 2008. 'Circular on the Matters concerning the Application of Chinese Vessels for Escort in the Gulf of Aden and Somali Sea Area'. 24 December 2008. In *People's Daily*. Online: http://military.people.com.cn/GB/1076/142153/8638178.html (accessed 7 January 2009).

Dodge, David and John Murray. 2006. 'The Evolving International Monetary Order and the Need for an Evolving IMF'. *Global Governance* 12(4): 361–71.

Duan Jielong. 2007. 'Statement on the Rule of Law at the National and International Levels'. *Chinese Journal of International Law* 6(1): 185–8.

Gao Yanping. 1995. 'International Dispute Settlement' [in Chinese]. In Wang Tieya (ed.), *International Law*, 568–613. Beijing: Law Press.

Halvorssen, Anita M. 2007. 'Climate Change Regime — Amending the Kyoto Protocol to Include Annex C and the Annex D Mitigation Fund'. *Colorado Journal of International Environmental Law and Policy* 18(2): 247–65.

ICISS. 2001. *The Responsibility to Protect: Report of the International Commission on Intervention and State Sovereignty*. Ottawa: International Commission on Intervention and State Sovereignty. Online: http://responsibilitytoprotect.org/ICISS%20Report.pdf (accessed 29 September 2011).

Ikenberry, G. John. 2008. 'The Rise of China and the Future of the West'. *Foreign Affairs* 87(1): 23–37.

Invest in China. 2007. '2006 National Economic and Social Development Statistical Announcement'. 30 April 2007. Invest in China, Investment Promotion Agency of MOFCOM. Online: http://www.fdi.gov.cn/pub/FDI/zgjj/tzhj/hgjj/gmjjyshfz/t20070430_77928.htm (accessed 8 July 2007).

Hu Jintao. 2009. 'President Hu Jintao's Speech at the Opening Plenary Session of the United Nations Summit on Climate Change'. 23 September 2009. Permanent Mission of the People's Republic of China to the UN. Online: http://www.china-un.org/eng/zt/hu2009summit/t606111.htm (accessed 2 November 2009).

Jia Qingguo. 2003. 'China'. In Watanabe Koji (ed.), *Humanitarian Intervention. The Evolving Asian* Debate, 19–32. Tokyo: Japan Center for International Exchange.

Koh, Tommy T. B. 1983. 'A Constitution for the Oceans'. (Remarks by Tommy T.B. Koh, of Singapore, President of the Third United Nations Conference on the Law of the Sea). In *The Law of the Sea: Official Text of the United Nations Convention on the Law of the Sea with Annexes and Index; Final Act of the Third United Nations Conference on the Law of the Sea; Introductory Material on the Convention and the Conference*. New York: United Nations.

Liu. 2009. 'Statement by Ambassador LIU Zhenmin on Scale of Assessments at the Fifth Committee of the 64th Session of the UNGA'. 5 October 2009. Permanent Mission of the People's Republic of China to the UN. Online: http://www.china-un.org/eng/hyyfy/t618422.htm (accessed 10 January 2011).

LOS Convention. 1982. 'United Nations Convention on the Law of the Sea'. United Nations. Online: http://www.un.org/Depts/los/convention_agreements/texts/unclos/unclos_e.pdf (accessed 20 December 2010).

Mu Yaping and Wang Yue. 2005. 'Crisis of International Humanitarian Law' [in Chinese]. *Journal of Political Science and Law* 22(2): 61–3.

National Intelligence Council. 2004. *Mapping the Global Future*. Report of the National Intelligence Council's 2020 Project. US National Intelligence Council. December.

NBSC. 2009. '2008 National Economic and Social Development Statistical Announcement' [in Chinese]. 26 February 2009. National Bureau of Statistics of China. Online: http://www.stats.gov.cn/tjgb/ndtjgb/qgndtjgb/t20090226_402540710.htm (accessed 5 July 2009).

NDRC. 2007. 'National Climate Change Programme'. prepared under the auspices of the National Development and Reform Commission. June 2007. National Development and Reform Commission, People's Republic of China. Online: http://en.ndrc.gov.cn/newsrelease/P020070604561191006823.pdf (accessed 22 July 2007).

People's Daily. 2007a. 'Wen Jiabao Chaired the First Meeting of the National Leading Work Group on Climate Change Adaptation, Energy Saving and Emission Reduction' [in Chinese]. *People's Daily*, 10 July: 1.

———. 2007b. 'Our Foreign Minister Expounds China's Position on the Issues of North Korean Nuclear and Climate Change' [in Chinese]. *People's Daily*, 2 August: 3.

———. 2009a. 'China Has Made Six Measures to Help Developing Countries' [in Chinese]. *People's Daily*, 22 September: 3.

_____. 2009b. 'World Bank and IMF Reiterate the Increase of Rights to Say for the Developing Countries' [in Chinese]. *People's Daily*, 6 October: 3.

ReCAAP. 2007. 'The Regional Cooperation Agreement on Combating Piracy and Armed Robbery against Ships in Asia'. (ReCAAP). Online: http://www.recaap.org/Portals/0/docs/About%20ReCAAP%20ISC/ReCAAP%20Agreement.pdf (accessed 19 October 2011).

Bush, George W. 2003. 'Remarks by the President to the People of Poland, Wawel Royal Castle, Krakow, Poland, May 31, 2003'. The White House. Online: http://www.whitehouse.gov/news/releases/2003/05/20030531-3.html (accessed 29 October 2005).

Shanghai Declaration. 2001. 'Declaration on the Establishment of the Shanghai Cooperation Organization'. Ministry of Foreign Affairs, the People's Republic of China. Online: http://www.fmprc.gov.cn/chn/pds/ziliao/1179/t4636.htm (accessed 20 October 2009).

Sino-India. 2006. 'Sino-India Joint Declaration'. 21 November 2006, New Delhi. Online: http://www.peacehall.com/news/gb/intl/2006/11/200611220052.shtml (accessed 22 November 2006).

UN Charter. 1945. *Charter of the United Nations*. United Nations. Online: http://www.un.org/en/documents/charter (accessed: 17 June 2008).

UNSC. 2001. United Nations Security Council Resolution 1373. 28 September 2001. S/RES/1373 (2001). United Nations. Online: http://www.un.org/Docs/scres/2001/sc2001.htm (accessed 10 January 2011).

_____. 2008. United Nations Security Council Resolution 1816. 2 June 2008. S/RES/1816 (2008). United Nations. Online: http://www.un.org/Docs/sc/unsc_resolutions08.htm (accessed 30 October 2008).

Wen Jiabao. 2004. 'Carrying Forward the Five Principles of Peaceful Coexistence in the Promotion of Peace and Development'. (Speech at the Rally Commemorating the 50th Anniversary of the Five Principles of Peaceful Coexistence, 28 June 2004). Ministry of Foreign Affairs, the People's Republic of China. Online: http://www.fmprc.gov.cn/eng/topics/seminaronfiveprinciples/t140777.htm (accessed 17 June 2008).

White Paper. 2009. 'White Paper on National Defense Published'. China.org.cn. Online: http://www.china.org.cn/government/central_government/2009-01/20/content_17155577_15.htm (accessed 26 October 2009).

WTO. 2009. 'Disputes by Country/Territory'. World Trade Organization. Online: http://www.wto.org/english/tratop_e/dispu_e/dispu_by_country_e.htm (accessed 30 October 2009).

Yuan, Jing-dong. 2008. 'The New Player in the Game: China, Arms Control, and Multilateralism'. In Guoguang Wu and Helen Lansdowne (eds), *China Turns to Multilateralism: Foreign Policy and Regional Security*, 51–72. London: Routledge.

Xue Hanqin. 2005. 'China's Open Policy and International Law'. *Chinese Journal of International Law* 4(1): 133–9.

_____. 2007. 'Chinese Observations on International Law'. *Chinese Journal of International Law* 6(1): 83–93.

Zeng Lingliang. 2006. 'ASEAN-China Relations: An International Law Perspective'. In John Wong, Zou Keyuan and Zeng Huaqun (eds), *China-ASEAN Relations: Economic and Legal Dimensions*, 33–55. Singapore: World Scientific.

Zhu Lijiang. 2009. 'Chinese Practice in Public International Law: 2008'. *Chinese Journal of International Law* 8(2): 493–551.

Zou Keyuan. 2009. 'New Developments in the International Law of Piracy'. *Chinese Journal of International Law* 8(2): 323–45.

Chapter 5

NON-USE OF FORCE, NON-INTERFERENCE AND SECURITY: THE CASE OF PACIFIC ASIA[1]

Ramses Amer

Purpose and Structure

The main purpose of the study is to investigate the linkages between some key dimensions of the Charter of the United Nations (UN) and the issue of security. This is done through an examination of two key norms of the charter: the prohibition of the threat or use of force in inter-state relations and the principle of non-interference in the internal affairs of states. The empirical application of these principles and their impact on regional security in the Pacific Asia region is examined through the study of the foreign policy of China and through the study of the principles governing the Association of Southeast Asian Nations (ASEAN). This is motivated by the fact that both China and ASEAN put strong emphasis on non-use of force in inter-state relations and on the principle of non-interference in the internal affairs of other states.

The study is structured in the following way. First, the key norms of the UN Charter relating the prohibition of the threat or use of force in inter-state relations and the principle of non-interference in the internal affairs of states are identified, followed by a presentation of the debate that they have generated. Second, the empirical application of these principles and their impact on regional security is in the Pacific Asia is examined through the foreign policy of China and the principles governing ASEAN. Third, the study is concluded by a broader discussion on the links between non-use of force, non-interference and security.

Key Norms of the Charter of the United Nations

Introduction

The two key clauses in the UN Charter that will be examined in the context of study are Article 2(4) relating to the prohibition of the threat or use of force, and Article 2(7) relating to the principle of non-interference in the internal affairs of member states. It is essential to look at what is literally stated in the two clauses.

Article 2(4) reads as follows:

> All Members shall refrain in their international relations from the threat or use of force against the territorial integrity or political independence of any state, or any other manner inconsistent with the purposes of the United Nations. (UN Charter 1945, art. 2)

Article 2(7) reads as follows:

> Nothing contained in the present Charter shall authorize the United Nations to intervene in matters which are essentially within the domestic jurisdiction of any state or shall require the Members to submit such matters to settlement under the present Charter; but this principle shall not prejudice the application of enforcement measures under Chapter VII. (UN Charter 1945, art. 2)

Article 2(4)[2]

The scholarly debate among international lawyers pertaining to the provisions of Article 2(4) of the charter displays considerable controversy as to how these provisions should be interpreted. This controversy can partly be ascribed to the wording of Article 2(4). The wording of this article, and for that matter the whole charter, was based on considerations and decisions among the original member states of the UN. It is the result of a series of compromises reached by these states after having reconciled each other's views. Consequently, the text is in some instances 'ambiguous' and 'unclear'.[3]

In the context of Article 2(4) the term 'force' has caused debate among scholars. A restrictive interpretation argues that 'force' refers to the threat or use of 'armed force' against the territorial integrity or political independence of a state. An extensive interpretation argues that 'force' refers to any 'action' or to any threat of 'action' initiated against the territorial integrity or political independence of a state.

The restrictive interpretation prohibits the threat or the use of 'armed force' but does not, in principle, prohibit an economic embargo directed at another state. Scholars adhering to such a restrictive interpretation usually point to the fact that forms of intervention in the internal affairs of a state other than 'armed force' are addressed by the provisions of Article 2(7) and the principle of non-interference. The extensive interpretation implies that the threat or the use of 'force' in whatever form in inter-state relations is prohibited, i.e., 'any' kind of interference which is not acceptable to the government of the target state.

Another point of disagreement is how the wording in Article 2(4), 'against the territorial integrity or political independence of any state', should be interpreted. A restrictive interpretation argues that only the threat or use of force that directly affects the territorial integrity or the political independence of a state is encompassed by the prohibition. An extensive interpretation centres on the argument that not only the threat or the use of force affecting the territorial integrity or the political independence of a state, but also any action against the political authority of a state is encompassed by the prohibition.

The interpretation of the wording in Article 2(4), 'against the territorial integrity or political independence of any state', has a bearing on the kind of inter-state behaviour that would fall under the phenomenon known as 'use of force'. Nevertheless, despite the divergent interpretations of Article 2(4) there is a consensus that this article provides a general prohibition of the threat or use of armed force in inter-state relations.

The scholarly interpretations of the provisions of Article 2(4) which restrict the use of 'force' in inter-state relations have their weaknesses.[4]

A restrictive interpretation of the term 'force' would not prohibit economic and political activities that could undermine the political stability in a state or create hardship for its population. Furthermore, it would not prohibit foreign interference in a state as long as such interference does not involve direct engagement of troops in the affected state.

A restrictive interpretation of the wording 'against the territorial integrity or political independence of any state' would imply that foreign interventions short of armed attacks would not be prohibited, notwithstanding their effects on the political structure of the target state.

To conclude, it is important to note that there are two exceptions to the prohibition of the threat or use of force: first, the inherent right of individual or collective self-defence if an armed attack occurs against a member of the UN as stated in Article 51 of the Charter of the United Nations (UN Charter 1945, art. 51);[5] and second, enforcement measures under Chapter VII of the charter.

Article 2(7)

In the case of Article 2(7) the interpretation of the wording has not led to the same debate as in the case of Article 2(4). It is generally acknowledged that Article 2(7) should be interpreted as stipulating that non-interference in the internal affairs of another state is not permitted. This is even reflected in the debate relating to Article 2(4) as exemplified above. The relationship between the principle of non-interference and the application of enforcement measures under Chapter VII is explicit in the wording of Article 2(7).

The debate in which Article 2(7) and the principle of non-interference has become an integral part is the one relating to 'non-intervention' versus 'humanitarian', 'pro-democratic', and 'pro–self-determination'[6] interventions. In fact, the principle of non-interference plays a central role in the 'non-intervention' line of argumentation. While proponents of 'humanitarian', 'pro-democratic' and 'pro–self-determination' interventions tend to minimize its importance and even the relevance of the principle of non-interference.[7]

In the post–Cold War era, these three types of intervention in particular have gained renewed 'popularity' and are at times almost looked upon as a remedy for all evils in the developing world.

Pro-democratic, pro–self-determination and humanitarian interventions can be carried out in response to human suffering of a twofold nature, the first involving the basic human rights of the citizens of the target state, and the second relating to the treatment of citizens of the intervening state residing in the target state. Both aspects could play a role in the same case of foreign intervention.

Proponents of humanitarian intervention are not unaware of the problems associated with such interventions and the risk of abuse.[8] By looking at the criteria listed by some proponents, one can see that the requirement of 'disinterestedness'[9] on the part of the intervening state is of particular concern. Some proponents do not address this requirement in a satisfactory manner since they accept that an intervening state can have motives other than purely humanitarian ones, as long as the humanitarian aspects are the most important. Such an approach complicates matters, and it raises the question of how it would be possible for third parties to assess the relative importance of the different motives put forward by the intervening state. Furthermore, to allow the intervening actor to have motives other than purely humanitarian ones would create a situation in which an intervening state may deliberately argue in humanitarian terms while carrying out the intervention for other reasons. Finally, by allowing other motives for an intervention one might legitimate any kind of interventionary behaviour as long as it is carried out under the banner of 'humanitarianism'.

If this line of argumentation is pursued then it is necessary to discuss if the intervening state claims of acting for humanitarian purposes and whether this can be accepted at face value. It is argued here that this it not necessarily the case. In fact, in order to properly address the issue of foreign interventions claimed to protect human rights, it is necessary to bear in mind that an intervention can be presented and portrayed as an intervention for humanitarian reasons by the intervening state, but it might prove to have been carried out for much less idealistic reasons. There is also a relationship of the opposite nature, namely that a military intervention can be carried out as a response to an armed attack from the target state or for other strategic reasons, but nevertheless put an end to or limit human suffering and human rights abuses in the target state. In other words, an intervention can primarily serve other purposes and still have positive humanitarian effects.

If the requirement of 'disinterestedness' was to be applied to these two different lines of motivating an intervention, the first line would result in the intervention being classified as a humanitarian one, whereas the second line would result in the intervention not being classified as humanitarian. Of course proponents of humanitarian intervention would argue that there are other requirements which would ensure that the abusive situation taking place in the first line of motivation would be addressed, and that such interventions would not be regarded as humanitarian.

The political reality in the world is that many governments have little or no respect for basic human rights, but this has not caused them to be 'removed' through foreign military intervention. If concern for the people of a state in which serious human rights violations are committed were a decisive factor, a much more consistent reaction to such violations through foreign military interventions could be expected. It can therefore be concluded that a decision to intervene militarily in another state solely on consideration of the protection of human rights is unlikely. This applies to an even higher degree when it comes to the way in which issues of human rights and democracy are used as foreign policy tools. The attention paid to any given country's human rights record is governed more by the economic, political and geo-strategic interests of foreign powers, thus resulting in a high degree of inconsistency in how the US, for one example, uses the criticism of foreign countries on their human rights records. It also creates a gap between the stated principles guiding the foreign policies of several so-called Western democracies and the foreign policy priorities that are made in practice. Economic considerations take precedence over human rights even for a country like Sweden. It can be argued that principles are often difficult to uphold when confronted with other priorities such as investment opportunities.

Returning to the concept of humanitarian intervention, it cannot be discussed without addressing the issues of self-determination and sovereignty. After all, a humanitarian intervention that is carried out without the consent of the target state has an impact on that state's internal affairs. The arguments for and against interventions to protect human rights can be summarized as follows. The proponents argue that violations of human rights are serious breaches of the Universal Declaration of Human Rights and that other states are duty bound to ensure, by any means necessary, that human rights are respected. One basic argument of the opponents is that the issue of human rights is internal and domestic, one which falls under the jurisdiction of each individual state, and as such cannot justify a foreign military intervention, no matter how extreme the human rights record is.

The two positions take into account two very different viewpoints with regard to the enforcement of respect for internationally recognized norms of human rights. Proponents subscribe to the notion that international responsibility for ensuring that norms pertaining to the respect for human rights are enforced supersedes the norm of non-interference in the internal affairs of a sovereign state. Opponents, on the other hand, stress the notion that non-interference in the internal affairs of a sovereign state takes precedence over the respect for human rights in a state. Thus, the basic disagreement in the scholarly debate is between those defending the sovereignty of the state and those who argue that such sovereignty is not absolute and that it is not the state but the people who have a right to self-determination. This debate raises the question of the continued relevance of the principle of non-interference.

An assessment of the merits of the arguments put forward by the proponents of intervention – for the purpose of promoting people's right to self-determination against the will of the state in which they live – has to begin with the legal aspects. The legal limitations of such intervention reside in the principle of non-intervention and the relevant provisions of the UN Charter, e.g., Articles 2(4) and 2(7). Proponents have a different interpretation of the provisions of the charter and choose to refer instead to Articles 1, 55 and 56.

The non-legal aspects can be formulated in a question: How is a people's right to self-determination best promoted? Proponents of foreign intervention would argue that if human rights are violated in a state, the self-determination of its people is denied. In order to rectify this situation they would hold the opinion that foreign intervention against the will of that state is permissible. This raises the issue of whether the self-determination of a people can be achieved through foreign military intervention. If a foreign power imposes a new political system, it can hardly be regarded as an act of enhancing the self-determination of the population in the target state. After all, the inhabitants of that state would not be given the opportunity to choose the new political system; in fact it would be imposed on them. Pursuant to this line of argumentation, it can be further argued that such a foreign military intervention would alter the political situation but would not alter the basic condition of the people's self-determination deprivation in the target state.

Thus far the discussion has been related to the concept of humanitarian intervention and the question of self-determination of people versus the sovereignty of the state, and the scholarly debate on these issues. Some basic problems have been highlighted by critically evaluating central aspects of the line of argumentation presented by proponents of humanitarian intervention and of the right to intervene to promote the self-determination of people in other states.

If attention is turned to a more political level, and to how state actors look at these issues, it can be noted that a change in attitude seems to have taken place in the post–Cold War era, indicated by the emergence of the new type of foreign intervention: 'peace enforcement'. In the early 1990s the Security Council begun to delegate the right of UN member states to carry out military interventions on their own. A higher degree of UN involvement in civil war situations is also an indication of a change in attitude. Did these changes imply a shift towards accepting humanitarian intervention against the will of the target state?

Proponents of humanitarian intervention would argue that they did, while opponents would point to the fact that all Security Council resolutions adopted under Chapter VII refer to threats to international peace and security as a basis for their adoption. Humanitarian concern might be mentioned but would not be the official reason for adopting a Chapter VII resolution.

Although it was possible to obtain the permission to carry out military interventions from the Security Council, the eagerness to do so even by the major 'Western' powers was considerably reduced by the mid-1990s, and in the case of Rwanda, the willingness to intervene displayed by France was in order to defend its own interests rather than to act against the genocide. The case of Rwanda prompted a process that would eventually lead to the establishment of the International Commission on Intervention and State Sovereignty which published its landmark report, 'The Responsibility to Protect', in 2001 (The Responsibility 2001).

By the end of the 1990s it became evident that the delegation of the right to carry out military interventions to member states of the UN was no longer supported by all the five permanent members of the Security Council as evidently displayed by the case of Kosovo in 1999. Members of the North Atlantic Treaty Organisation (NATO) carried out their military intervention without a mandate from the Security Council, due to opposition by Russia and China. Also in the case of Iraq in 2003, the US and UK intervened militarily without Security Council authorization due to opposition by China, France and Russia. In fact, the US-led military intervention in Afghanistan beginning in 2001 was also carried out without explicit authorization by the Security Council. Although in this case, prior authorization was not sought by the intervening actors.[10]

In terms of the UN's reactions to foreign military interventions, recent research shows that in the post–Cold War era, the cases of Kuwait in 1990 on the one hand, and the cases of Afghanistan in 2001 and Iraq in 2003 on the other, clearly illustrate the full extent of inconsistency. In the early 1990s the UN's reaction to Iraq's intervention in Kuwait was hailed as an example of how the UN should react to breaches of the provisions of the UN Charter and it was said to herald a new era when breaches of the charter would no longer be tolerated. In contrast, the UN's reactions to the interventions in Afghanistan in 2001 and in Iraq in 2003 are examples of the diametrically opposite trend, namely, a weaker response which could be seen as setting a trend of legitimizing the outcome of actions that breach the provisions of the charter, indicating a shift towards a loosening of the prohibition of the use of force, as well as a weakening of the principle of non-interference.[11]

The developments in Libya in 2011 have provoked renewed debate relating to the questions of non-interference and foreign military intervention in the context of an internal crisis in a country. Of particular interest was the adoption of Security Council Resolution 1973 on 17 March 2011 under Chapter VII of the Charter of the United Nations. In operative paragraph 4 of the resolution, it is stated that the Security Council:

> *Authorizes* Member States that have notified the Secretary-General, acting nationally or through regional organizations or arrangements, and acting in cooperation with the Secretary-General, to take all necessary measures, notwithstanding paragraph 9 of resolution 1970 (2011), to protect civilians and civilian populated areas under threat of attack in the Libyan Arab Jamahiriya, including Benghazi, while excluding a foreign occupation force of any form on any part of Libyan territory, and *requests* the Member States concerned to inform the Secretary-General immediately of the measures they take pursuant to the authorization conferred by this paragraph which shall be immediately reported to the Security Council. (UNSC 2011b, italics in the original)

The wording 'all necessary measures' implies that the use of force by outside powers to 'protect civilians and civilian populated areas' in Libya is permitted, but 'a foreign occupation force of any form on any part of Libyan territory' is not permitted. The air campaign launched after the resolution was passed spearheaded by some of the members of NATO – most notably France, the UK and the US – has received active support by several countries also outside NATO while it has been criticized by China and Russia – who both abstained in the vote in the Security Council – and by some developing countries. The broader ramifications of the case of Libya and its longer-term impact cannot be grasped at this stage.

It can be observed that the strongest opposition to humanitarian intervention and to foreign military interventionary behaviour in general comes from the developing world; how might this be explained? Could it be attributed to disparate human rights values? In the context of this analysis it will be argued that this is not necessarily the case, but that there could very well be differences between the North and the South in the importance given to different forms of human rights. The debate of the 1990s between proponents of the so-called 'Asian values', who put more emphasis on economic and social rights, and proponents of primarily promoting individual and political rights, such as Australia and the US, indicates that differences in perception exist.

More importantly, most foreign interventions are carried out in third world states, and the examples in the literature of the need for humanitarian intervention often refer to the situation in the third world (e.g., Reisman 1990, 869–74; Hoffmann 1995–96, 37–49). One cannot expect the leaders of third world states to stand up and support interventions that could contribute to their downfall or in fact aim directly at overthrowing them. Not surprisingly, most third world states are keen to uphold the principles of non-intervention and non-interference in the internal affairs of other states. However, this does not mean that they would not themselves carry out military interventions in other states if they felt that they had legitimate reasons to do so, e.g., India in former East Pakistan (now Bangladesh) in the early 1970s, and Vietnam in Cambodia and Tanzania in Uganda both in the late 1970s. Hoffmann sees such behaviour as weakening their position as opponents to interventions in general (1995–96, 36). An alternative line of argumentation is that such states are no different from states in North America and Western Europe, but since they fear becoming victims of foreign interventions, they oppose such behaviour when other states resort to it. After all, no leadership of a state in the world would, on a voluntary basis, welcome a foreign intervention that is hostile to it.

In other words, even countries supporting interventionism in other countries would not accept being the target of a hostile intervention themselves. In examining the positions taken by China and ASEAN, this aspect will be taken into consideration with regard to the principle of non-interference.

Chinese Foreign Policy

Chinese foreign policy is still governed by the 'Five Principles of Peaceful Coexistence' which were formulated for the first time in agreement between China and India on 29 April 1954. These principles are fundamental not only to China's overall foreign policy but also to China's bilateral relations with several countries. The essence of the five principles have been summarized as follows by Zou:

> (1) respect for each other's sovereignty and territorial integrity, (2) non-aggression, (3) non-interference in each other's internal affairs, (4) equality and mutual benefit and (5) peaceful coexistence. (Zou 2009, 25)

Respect for sovereignty and non-interference display strong commitment to Article 2(7) of the UN Charter. Non-aggression is in line with the prohibition of the threat or use of force since it rules out attacking another country. Peaceful coexistence implies that a country does not threaten or use force against another country. Thus, although the People's Republic of China (PRC) was not representing 'China' in the UN in 1954 – the Republic of China (Taiwan) did so until 1971 – the foreign policy of the PRC was in tune with key aspects and principles of the UN Charter. Since the PRC gained control of China's seat in the UN and of the permanent membership in the UN Security Council, it has pursued a foreign policy adhering to the five principles and thus in line with key aspects and principles of the charter.

Given the principles governing China's foreign policy, it has taken a negative stand against foreign military interventions in the international system. China has been highly critical of US military interventions and even actively opposed the US intervention in the Second Indochina Conflict (the Vietnam War). During the Sino–Soviet conflict China also opposed Soviet-led interventions. China continues to be opposed to foreign military interventions also in the post–Cold War era, in particular those carried out by other major powers without explicit Security Council authorization, i.e., in Kosovo in 1999 and Iraq in 2003. The extent – both in terms of intensity and in length of time – to which China will criticize an intervention and possibly act against it depends on the direct or indirect impact on China, and also on which principles are being negatively affected by the interventionary behaviour. In this context the case of Kosovo is important both because China was directly targeted when its embassy in Belgrade was bombed, and because the intervention violated both the principle of non-interference and the prohibition of the threat or use of force. Other aspects also played a role, such as the 'humanitarian' debate that surrounded the intervention and the challenge to the principle of territorial integrity. Both aspects prompted China to respond negatively and to oppose the intervention.[12]

China's stand on Libya in 2011 has reflected the pragmatism and flexibility with which China pursues its policies of non-interference, and it appears that China considers that abstaining from the vote on Security Council Resolution 1973 should be understood as China not supporting it. After the vote in the Security Council the representative of China – the then president of the Security Council – made a statement in which he outlined China's position:

> China is always against the use of force in international relations. In the Security Council's consultations on resolution 1973 (2011), we and other Council members asked specific questions. However, regrettably, many of those questions failed to be clarified or answered. China has serious difficulty with parts of the resolution. (UNSC 2011a, 10)

Given this opposition to a key aspect of the resolution, there appears to be a contradiction between China's stated position and the fact that by not casting its veto against the resolution China allowed it to be adopted (UNSC 2011b).

China was also initially reluctant to both support and participate in peacekeeping operations. There has been a change in China's attitude towards peacekeeping, and it has gradually come not only to openly support such operations through its voting behaviour in the Security Council, but also through direct active Chinese participation in peacekeeping operations.[13] It appears as though China can reconcile its stance on non-interference with peacekeeping operation as long as the existing government in the target country welcomes an operation.

If the above developments and observations are taken into account, it appears as though China is consistently guided by the Five Principles of Peaceful Coexistence and that principles such as non-interference in the internal affairs of other countries and respect for state sovereignty and territorial integrity are very important to China and evident in China's foreign policy. However, the way in which China responds to breaches of these principles by other countries seems to be guided by China's national interest and how they affect China directly or indirectly. Thus, China is pragmatic in its approach and flexible, but would not act in such a way as to compromise its own national interest. Nevertheless, this should not be interpreted as though China has abandoned the basic principles guiding its foreign policy.

Principles Governing ASEAN

Introduction

Six key ASEAN documents are examined in the context of this study to identify the importance of non-interference within the ASEAN framework.

The six documents are: 'The ASEAN Declaration'; the 'Declaration of ASEAN Concord'; the 'Treaty of Amity and Cooperation' (TAC); the 'Declaration of ASEAN Concord II'; the 'ASEAN Security Community Plan of Action' (ASCPA); and the 'Charter of the Association of Southeast Asian Nations' (ASEAN Charter). These key documents are examined in chronological order based on the dates of adoption by ASEAN.

The ASEAN Declaration

The ASEAN Declaration, adopted on 8 August 1967, spells out the overall goals and aims of ASEAN and sets the stage for a process aimed at defining the way in which the association should function and the mechanisms by which the goals and aims of the association should be achieved. The importance of non-interference is explicit as outlined in the preamble of the declaration:

> CONSIDERING that the countries of SouthEast Asia [sic] share a primary responsibility for strengthening the economic and social stability of the region and ensuring their peacefull [sic] and progressive national development, and that they are determined to ensure their stability and security from external interference in any form or manifestation in order to preserve their national identities in accordance with the ideals and aspirations of their peoples. (ASEAN Declaration 1967)

The importance of the UN Charter in the context of promoting regional peace and the commitment of the member states of ASEAN to the charter is also explicit as displayed in the following:

> To promote regional peace and stability through abiding respect for justice and the rule of law in the relationship among countries of the region and adherence to the principles of the United Nations Charter. (ASEAN Declaration 1967)

The Declaration of ASEAN Concord

The evolution that followed during the so-called 'formative years' (i.e., 1967 to 1976) led to the signing of the Declaration of ASEAN Concord on 24 February 1976, in connection with the First Summit Meeting of ASEAN held in Bali.[14]

The Declaration of ASEAN Concord relates to the member states of ASEAN; it contains both general principles relating to the overall goals of the association and principles relating to the specific goal of managing disputes and expanding cooperation among the member states. Emphasis is put on the respect for the principles of 'self-determination, sovereign equality and non-interference in the internal affairs of nations' (ASEAN Concord 1976).

In order to achieve its overall goals, the Declaration of ASEAN Concord includes a programme of action which constitutes a framework for ASEAN cooperation in the following fields: political, economic, social, cultural and informational, security, and the improvement of the ASEAN machinery (ASEAN Concord 1976).

The Treaty of Amity and Cooperation

The TAC was also adopted on 24 February 1976 in Bali. In Chapter I, dealing with 'purpose and principles', Article 2 outlines the fundamental principles that should guide the relations between the signatories to the treaty. The principles are

a. Mutual respect for the independence, sovereignty, equality, territorial integrity and national identity of all nations;
b. The right of every State to lead its national existence free from external interference, subversion or coercion;
c. Non-interference in the internal affairs of one another;
d. Settlement of differences or disputes by peaceful means;
e. Renunciation of the threat or use of force;
f. Effective co-operation among themselves. (TAC 1976)

The principles include three main factors for managing inter-state relations: non-interference in the internal affairs of other countries, peaceful settlement of disputes and overall cooperation.

In Chapter III, dealing with 'cooperation', the areas in which mutual cooperation can be established and expanded are outlined, and the linkages between cooperation, peaceful relations and non-interference are displayed. The later is most evidently shown in Article 12, which states that, the signatories

in their efforts to achieve regional prosperity and security, shall endeavour to cooperate in all fields for the promotion of regional resilience, based on the principles of self-confidence, self-reliance, mutual respect, co-operation and solidarity which will constitute the foundation for a strong and viable community of nations in Southeast Asia. (TAC 1976)

The Declaration of ASEAN Concord II

The Declaration ASEAN Concord II, adopted on 7 October 2003 in connection with the Ninth ASEAN Summit held in Bali, displays a continuity in the development of collaboration within ASEAN. In its preamble it is confirmed that the fundamental values and principles are still very much in evidence, as displayed by the fact that it is stated that the member states are: 'Reaffirming the fundamental importance of adhering to the principle of non-interference and consensus in ASEAN Cooperation' (ASEAN Concord 2003).

The Declaration of ASEAN Concord II also includes a part in which the member states adopt a framework to achieve a 'dynamic, cohesive, resilient and integrated ASEAN community'. To achieve this overarching goal the association will strive to create an 'ASEAN Security Community (ASC)', an 'ASEAN Economic Community (AEC)', and an 'ASEAN Socio-Cultural Community (ASSC)' (ASEAN Concord 2003).

In the part relating to the ASC, Point 3 outlines that ASEAN shall continue to promote regional solidarity and cooperation, and in this context it is stated that: 'member countries shall exercise their rights to lead their national existence free from outside interference in their internal affairs.' Point 4 also relates to this dimension, but is more general and states that

> The ASEAN Security Community shall abide by the UN Charter and other principles of international law and uphold ASEAN's principles of non-interference, consensus based decision-making, national and regional resilience, respect for national sovereignty, the renunciation of the threat or use of force, and peaceful settlement of differences and disputes. (ASEAN Concord 2003)

Thus, both points confirm the continued relevance and importance of the principle of non-interference in the ASEAN framework for regional collaboration, and in relation to the prohibition of the threat or use of force.

The ASEAN Security Community Plan of Action[15]

The process aiming at establishing the ASC was reinforced at the Tenth ASEAN Summit held in Vientiane in late November 2004 when ASEAN adopted the ASCPA. The ASCPA outlines that the ASC should be based on 'shared norms and rules of good conduct in inter-state relations; effective conflict prevention and resolution mechanisms; and post-conflict peace building activities.'

The ASCPA also stresses that the ASC process shall be 'progressive' and that it shall be guided by

> well-established principles of non-interference, consensus based decision-making, national and regional resilience, respect for the national sovereignty, the renunciation of the threat or the use of force, and peaceful settlement of differences and disputes which has served as the foundation of ASEAN cooperation. (ASEAN Security 2004)

Thus, the ASCPA clearly displays a high degree of continuity and adherence to established principles for inter-state collaboration in ASEAN. It also states that ASEAN shall not only strengthen existing 'initiatives' but also launch new ones and set 'appropriate implementation frameworks'.

The ASCPA includes seven sections: 'I. Political Development', 'II. Shaping and Sharing of Norms', 'III. Conflict Prevention', 'IV. Conflict Resolution', 'V. Post-conflict Peace Building', 'VI. Implementing Mechanisms', and 'VII. Areas of Activities'.

In the section on shaping norms it is stated that the aim is to achieve a standard of 'common adherence to norms of good conduct among the members of the ASEAN Community' in any norm setting activity the following principles must be adhered to:

1. Non-alignment,
2. Fostering of peace-oriented attitudes of ASEAN Member Countries;
3. Conflict Resolution through non-violent means;
4. Renunciation of nuclear weapons and other weapons of mass destruction and avoidance of arms race in Southeast Asia; and
5. Renunciation of the threat or the use of force. (ASEAN Security 2004)

The ASCPA explicitly put emphasis on such core principles as non-interference, renunciation of the threat or the use of force and peace settlement of disputes.

The ASEAN Charter[16]

The ASEAN Charter – adopted on 20 November 2007 in Singapore – reaffirms a number of fundamental principles governing inter-state relations among its member states. In paragraph 7 of the preamble it is stated: 'Respecting the fundamental importance of amity and cooperation, and the principles of sovereignty, equality, territorial integrity, non-interference, consensus and unity in diversity' (ASEAN Charter 2007, 2).

In Article 2, 'principles' of non-interference, peace and dispute settlement are highlighted, as articulated in the following principles that ASEAN member states should 'act in accordance with'

(a) respect for the independence, sovereignty, equality, territorial integrity and national identity of all ASEAN Member States;
(b) shared commitment and collective responsibility in enhancing regional peace, security and prosperity;
(c) renunciation of aggression and the threat or use of force or other actions in any manner inconsistent with international law;
(d) reliance of peaceful settlement of dispute;
(e) non-interference in the internal affairs of ASEAN member-states;
(f) respect for the right of every Member State to lead its national existence free from external interference, subversion and coercion;
[…]
(k) abstention from participation in any policy or activity, including the use of its territory, pursued by any ASEAN Member State or non-ASEAN State or any non-State actor, which threatens the sovereignty, territorial integrity or political and economic stability of ASEAN Member States. (ASEAN Charter 2007, 5–6)

The non-interference dimension is extensive and explicit in these principles. The strict adherence to the provisions on the UN Charter relating to the prohibition of the 'threat or use of force' in inter-state relations is also notable.

Concluding Remarks

Both China and ASEAN pursue policies that are strongly in favour the principle of non-interference in the internal affairs of other countries. They also pursue policies that adhere to the prohibition of the threat or use of force. Furthermore, both China and ASEAN are committed to the peaceful settlements of disputes.

The principle of non-interference has been a cornerstone of China's foreign policy since the 1950s, as enshrined in the 'Five Principles of Peaceful Coexistence' (Jia 2003, 20–1). However, the increased number of resolutions adopted by the Security Council since the end of the Cold War involving the authorization of the use of force and expanded peacekeeping mandates indicates a more flexible stand on interventionism on China's part. Recent research findings support that notion and trend (Carlsson 2004, 9–27; Gill and

Huang 2009; Stähle; 2008, 631–55; Zou 2009, 21–42). Nevertheless, as argued in this study, this does not imply that China has altered its basic stand on the principle of non-interference. China would not tolerate any such action directly affecting China, and it strongly reacts when its national interests are threatened by actions carried out elsewhere in the international system.

The fundamental importance of non-interference within ASEAN has been confirmed through research since the association was established. Following an internal debate in the late 1990s on proposals that the non-interference principle ought to be relaxed, ASEAN opted not to change its policy and re-affirmed the primacy of the principle of non-interference (Ramcharan 2000, 60–88). The importance of that principle as part of the regional collaborative structure was displayed during the expansion of the association in the 1990s (Amer 1999, 1031–45). As displayed by the overview of six key ASEAN documents, non-interference is a cornerstone within the ASEAN framework for regional collaboration. Furthermore, the peaceful settlement of inter-state disputes and the prohibition of the threat or use of force are also fundamental aspects of the ASEAN framework.

Within ASEAN the principle of non-interference in the internal affairs of other states prevents member states from intervening in the internal conflicts of other member states. This implies that only if a member state requests the assistance or intervention of ASEAN, a group of selected member states, and/or individual member states, can they intervene. The nature of such intervention can differ depending on the request and on the role that ASEAN or the member states are willing to provide.

As in the case of China, the individual member states of ASEAN display more flexible policies towards interventionism and peacekeeping outside the region. Each member state pursues its own independent foreign policy, and given the differences in history, politics and economics among the ASEAN members, the foreign policies and the foreign policy priorities outside the ASEAN context varies considerably. However, none of the ten member states of ASEAN would accept being the target of a hostile foreign intervention.

In the context of regional security, the strong emphasis on non-interference, non-threat and non-use of force, and peaceful dispute settlement in both China's foreign policy and within the framework of ASEAN regional collaboration contribute to the enhancement of regional security and stability. Non-interference reduces the risk of neighbouring countries intervening in disputes within other countries. The adherence to the prohibition of threat or use of force in inter-state relations diminishes the risk of militarized inter-state disputes and conflicts between the countries of the region. The stated preference for the peaceful settlement of disputes further diminishes the risk of disputes leading to militarized conflicts between the countries of the region.

An adherence to theses principles has further implications, namely, that it not only reduces, but de facto removes the option of directly influencing neighbouring countries through a potential threat of military action. This would only apply in a situation when a neighbouring country would not conduct itself in line with the priorities and preferences of a potential intervening power. This aspect is most relevant in the relationships between more powerful countries and weaker neighbours. In the case of China it implies that although China can wield considerable economic and political influence over some countries that are heavily dependent on China, it does not necessarily translate into a direct Chinese capability to influence the way those countries, e.g., North Korea or Myanmar, behave internationally or domestically. It appears that the prohibition of the threat or use of force to bring pressure to bear on neighbouring countries to change their policies implies that China has limited influence in relation to other states' dependence on China, e.g., North Korea and Myanmar. It also limits China's options in the South China Sea, since it would be counter-productive for China to provoke a military confrontation with other claimants as it would seriously harm its relations both with individual Southeast Asian countries and with ASEAN. The principle of non-interference also plays a role here since it essentially rules out trying to alter the political leadership in a neighbouring country against the will of the leadership in order to bring to power a leadership that that is more amenable to China's interests and policies.

To conclude, it can be observed that although China and ASEAN so strongly adhere to the principle of non-interference, it is notable that they were not part of the process of drafting the Charter of the United Nations. The PRC was not yet established, and of the current ten member states of ASEAN, only Thailand was independent at the time. In fact, the principle of non-interference was put firmly on the agenda by the Latin American countries where opposition to US interventionism had led to the formulation of the principles of non-interference and non-intervention, and to the emergence of widespread support for these principles. A number of Latin American countries took part in the drafting of the charter and could influence its content together with like-minded countries, and so could push for the inclusion of a principle like non-interference. In other words, although China and ASEAN nowadays strongly support the principle of non-interference, both the concept and the principle have their roots elsewhere.

Notes

1 This study forms part of that author's ongoing research on Asian perspectives and policies on interventionism. It also draws on the author's research on the regional collaboration in Southeast Asia and the wider Pacific Asia as well as on the

United Nations and military intervention. It is a revised version of a paper prepared for The 2009 Conference of the Swedish Network of Peace, Conflict and Development Research – 'The Development and Security Nexus', hosted by the Center for Pacific Asia Studies (CPAS), Department of Oriental Languages, Stockholm University, Stockholm, Sweden, 6–7 November 2009.

2 This section is adapted from Amer (2007b, 39–46) and from Johansson and Amer (2009, 40–2). The overview of the scholarly debate also draws on Amer (1994, 22–30; 1994b, 428–30; 2007a, 5–7).

3 References to the discussions about Article 2(4) can be found in: Asrat (1991, 38–40, 199–200), Bowett (1955–6, 131), Brownlie (1962, 223–33). The continued relevance of the study of the legal regulations of the use of force in international law can be seen from recent studies such as Brownlie (2001, 21–37), Gazzini (2005) and O'Conelll (2007).

4 In this context the listed weaknesses are only seen from the perspective of the provisions of the UN Charter, and they do not take into consideration whether customary international law or General Assembly Resolutions address these weaknesses.

5 For overviews of the debate relating to the interpretation of the provisions of Article 51, see Amer (1994, 429–30) and Johansson and Amer (2009, 42–4).

6 W. Michael Reisman has played a prominent role in the more general debate on these issues. In his article on the interplay between sovereignty and human rights in contemporary international law, Reisman (1990) argues in favour of defining 'sovereignty' as the right of people rather than the right of the 'sovereign', following what he believes to be a change in the generally accepted meaning of the term. For a critical assessment of the issues and their implications see Ryan (1991, 55–71).

7 The doctrinal debate relating to the key concepts 'pro-democratic', 'pro–self-determination' and 'humanitarian' interventions is not included in this study nor is a overview of how to define external involvement and various forms of foreign intervention. For two such overviews, see Amer (2007c; 1997, 17–60).

8 This awareness and the emphasis put on criteria such as proportionality and limited duration of the intervention can also be seen in the way that proponents of an extensive interpretation of the provisions of Article 51 of the UN Charter and the right to use force in self-defence are formulating criteria to minimize the risk of abuse. For overviews of the debate relating to the interpretation of the provisions of Article 51 see Amer (1994, 429–30), Johansson and Amer (2009, 42–4).

9 Tesón (1988, 115–20) sets up three basic criteria to be fulfilled in order to make an intervention a humanitarian one. The first criterion is that the purpose of the intervention must be 'truly' humanitarian to be justified, in other words the intervening states have to fulfil the requirement of 'disinterestedness'. The second criterion is that the intervention has to be proportionate both to the gravity of the human rights abuses and to the probability of remedying the situation. Furthermore, military intervention should only be resorted to when all peaceful means have failed or are 'likely' to fail. The third criterion is that the victims of the human rights abuses in target states must welcome the foreign intervention and this requirement is met when the victims are 'actually willing to revolt' against the oppressive government.

10 For a detailed analysis of three cases of unauthorized military intervention and the UN, see Amer (2009, 17–38).

11 For a detailed analysis of the UN's response to the use of force in inter-state relations see Johansson and Amer (2009, 39–65).

12 The case of Kosovo is discussed by both Zou (2009, 28) and Carlson (2004, 9–27). Carlson examines China's recent stance on both sovereignty and 'Multilateral Intervention', ranging from non–UN-authorized to peacekeeping operations.
13 For two detailed studies on China's attitude towards peacekeeping, see Gill and Huang (2009) and Stähle (2008, 631–55).
14 Askandar (1994, 68) argues that the First Summit Meeting marked the end of the 'formative stage' of ASEAN regionalism and that the signing of the Declaration of ASEAN Concord and the TAC marked the beginning of the 'second phase'.
15 Unless otherwise stated, all factual information in this section is derived from the text of 'ASEAN Security Community Plan of Action' (ASEAN Security 2004) and 'ANNEX for ASEAN Security Community Plan of Action' (ASEAN Security Annex 2004).
16 Unless otherwise stated, all factual information in this section is derived from the text of 'The Charter of the Association of Southeast Asian Nations' (ASEAN Charter 2007).

References

Amer, Ramses. 1994a. *The United Nations and Foreign Military Interventions. A Comparative Study of the Application of the Charter.* Second Edition, Report 33. Uppsala: Department of Peace and Conflict Research, Uppsala University.

_____. 1994b. 'The United Nations' Reactions to Foreign Military Interventions'. *Journal of Peace Research* 31(2): 425–44.

_____. 1997. 'The Intervention Debate: New or Old Concepts?'. In Peter Wallensteen (ed.), *International Intervention: New Norms in the Post-Cold War Era?*, 17–60. Report 45. Uppsala: Department of Peace and Conflict Research, Uppsala University.

_____. 1999. 'Conflict Management and Constructive Engagement in ASEAN's Expansion'. *Third World Quarterly* (Special Issue on New Regionalisms) 20(5): 1031–48.

_____. 2007a. The United Nations' reactions to foreign military interventions: A comparative case study analysis. Umeå Working Papers in Peace and Conflict Studies 2. Umeå: Department of Political Science, Umeå University.

_____. 2007b. 'Pre-emptive Self-Defence New Legal Principle or Political Action?'. In Ashok Swain, Ramses Amer and Joakim Öjendal (eds), *Globalization and Challenges to Building Peace*, 39–54. London, New York and Delhi: Anthem Press.

_____. 2007c. Democracy from the outside: A contested phenomenon. Paper prepared for the panel on 'Democratic Alternatives in Asia'. (Sponsored by Konrad Adenauer Stiftung, 3rd Congress of the Asian Political and International Studies Association (APISA); Organized by Developing Countries Research Centre, University of Delhi, New Delhi.) 23–5 November.

_____. 2009. 'Non-Authorized Military Interventions and Legitimization by the United Nations'. In Ashok Swain, Ramses Amer and Joakim Öjendal (eds), *The Democratization Project: Opportunities and Challenges*, 17–38. London and New York: Anthem Press.

ASEAN Charter. 2007. *The Charter of the Association of Southeast Asian Nations.* Association of Southeast Asian Nations. Online: http://www.aseansec.org/21069.pdf (accessed 11 November 2008).

ASEAN Concord. 1976. *Declaration of ASEAN Concord.* Association of Southeast Asian Nations. Online: http://www.asesansec.org/3630.htm (accessed 13 November 2008).

ASEAN Concord. 2003. *Declaration of ASEAN Concord II (Bali Concord II).* Association of Southeast Asian Nations. Online: http://www.asesansec.org/15159.htm (accessed 13 November 2008).

ASEAN Declaration. 1967. *The ASEAN Declaration (Bangkok Declaration) Bangkok, 8 August 1967*. Association of Southeast Asian Nations. Online: http://www.aseansec.org/1212. htm (accessed 13 November 2008).

ASEAN Security. 2004. *ASEAN Security Community Plan of Action*. Association of Southeast Asian Nations. Online: http://www.asesansec.org/16826.htm (accessed 13 November 2008).

ASEAN Security Annex. 2004. *ANNEX for ASEAN Security Community Plan of Action*. Association of Southeast Asian Nations. Online: http://www.asesansec.org/16829.htm (accessed 13 November 2008).

Askandar, Kamarulzaman. 1994. 'ASEAN and Conflict Management: The Formative Years of 1967–1976'. *Pacifica Review* 6(2): 43–56.

Asrat, Belatchew. 1991. *Prohibition of Force Under the UN Charter: A Study of Art. 2 (4)*. Studies in International Law 10. Uppsala University, Swedish Institute of International Law. Uppsala: IUSTUS förlag.

Bowett, D. W. 1955–6. 'Collective Self-Defence Under the Charter of the United Nations'. *British Yearbook of International Law*, 32: 130–61.

Brownlie, Ian. 1962. 'The Use of Force in Self-Defence'. *British Yearbook of International Law*, 37: 183–268.

———. 2001. '*International Law and the Use of Force by States* Revisited'. *The Australian Year Book of International Law*, 21: 21–37.

Carlsson, Allen. 2004. 'Helping to Keep the Peace (Albeit Reluctantly): China's Recent Stance on Sovereignty and Multilateral Intervention'. *Pacific Affairs* 7(1): 9–27.

Gazzini, Tarcisio. 2005. *The Changing Rules on the Use of Force in International Law*. Manchester: Manchester University Press.

Gill, Bates and Huang Chin-Hao. 2009. *China's Expanding Role in Peacekeeping: Prospects and Policy Implications*. SIPRI Policy Paper 25 (November). Stockholm: Stockholm International Peace Research Institute.

Hoffmann, Stanley. 1995–6. 'The Politics and Ethics of Military Intervention'. *Survival* 37(4): 29–51.

ICISS. 2001. *The Responsibility to Protect: Report of the International Commission on Intervention and State Sovereignty*. Ottawa: International Commission on Intervention and State Sovereignty. Online: http://responsibilitytoprotect.org/ICISS%20Report.pdf (accessed 29 September 2011).

Jia Qingguo. 2003. 'China'. In Watanabe Koji (ed.), *Humanitarian Intervention. The Evolving Asian Debate*, 19–32. Tokyo: Japan Center for International Exchange.

Johansson, Patrik and Ramses Amer. 2009. 'From Condemnation to Legitimization of Outcome: The United Nations and the Use of Force in Inter-State Relations'. In Ashok Swain, Ramses Amer and Joakim Öjendal (eds), *The Democratization Project: Opportunities and Challenges*, 39–65. London and New York: Anthem Press.

O'Connell, Mary Ellen. 2007. *International Law and the 'Global War on Terror'*. Cours et travaux 10. Université Panthéon-Assas (Paris II), Institute des hautes études internationales de Paris. Paris: Editions A. Pedone.

Ramcharan, Robin. 2000. 'ASEAN and Non-interference: A Principle Maintained'. *Contemporary Southeast Asia* 22(1): 60–88.

Reisman, W. Michael. 1990. 'Sovereignty and Human Rights in Contemporary International Law'. *American Journal of International Law* 84(4): 866–76.

Ryan, Kevin. 1991. 'Rights, Intervention, and Self-Determination'. *Denver Journal of International Law and Policy* 20(1): 55–71.

Stähle, Stefan. 2008. 'China's Shifting Attitude towards United Nations Peacekeeping Operations'. *The China Quarterly* (195): 631–55.

TAC. 1976. *Treaty of Amity and Cooperation in Southeast Asia.* Association of Southeast Asian Nations. Online: http://www.asesansec.org/1217.htm (accessed 13 November 2008).

Tesón, Fernando. 1988. *Humanitarian Intervention: An Inquiry Into Law and Morality.* New York: Transnational Publishers.

UN Charter. 1945. *Charter of the United Nations.* United Nations. Online: http://www.un.org/en/documents/charter (accessed 20 September 2010).

UNSC. 2011a. United Nations Security Council Record S/PV.6498. (Sixty-sixth year, 6498th meeting, 17 March 2011.) United Nations. Online: http://www.un.org/Depts/dhl/resguide/scact2011.htm (accessed 1 April 2011).

UNSC. 2011b. United Nations Security Council Resolution 1973. (Adopted by the Security Council at its 6498th meeting, 17 March 2011). S/RES/1973 (2011). United Nations. Online: http://www.un.org/Docs/sc/unsc_resolutions11.htm (accessed 20 March 2011).

Zou Keyuan. 2009. *China-ASEAN Relations and International Law.* Oxford and Cambridge: Chandos.

Chapter 6

INTERNATIONAL DIMENSIONS OF PEACE PROCESSES IN ACEH AND SRI LANKA: THE ROLE OF INTERMEDIARIES IN THE 2000s[1]

Malin Åkebo

Introduction

When the government of Indonesia and the Free Aceh Movement (Gerakan Aceh Merdeka, GAM) signed the Helsinki peace agreement in 2005, as many as thirty years had passed since the armed conflict in Aceh started. Likewise in Sri Lanka, the civil war between the government and the Liberation Tigers of Tamil Eelam (LTTE) had been raging for more than two and a half decades when the government declared victory in 2009. The prolonging of these two conflicts is striking, and still they are merely two out of a number of civil wars that have lasted for several decades, causing widespread human suffering with numerous casualties and socio-economic losses.

As many of today's armed conflicts tend to be long lasting, they often have a noteworthy track record of peace attempts. At an international glance, efforts to reach a negotiated settlement to armed conflicts have increased in the last decades and nowadays engage a variety of both state and non-state actors (see Ramsbotham, Woodhouse and Miall 2005; Wallensteen 2007). In Aceh, however, it was not until the beginning of the 2000s – more than two decades after the armed conflict started – that the conflict gained international attention while carrying out peace attempts. Also in Sri Lanka, the peace attempts made in the 2000s reached a new dimension of internationalization (Goodhand and Klem 2005, 88). Notwithstanding these initiatives, however, together with several other civil wars in the Asian region these two conflicts have attracted comparatively low levels of international attention and third party conflict management efforts (Möller et al. 2007). How then can this comparatively modest international attention be understood? And what made the internationally influenced peace processes in Aceh and Sri Lanka possible in the 2000s? What role did external actors play in these peace attempts? This chapter aims to address these overarching questions by exploring the rationale for international involvement in managing peace processes in the protracted internal conflicts in Aceh and Sri Lanka.

The chapter begins by introducing some tools for analysing the management of peace processes in contemporary intra-state conflicts. From there on, it will be structured around two main sections that address the cases of Aceh and Sri Lanka. After a brief background presentation on the armed conflicts, the main parts of these sections constitute an overview of significant peace attempts with a focus on the initiation of peace processes and on the role external actors have played in these peace attempts. The chapter finally ends with some concluding reflections and comparisons.

Contemporary Conflicts and the Management of Peace Processes: Analytical Tools

The features of war – as well as the enterprise to manage them – are constantly in change. While most parts of the twentieth century were characterized by the World Wars and the subsequent Cold War, the challenges facing the world today are different in many respects (Aggestam and Björkdahl 2009, 15). As is widely recognized, almost all armed conflicts today take place within states and involve a government and one or several non-state groups as the main warring parties. Many of these intra-state conflicts are located in developing countries and share a history of colonial rule and of competing nation-building projects with devastating outcomes. Concepts like 'intractable' and 'protracted' conflicts are often used to describe these long-lasting civil wars, thus indicating the difficulties in reaching a solution (see Azar 1990; Crocker, Hampson and Aall 2005).

In the aftermath of the Cold War it has become all the more common for warring parties to engage in peace processes, which refer to repeated initiatives with the purpose of ending conflicts peacefully through mutual agreements (Darby and Mac Ginty 2003, 2008). Many of today's intra-state peace processes can be described as internally rather than externally driven. Nevertheless, in order to begin and carry through peace attempts, nearly all peace processes to a varying extent involve external actors as intermediaries (Mitchell 2008, 94).[2] Such external actors can broadly be categorized as ranging from international organizations to states, to non-governmental organizations (NGOs), to individuals. Dayton (2009, 68) stresses that states have traditionally been the most common primary external actor engaging in intra-state peace processes. However, other types of actors increasingly play a vital role in many peace processes, notably various NGOs (Aggestam and Björkdahl 2009, 20–1).

External actors can use different approaches and strategies in order to influence or facilitate a settlement between conflicting parties. Dayton (2009, 64–7) lists a number of intermediary functions in managing violent conflicts (see Table 6.1 for a summary), in which various activities are being used and where different degrees of leverage and coercion are being exercised. At one end of the spectrum we have activities where coercive means are explicitly used with the intent to stall acts of violence, for example when using military force in peacekeeping operations, by providing either side with resources (such as arms or expertise), or by imposing various kinds of sanctions (Dayton 2009, 62). Still, as many peace processes can be described as largely internally driven by the conflicting parties, the primary role for external actors in intra-state peace processes often focuses more on assisting the conflicting parties in a less coercive manner. One commonly used function, which generally also gains a great deal of public attention, is to mediate agreements between the conflicting parties. Such engagement is usually based on a request by the warring parties or on an offer by the external actor. A mediator can, for example, channel and facilitate communication between the parties, create venues for talks, or formulate proposals for the parties to consider – albeit with different levels of influence being exercised (Bercovitch 2002, 14–16). Besides mediating elite talks, external actors can also use so-called 'track two' diplomacy and address community groups with an intent to transform relationships, or to provide conflict resolution training either to leaders or to the general public (Dayton 2009, 65–7). Furthermore, intermediaries might serve a monitoring function in peace processes by overseeing the compliance of agreements and accordingly provide both the warring parties as well as the public with information and early warning signs of conflict escalation.

Table 6.1. The functions intermediaries perform when addressing intra-state violent conflicts as suggested by Dayton (2009)

Intermediary functions:	Using coercion to halt violence
	Mediating agreements
	Transforming relationships between communities in conflict
	Providing consultation and conflict resolution training
	Providing early warning and post-conflict monitoring services
	Addressing the structural sources of the conflict

Dayton (2009, 66) also emphasizes that external actors can use various measures to address the structural sources of conflicts, which can include financial assistance in order to strengthen political, economic and legal institutions, (re)build infrastructure, support educational systems, etc.

Many observers emphasize that, in addition to the increase of international initiatives in peace processes, there has also been a widening scope for outside involvement with a more 'ambitious agenda' being employed (Aggestam and Björkdahl 2009, 19). Particularly, notions of the relationship between development and security and its relevance for peace attempts have gained an increasing influence both among academics and in policy circles (Mac Ginty and Williams 2009, 2). Thus, many external interventions are nowadays characterized by 'multi-mandate responses' that comprise diplomatic engagements with military, development and humanitarian components in what Goodhand and Klem (2005, 65) describe as a 'convergence of development and security concerns'.

The tendency of an overall increase in and widening scope for international peace efforts has, however, not been equally evident in all conflict-affected areas. Looking first at the geographic distribution of armed conflicts, Möller et al. (2007, 374) suggest that many of the contemporary civil wars that tend to be the most long lasting and show a pattern of recurrence can be found in the Asian region,[3] in many of which, regionally based groups are fighting for secession of a territory in a bordering area of the state. And yet, while civil wars in Asia thus tend to last longer than conflicts in other regions of the world, the instances of engagement by outside parties in peace efforts have been comparatively few in number and modest in scale (Wallensteen et al. 2009, 258). This makes intra-state conflicts in the region particularly interesting for an enquiry into peace attempts in which external involvements have taken place in spite of these limiting conditions, as well as for an analysis of how such initiatives were made possible and how they have been manifested. This chapter hence takes a closer look at peace processes in two such intra-state Asian conflicts – Aceh and Sri Lanka. Through an overview of peace attempts in these conflicts the chapter explores what role external actors have played in these attempts, who have been involved, and what strategies and activities have been used. Furthermore, in order to understand the rationale behind these internationally influenced peace processes and the contexts and dynamics that made them possible, consideration will be given to internal political dynamics, changes in the relationship between the warring parties, and changes at the international and regional level.[4] The overview is limited to the examination of peace efforts and intermediary activities at the elite level. Furthermore, most attention will be paid to the main external parties' roles and activities, although the involvement of other external actors is also considered in order to gain a better understanding of the international dimension of the peace processes.

Aceh – The Conflict and Peace Attempts

Background to the Armed Conflict

The conflict between the government of Indonesia and GAM started in 1976 when GAM declared the independence of Aceh – a region located in the northernmost part of the island of Sumatra. Already in the 1950s the Darul Islam rebellion had been active in Aceh (Miller 2008, 13). A new rebellion erupted in the mid-1970s at a point when the Indonesian government changed its policy regarding the amount of autonomy to allow Aceh after Indonesia's independence from colonial rule in 1949 (Large and Aguswandi 2008, 8). This, combined with an overall growing discontent over the uneven economic distribution of regional resources and the lack of influence over local government and religion, laid the ground for the forthcoming protracted armed conflict.

When Hasan di Tiro, founder of GAM, officially declared the movement's demands to the Indonesian government in the mid-1970s, the Indonesian military under President Suharto launched a counter-insurgency operation to repress the GAM rebellion (Large and Aguswandi 2008, 99). Numerous GAM members were thus either arrested, killed or forced to exile, and GAM's leader di Tiro was himself exiled. From the early 1980s di Tiro ran a 'government-in-exile' from Sweden and made preparations for a renewed struggle in Aceh. The second phase of the violent conflict was initiated in 1989 when GAM launched guerrilla operations in Aceh, to which the government responded by turning Aceh into a 'military operation zone' (Aceh DOM) (Aspinall and Crouch 2003, 5). During the following years many Acehnese civilians were killed in the armed conflict and severe violations of human rights were committed by both sides. While speculations were made that GAM was defeated, di Tiro continued to lead the fragmented group from Sweden, and in the second half of the 1990s the group gained increased territorial control to the extent that they set up local administrations in parts of the region (UCDP 2011).

While the conflict between the Indonesian government and GAM remained unresolved throughout the 1990s, the end of the decade witnessed a number of significant changes in Indonesia's political landscape, with the breakdown of President Suharto's regime in 1998, followed by reforms introduced first by President Habibie in 1998–9 and later on by President Wahid from 1999. In this context, opportunities opened up for peace attempts between the conflicting parties and after two major efforts, a comprehensive peace accord was finally signed in 2005.

Peace Attempts in the 2000s: The First Efforts

Initiating the Peace Process: Context and Dynamics

The initiation of the first peace process in Aceh can be traced back to the late 1990s, more than two decades after the initiation of armed conflict. In 1998 there was a presidential shift in Indonesia; Suharto left this post after 21 years in power and democratic reforms were introduced by the new President Habibie. The military operation area in Aceh was stopped, and some restrictions on the media lifted (Large and Aguswandi 2008, 99). Furthermore, symbolic statements were made by influential leaders in Jakarta, with the military chief General Wiranto apologizing for abuses committed by 'individual soldiers' in Aceh (Huber 2008, 17). President Habibie also made a public apology to the Acehnese for atrocities and human rights violations committed by the military (Large and Aguswandi 2008, 99). The new political approach pushed by Habibie had, however, taken on more far-reaching expressions elsewhere. Significantly, the president had given approval for another regional territory, East Timor, to hold a referendum in order to determine the future status of the region, in which they voted for independence in 1999. Through extensive demonstrations, calls were made for a similar referendum in Aceh. However, the Indonesian government rejected the demands for a referendum in Aceh and yet again the disturbances in the region escalated (Aspinall and Crouch 2003, 6). The government feared that holding a referendum on Aceh's future would provoke similar demands in other regions of the country, which eventually could lead to a break-up of the state. The Aceh region also contained valuable economic assets for the state such as oil and natural gas (Aspinall and Crouch 2003, 2).

After the fall of Suharto and with the East Timor independence, GAM intensified their political strategy and called for international negotiations under the United Nations. The group also increased its political activities in Aceh by, for example, arranging gatherings for people in mosques, alongside the continuous guerrilla warfare (Schulze 2006, 236–7). However, while the group had gained some strength during the previous years, the leadership in Sweden faced difficulties in efforts to gain international attention for their cause. At the same time, the Indonesian military was still trying to get back on its feet after the breakdown of the Suharto regime. The state had also suffered from the Asian financial crisis and the government faced harsh international critique for its handling of East Timor's independence (Aspinall and Crouch 2003, 8). Despite resistance from some officials within the Indonesian government as well as the military, President Wahid, who assumed office in October 1999, decided to explore an approach based on dialogue with GAM (Huber 2008, 17).

In the beginning of 2000, peace talks were hence conducted between representatives from the government of Indonesia and GAM. Mediating this first dialogue process was the Swiss-based NGO, Henry Dunant Centre – later known as the Centre for Humanitarian Dialogue (HD Centre[5]) – a new and low-profile organization established in August 1999 (HD Centre 2009). A representative from the HD Centre met with President Wahid in Jakarta and offered to facilitate contacts with GAM. Wahid supported this offer even though the idea of talks had been met with critique from Indonesian nationalists and the military who opposed foreign interference in an internal matter. For GAM the involvement of HD Centre was perceived as an opportunity to gain international recognition as the legitimate representative of the Acehnese people (Aspinall and Crouch 2003, 10). Schulze (2006, 237) points out that the use of internationalization as a political strategy had long been a central idea within the GAM leadership, but earlier efforts to approach important international actors like the US, UN or Islamic states – from which they hoped to gain sympathy and support – had not had any significant impact.

The Role of Intermediaries: Strategies and Activities

The HD Centre was formed by former humanitarian practitioners with an aim to support solutions to armed conflicts by mediation, in order to protect civilians suffering from these conflicts (Huber 2008, 17). As a mediator between the government and GAM, the core of HD Centre's strategy was that the peace process itself and a dialogue focusing on humanitarian issues would pave the way for future discussions on a political solution (Schulze 2006, 259). Huber (2008, 17) points out that while the HD Centre had never expected to play such a big role as third party between the Indonesian government and GAM, their involvement turned out to be vital for facilitating communication and mediating agreements between the conflicting parties. Parallel to the peace talks held in Geneva, meetings also took place on the ground in Aceh between Indonesian government officials and GAM.

As an intermediary, the HD Centre mediated two ceasefire agreements and a provisional understanding on political issues. The first agreement was the Joint Understanding on a Humanitarian Pause, which was signed in Switzerland in May 2000 (Humanitarian Pause 2000). As part of the agreement, a Joint Forum was created and two committees were established in order to enable its implementation, the Joint Committee on Humanitarian Action and the Joint Committee on Security Modalities. While the former committee primarily aimed to facilitate the coordination and distribution of humanitarian assistance, the latter mainly focused on assuring that no military confrontations were initiated and that violence would not erupt.

Furthermore, in 2001 a Provisional Understanding was mediated based on the first exploratory talks on a political solution to the protracted conflict (HD Centre 2009). The Provisional Understanding comprised a list of elements to be included in such a solution, which took into account the democratic process, human rights and humanitarian law, socio-economic development and security arrangements (Provisional Understanding 2001). After a period of increased violence and a change of presidency in Indonesia, the second ceasefire agreement during HD Centre's mediation came about: the Cessation of Hostilities Agreement, which was signed by the government under President Megawati Sukarnoputri and GAM in December 2002 (CoHA 2002). This agreement was also preceded by talks in Geneva, this time facilitated by an extended mediation team consisting of international officials referred to as the 'wise men' (Huber 2008, 18). This team was formed by the HD Centre and constituted former senior diplomats: a retired marine general from the US, a former foreign minister from Thailand and the former Yugoslav ambassador to Indonesia. A former Swedish diplomat later also joined the group (Aspinall and Crouch 2003, 27). GAM had made demands for an increased international involvement in order to return to negotiations, as well as for the talks to be located outside of Indonesia. Holding meetings outside Indonesia was perceived as important in order to gain international legitimacy and draw attention from influential actors on the international scene (Schulze 2006, 240–1). The Indonesian government had given its approval for the 'wise men' team members to participate under the condition that they were not to be regarded as representatives from their own countries (Aspinall and Crouch 2003, 27).

Besides facilitating talks and mediating agreements, external actors also played a function in ceasefire monitoring. In the first ceasefire agreement during these peace attempts (the Humanitarian Pause), however, only a small monitoring team with members chosen by GAM and the Indonesian government was appointed to supervise its compliance. This ceasefire was initially signed for three months, and during this time the violence in Aceh was temporarily reduced, though not ceased. Wiratmadinata (2009, 65–7) concludes that the agreement did not in any significant way contribute to the search for a peaceful settlement of the armed conflict, nor did the prolonging of the pause for another three months. In both these periods of ceasefire, mistrust between the parties prevailed along with continuous violence and human rights abuses. In the subsequent Cessation of Hostilities Agreement on the other hand, international monitors were brought in. The agreement resulted in the creation of a Joint Security Committee and the establishment of peace zones in Aceh. The international monitors invited to observe compliance with the agreement, alongside monitors from GAM and from the army, came from Thailand and the Philippines (Huber 2008, 19). However, the international monitors were few in number – only 50 persons – and their mandate was limited. Furthermore, just as with the extended mediation team of the 'wise men', the Indonesian government emphasized that the foreign monitors were not to be regarded as representatives from their own countries but to serve as responsible to the HD Centre (Aspinall and Crouch 2003, 33).

While the HD Centre held the central intermediary role in these peace efforts, alongside their involvement other actors, most notably the US, EU, Japan, Canada and the World Bank, used economic rehabilitation of Aceh as an incentive to bring about an agreement (Schulze 2006, 259). Japan engaged as host of two donor conferences aimed to push for progress in the peace process. Furthermore, Norway was crucial in financially supporting the initial mediation efforts as well as the ceasefire monitoring (Huber 2004, 60–6). However, Aspinall and Crouch (2003, 50) argue that many international leaders were unwilling to jeopardize their relationships with the government in Jakarta because of the 'war on terror', and that the UN's recent experiences in East Timor and its impact on the relationship with Jakarta further complicated an involvement in Aceh.[6] Thus, no state or international organization took a leading role in the process alongside the HD Centre; rather, international actors supported the mediator's peace attempts more from behind the scenes.

However, despite these peace efforts, GAM kept insisting on independence for Aceh and the government on maintaining a unitary state (Aspinall and Crouch 2003, 10). Furthermore, Indonesian government officials argued that participation in the peace talks should not be seen as recognition of GAM as a legitimate actor in the international arena, and criticism came from the national council that agreements were signed abroad. Parallels were also made to East Timor, with the anxiety raised that the international community would intervene if the process failed to provide security in the region. On the other side, groups associated with GAM called for a stronger international role and for attention from the UN (Aspinall and Crouch 2003, 16–17). Consequently, the process eventually derailed in 2003. Subsequently, the Indonesian government imposed martial law in Aceh (Huber 2008, 19).

Peace Attempts in the 2000s: The Second Efforts

Initiating the Peace Process: Context and Dynamics

With martial law imposed in Aceh in 2003, the largest military operation yet was launched in the region, and GAM's military position further declined. In 2004 new political changes took place in Jakarta with President Susilo Bambang Yudhoyono assuming office in October 2004 after winning the first direct presidential elections ever to be held in Indonesia (Huber 2008, 19). Yudhoyono's military background proved to be important in order for him to legitimately state that the conflict could not be solved with military means, as well as to protect the peace process from potential spoilers through contacts within the army. Another important government actor was Vice President Jusuf Kalla (Large and Aguswandi 2008, 92–7). Kalla and Yudhoyono had both been part of the previous government – Kalla as President Megawati's coordinating minister of people's welfare and Yudhoyono as her coordinating minister for security and politics – and they were hence familiar with the issues of negotiations as well as the difficulties faced in earlier attempts (Huber 2008, 17). Even before gaining the post of vice president, Kalla had also secretly contacted 'moderate' Acehnese in order to lay the ground for a new dialogue process (Huber 2008, 20).

On 26 December 2004 Aceh was hit by the devastating tsunami that killed approximately 160,000 in Aceh alone and left numerous Acehnese homeless (Large and Aguswandi 2008, 101). The day following the tsunami GAM declared a unilateral ceasefire. Major international attention was turned towards the region for humanitarian relief and reconstruction, and both donor states and relief organizations increasingly started to put pressure on the parties to resume negotiations. This time around another fairly new European-based NGO – the Crisis Management Initiative (CMI) – with its chairman Martti Ahtisaari, was asked to mediate between the government and GAM. The CMI was established in 2000, based in Helsinki and led by its founder, Ahtisaari. Although the new peace process did not gain momentum until after the tsunami catastrophe, contacts had been initiated earlier by a Finnish businessman, Juha Christensen, who himself started discussions with the parties. Ahtisaari was thereafter introduced in late 2004, just prior to the tsunami (Ahtisaari 2008a, 10).

The Role of Intermediaries: Strategies and Activities

With the former president and well-known diplomat Ahtisaari as a front figure, the CMI had more authority as a mediator than the previous HD Centre (Aspinall 2005, 4). From the end of January until mid-July 2005 five rounds of talks took place in Finland, mediated by Ahtisaari and the CMI. A month after the fifth round, on August 15, the Indonesian government and GAM signed the Memorandum of Understanding – a 'final' peace accord (Crisis Management Initiative 2011). CMI's strategy differed from the one used by HD Centre in the earlier peace process; instead of agreeing on a ceasefire in order to build confidence and pave the way for political negotiations, the peace talks focused on reaching agreements on substantial political issues before a ceasefire was put into effect, based on the formula that 'nothing is agreed until everything is agreed' (Ahtisaari 2008a, 10). The Memorandum of Understanding was thus to be perceived as a final 'comprehensive peace settlement', that dealt with the future relationship between GAM and the Indonesian state in terms of socio-economic, political and security related matters (MoU 2005). Hence, for the first time, GAM came to accept a solution on the governing of Aceh within the intact Indonesian state. The government agreed to enable the legalization of local political parties in Aceh, which allowed for GAM to transform into a non-violent political party (Huber 2008, 20). Furthermore, the security situation was addressed in the Memorandum of Understanding by the establishment of a monitoring team, a programme for Demobilization, Disarmament and Reintegration (DDR), and a Commission of the Security Arrangement aimed at settling potential disputes over the agreement. An Aceh Peace and Reintegration Agency (BRA) was eventually set up to deal with socio-economic and political matters such as poverty reduction, political participation, legal issues, and other essential matters related to the process of reintegrating GAM combatants into society, and to address civilian victims of the protracted conflict in accordance with the peace agreement (Wiratmadinata 2009, 70–1).

A part of CMI's third party strategy was furthermore to make sure that their own engagement would be limited in terms of depth and duration (Ahtisaari 2008a, 14). The assignment to monitor and follow up on the agreement through the Aceh Monitoring Mission (AMM) was thus undertaken by the EU, five contributing countries from the Association of Southeast Asian Nations (ASEAN) – Thailand, Malaysia, Brunei, the Philippines and Singapore – in addition to Norway and Switzerland (Wiratmadinata 2009, 78). A UN mission was not considered an option after the East Timor experiences and with the Indonesian government not wanting to 'internationalize' the matter. Hence, an EU–ASEAN team became an acceptable solution for both parties (Ahtisaaari 2008b, 24). In order to restrain new outbreaks of violence and to create conditions favourable for post-conflict reconstruction the team had a mandate to stay for one and a half year. Hence, in the immediate aftermath of the settlement, the focus for the AMM was on security and DDR rather than comprehensive long-term measures (Wiratmadinata 2009, 78). The AMM monitoring mission, however, had a more comprehensive mandate than in the 2002 Cessation of Hostilities Agreement. For example, the monitors now had power to make binding decisions for the parties (Aspinall 2005, 6). Importantly though, the presence of the international monitors was based on a formal invitation by the Indonesian government with the full support of GAM, and its main purpose was assisting the two warring parties to implement the peace agreement (Wiratmadinata 2009, 78).

Aspinall (2005, 21) argues that Athisaari and the CMI had taken in account during the peace process that Indonesia was a 'powerful sovereign state' and that many important domestic actors were hostile towards any international involvement. Hence, the peace process was, to a large extent, to be carried out on the Indonesian government's terms. Still, in comparison to the earlier peace attempts in Aceh with the HD Centre, the acceptance of international involvement was greater this second time around. Among other things, the Indonesian government saw how the international reconstruction of areas damaged from the natural disaster would increase with a peace process. In this respect, it is important to emphasize the vital role played by the EU alongside the CMI in the 2005 peace process, by providing financial support for the CMI mediation; funding and employing the AMM; supporting the reintegration of ex-GAM combatants, rule of law and democracy; as well as through assistance in the elections arranged after the peace agreement (Aguswandi and Large 2008, 97). Hence, while initiatives for a new externally mediated dialogue were initiated prior to the tsunami, it is essential to take into account that the peace process took place in the context of a natural catastrophe. Estimations from the World Bank suggest that – in addition to the enormous number of casualties – 500,000 people lost their homes in the tsunami, and roads, buildings and thousands of hectares farmland were damaged. A substantial amount of tsunami aid was delivered partially from Indonesia but mainly from abroad (Barron 2008, 59). As Frödin (2008, 56) points out, aid for tsunami reconstruction and for post-conflict reconstruction was hence handed out simultaneously but in parallel processes, and with more resources for the former this led to an uneven development between the coastline areas most struck by the tsunami and the most conflict-affected north and central regions. Thus, while the internationally supported peace process and tsunami reconstruction had an essential impact on peace in Aceh and improved the living conditions for many after decades of violent conflict, there were still many challenges to manage as international attention was phased out.

Sri Lanka – The Conflict and Peace Attempts

Background to the Armed Conflict

The armed conflict between the government of Sri Lanka and the LTTE has been one of the most severe contemporary civil wars, both in terms of casualties and duration. The background to the conflict is often described in the context of a marginalization of the Tamil minority that began after the country's independence from the British colonial rule in 1948 (Nissan 1998, 10).

The centralized government that was established and ruled with support from the Sinhalese majority introduced different linguistic and religious restrictions that had severe consequences for the Tamil minority. This discrimination is often described as a reaction from the Sinhalese majority against the Tamils' former privileged situation during the British colonial period, as an attempt to protect and give prominence to the Sinhala culture (Höglund 2004, 155). Tamils began to demand a right to self-determination for Tamils in the north and east – a demand that in the beginning only involved non-violent methods but later on evolved into an armed struggle led by the militant organization, the LTTE (Rupesinghe 2006a, xvi).

The government and the LTTE have been the main belligerent parties in the armed conflict that raged on the island for more than two and a half decades. The conflict has an ethnic dimension, with the main conflicting parties identifying themselves with ethnic groups. The Tamil minority in Sri Lanka makes up 18 per cent of the population, of which a major part live in the north and east (Höglund 2004, 154). Although the LTTE have claimed themselves to be the sole representatives of the Tamil people, it has been difficult throughout the conflict to estimate how extensive the support of the organization has been. The LTTE was founded in the 1970s by Velupillai Prabhakaran. The movement became known for its guerrilla warfare and from the early 1990s the movement controlled parts of northern Sri Lanka (Orjuela 2009, 253). The Sinhalese majority, which makes up 74 per cent of the total population, has since independence dominated the country's government. The domestic politics in Sri Lanka are very dynamic, with frequent changes in government between the major political parties. Notable among the important actors in Sri Lanka is also the Muslim minority, which makes up seven per cent of the population and mainly lives in the eastern parts of the island, claimed by the LTTE (Höglund 2004, 154).

Outbreaks of violence against Tamils in 1983 are usually seen to mark the official start of the armed conflict between the government and the LTTE. Throughout the conflict both parties expressed strong confidence in their own military capacity, while the civilian population was severely affected by the military activities. The war was officially ended in May 2009, after the government took control over former LTTE-controlled areas and with the death of the LTTE leader Prabhakaran (International Crisis Group 2009).

Earlier Peace Attempts

In order to understand the peace attempts in Sri Lanka in the 2000s and its international dimensions, it is essential to first briefly review earlier major efforts.[7] The first attempts to negotiate an end to the armed conflict in

Sri Lanka was initiated a few years after the violence had started, and involved Sri Lanka's powerful neighbouring state, India. India first became involved as a mediator in 1985 and two years later the Indo-Sri Lanka Accord was signed by the Sri Lankan President Jayewardene and the Indian Prime Minister Rajiv Gandhi (Uyangoda 2005, 5). Tamil groups were not, however, a party of the agreement. Furthermore, in order to oversee the implementation of the accord, Indian Peace Keeping Forces (IPKF) were stationed in the northern and northeastern parts of the island (de Silva 1998, 232–3). However, these attempts turned out to be a failure as the Indian peacekeeping troops themselves got involved in fighting with the LTTE, and meanwhile protests against India's intervention and its challenge to the territorial integrity of Sri Lanka came from the southern parts of the island (Nissan 1998, 19). As a result the Sri Lankan President Premadasa invited the LTTE to negotiate in 1989, mainly on how to get the Indian peacekeeping troops out of the country. Consequently, the IPKF was forced to leave Sri Lanka in 1990, but the negotiations between the government and the LTTE broke down once they had achieved this commonly held cause (Uyangoda 2007, 33).

The troublesome experience with India's outside involvement caused the government and the LTTE to engage in bilateral negotiations without any external third party when new peace attempts were made in 1994. At this point, India had decided to ban the LTTE as a response to the assassination of India's Prime Minister Rajiv Gandhi, and hence the organization was weakened and experienced difficulties gaining international support. Four rounds of talks were conducted between the government and the LTTE, and over 40 letters were exchanged (Samuel 1998, 20–1). According to Höglund (2004, 156–7), the parties, however, had different opinions of how the negotiation process should go; the LTTE demanded a permanent ceasefire and humanitarian improvements in the war-torn area before talks on substantive issues could start; the government on the other hand wanted to simultaneously negotiate issues concerning reconstruction and a political solution. Nevertheless, a Declaration on Cessation of Hostilities was signed in January 1995, which lasted for three months. Foreign experts had come to supervise the implementation of the agreement but they never got a chance to begin their work, since the LTTE had contested the functioning of the monitoring committees (Höglund 2004, 168). The LTTE was also concerned about the government's proposal to involve a foreign mediator – a retired French diplomat – in the peace process which the LTTE opposed (Uyangoda 2007, 34). Thus, these negotiations also faltered and there was an escalation rather than a decrease in violence.

Peace Attempts in the 2000s

Initiating the Peace Process: Context and Dynamics

The period following the failed 1994–5 negotiations became the most intense period of fighting since the war had started. President Chandrika Kumaratunga – once elected in 1994 on promises of democratic reforms and negotiations with the LTTE – had changed her approach towards a 'War for Peace' strategy (Höglund and Svensson 2002, 108). The intensified warfare and worsening situation caused widespread war weariness in the country. The government and the LTTE thus cautiously approached each other again in 1999, but regardless of these initiatives both conflicting parties continued to pursue their hostile and military operations. In 2000 the LTTE advanced their military position by taking control over important territories in the north. This was followed by an escalation of violent attacks between the adversaries in the north and east as well as terror incidents in the south, resulting in numerous casualties and displacements (Ganguly 2004, 904). Furthermore, the continuous violence also had severe economic consequences for the state, with a decrease in tourism and foreign investment, which resulted in criticism of President Kumaratunga (Höglund and Svensson 2002, 108). Notwithstanding some military victories the LTTE also faced difficulties. As several important states had decided to classify the LTTE as a terrorist organization, vital financial support from diasporas was reduced. Furthermore, the group met harsh critique from abroad due to its recruitment of child soldiers. Thus, in addition to financial constrains and the overall increased costs of war, the terrorist label and the human rights critique made it more difficult for the LTTE to be internationally recognized as a legitimate actor (Nadarajah 2003, 25–7).

A shift in government in December 2001, however, opened up new opportunities for peace initiatives. The new prime minister – the opposition party leader Ranil Wickremesinghe – had prior to the election declared his intention to abandon the 'War for Peace' strategy in favour of a compromising approach and engage in talks with the LTTE. At the same time, the LTTE had explicitly lowered their earlier demands for an independent state and declared themselves prepared to discuss alternative solutions with the government (Höglund and Svensson 2002, 113). Despite resistance from some opposition parties in the south, Wickremesinghe also agreed to lift an embargo on goods imposed on the LTTE-controlled areas, as well as to accept the recognition of the group as the sole representative for the Tamil people in the peace process (Ganguly 2004, 905).

With the problems of earlier peace attempts still vividly in mind, the parties agreed to engage the state of Norway as a facilitator to assist them in peace efforts. The involvement of Norway had begun already in the late 1990s when President Kumaratunga and the LTTE briefly started to discuss the holding of negotiations (Rupesinghe 2006a, xxxvii). A number of reasons can be given to explain why the state of Norway was approached to become a facilitator in this peace process. By being a fairly small state located far away from Sri Lanka, the conflicting parties neither perceived Norway as a threat, with power to force a given solution upon the parties, nor to have an interest of its own in the region. Furthermore, since both parties had agreed to enter into negotiations as equals, it was important that both of them, as well as India, would accept the choice.[8] Engaging as a third party in peace processes has also become a widely recognized feature of Norway's foreign policy, and from these previous involvements they had become known for using a facilitative method, which was seen as appropriate given the problems with India's intervention. Furthermore, with a long history of engagement in different development projects in Sri Lanka, many personal networks had been created that proved favourable for an involvement (Moolakkattu 2005, 391–2).

The Role of Intermediaries: Strategies and Activities

In their approach as third party, Norway was largely to be perceived as a low profile actor, keeping a limited agenda rather than operating as a driving force. In order to emphasize the third party's limited commission, both Norway and the conflicting parties consistently referred to the Norwegian's role in the peace process as *facilitation* instead of *mediation*. This was indicative of their strategy in the process, which was foremost to facilitate communication and enable the participation of both parties.[9] Thus, there was an emphasis on impartiality, and it was stressed that the ownership of the process rested on the main parties of the conflict – the Sri Lankan government and the LTTE – while the Norwegians assisted them in this process. According to the facilitator Erik Solheim, the Norwegians were also involved in the drafting of agreements on the request of both parties (interview in Rupesinghe 2006b, 346). Furthermore, the facilitators were essential in finding venues for peace talks and for bringing together international support for the peace process (Höglund and Svensson 2009, 150). Six rounds of peace talks were facilitated by Norway in 2002–03. These all took place at foreign venues in Thailand, Norway, Germany and Japan. On 22 February 2002, the parties signed the Ceasefire Agreement (CFA), which essentially structured the subsequent peace process. According to the special envoy of the Norwegian government Eric Solheim, the document was drafted by him during a period of approximately two months and was based on the parties' requirements (interview in Rupesinghe 2006b, 346).[10] The main objective of the agreement was expressed as 'find[ing] a negotiated solution to the ongoing ethnic conflict in Sri Lanka' and 'establishing a positive atmosphere in which further steps towards a lasting solution can be taken'. The agreement focused on the cessation of military operations, the restoration of normalcy in war affected areas, the establishment of a Nordic monitoring group referred to as the Sri Lanka Monitoring Mission (SLMM), and an agreement on the principles for the agreement's validity (Ceasefire Agreement 2002).

Thus with the SLMM monitoring group – constituted by monitors from Denmark, Finland, Iceland, Norway and Sweden – external actors also had the function in the peace process of overseeing the compliance with the CFA. The mission differed significantly from that of the former Indian peacekeepers, as it did not have a peacekeeping mandate or a means to enforce compliance (Goodhand and Klem 2005, 70). The CFA is often highlighted as the mediator's main achievement, as it considerably reduced the violence. During this period the parties undertook a number of measures which, at least temporary, led to security and humanitarian improvements. Joint committees were created – the Sub-Committee for Immediate Humanitarian and Rehabilitation Needs (SIRHAN), a political affairs committee, and a Gender Sub-Committee – and the parties briefly began to discuss a political solution to the conflict based on federalism (Uyangoda 2005, 19). Leaders both from the government and the LTTE also made a number of public statements to affirm their commitment to the peace process. Notably, many observers emphasized it as an important symbolic gesture when the LTTE leader Prabhakaran left his military uniform behind and stepped out of the jungle to hold a press conference in April 2002 (Höglund and Svensson 2002, 111). As the process proceeded, however, many issues regarding the ceasefire also got caught up in the political struggle. Furthermore, criticism was directed towards Norway's dual role in the process, as the monitoring mission that was to report on violations against the truce involved Norwegian monitors and also had a Norwegian as head of mission. While the Norwegians stressed the clear distinction between the peace talks and the monitoring assignment, the difference was not all that clear to the public and was used as an argument against the peace process by critics in the south (Goodhand and Klem 2005, 70).

As an intermediary in the Sri Lankan peace process, Norway also played a role in seeking international support for the peace attempts as one of the donor co-chairs together with the EU, US and Japan (Höglund and Svensson 2009, 150). International donor conferences were initially held in Norway and Japan where pledges were made to support the peace process. Japan has been the largest aid donor to Sri Lanka, which can explain their role as co-chair, while the roles of the other donors – the US and the EU – had a more explicit political dimension in putting pressure on the parties of the peace process (Goodhand

and Klem 2005, 68–9). Thus, in comparison to earlier peace attempts, this peace process had the organized involvement of the international community (Noyahr 2006, 355). Goodhand and Klem (2005, 78) argue that while donors had previously tried to 'work "around" conflicts' and view them as 'political concerns', the peace process in the 2000s differed in that respect. Instead, donors tried to exert influence on the peace attempts by applying conditions for reconstruction and development aid, as well as by attempting to address the causes and consequences of conflict. The peak in pledges came during the Tokyo conference in 2003 where pledges were made for a total of $4.5 billion. While the international engagement was largely perceived by the LTTE as a way to gain recognition as a legitimate actor, the government referred to it as an international 'safety net' that was in place to guarantee security and economic funding (Goodhand and Klem 2005, 72–3).

However, as the process evolved, critical voices became increasingly louder, notably among southern nationalists and Buddhist monks who questioned the peace talks in general and the involvement by Norway in particular (Frydenlund 2005, 20–5). Furthermore, after the sixth round of talks the LTTE decided to abandon the negotiation process, with the justification that the decisions taken during the negotiations were not being implemented to their satisfaction. The group also expressed discontent for being excluded from a donor conference in Washington, a decision they believed disrupted the perceived parity between the parties (Balasingham 2004, 430). The LTTE still maintained their commitment to the CFA but it was heavily violated. Meanwhile, the establishment of joint committees was put on hold (Rupesinghe 2006a, 100–1). As Uyangoda (2005, 17) emphasizes, pledges for reconstruction and development made by the international community during a donor meeting in Tokyo after the peace talks had stalled did not prove enough to bring the parties back to the negation table. Furthermore, monitoring the ceasefire agreement that was still in place became an all the more challenging task for the Nordic monitoring group. In 2006, the monitoring mission was further constrained when the LTTE required monitors from EU-member countries to resign, as a reaction to the EU's banning of the LTTE as a terrorist group (SLMM 2006).

After the peace talks stalled the Norwegian facilitators tried to make the parties return to the negotiation table. However, such attempts were hindered both by changes in the political environment in Colombo, with Kamaratunga dissolving parliament and a coalition of the People's Alliance (PA) and nationalist Janatha Vimukthi Peramuna (JVP) winning a majority, as well as by disturbances within the LTTE, with the breaking away of the eastern leader Karuna. Furthermore, there were difficulties for the parties to agree on an agenda: the LTTE wanted to discuss their Interim

Self-Governing Authority proposal (ISGA), a demand that the government rejected (Social Scientists' Association 2004). After the tsunami catastrophe that severely affected Sri Lanka in 2004, a joint mechanism to handle post-tsunami reconstruction was formulated with assistance from the Norwegian facilitators. Initially, there were high hopes that the natural disaster would force the parties together and, despite all its misery, create an environment favourable to peace. However, the joint agreement was not implemented, partly due to the Supreme Court's ruling about the agreement's legacy (Goodhand and Klem 2005, 21–2). Furthermore, the large amount of tsunami aid that came into the country led in many respects to a worsening of the conflict as new disputes erupted over aid distribution (Orjuela 2007, 127–32). In 2005, Mahinda Rajapaksa from the United People's Freedom Alliance (UPFA) became the new president of Sri Lanka and the following year the government and the LTTE once again agreed to commence talks in Geneva, also this time facilitated by Norway. While the first round of talks took place in Geneva in February 2006, the second round, scheduled for the end of April, was never held (*Lanka Academic* 2006).

After years of increased hostilities, the Sri Lankan government officially withdrew from the ceasefire agreement in 2008, and in April 2009 – during an intensive military offensive – the Norwegian facilitation was also announced as having come to an end (BBC 2009). The following month the government declared its victory in the war through a military defeat over the LTTE and by the death of the LTTE leadership. International access into the formerly LTTE-controlled areas where the last battles had taken place was to large extent limited, and the Sri Lankan government strongly resisted, and rejected the results of, an investigation on accountability commissioned by the United Nations secretary-general Ban Ki-Moon (BBC 2011). For the post-war Sri Lanka entering a new decade, the context of international influences has changed notably as compared to the early phases of peace initiatives in the beginning of the 2000s. As Höglund and Orjuela (2011, 25) stress 'the power and legitimacy of the West to influence the Sri Lankan government has diminished' while some Asian states, in particular China, are further developing and strengthening their economic and military relations with Sri Lanka – states that seldom question Sri Lankan politics or put conflict sensitivity as a condition for donor support (Höglund and Orjuela 2011, 32).

Conclusions

The aim of this chapter has been to explore the rationale for international involvements in managing peace processes in the two intra-state armed conflicts of Aceh and Sri Lanka. The study has focused on peace attempts in the 2000s in order to analyse how the internationally influenced peace processes were made possible, and how the roles of external actors in these processes can be understood. The conflicts in Aceh and Sri Lanka are both situated in a region that on the whole has attracted low levels of international attention in peace efforts, and where the norms of sovereignty and non-interference in internal matters are strongly emphasized among states. The peace attempts that Aceh and Sri Lanka experienced in the 2000s – mediated by HD Centre and CMI in Aceh, and by Norway in Sri Lanka – therefore meant a new dimension of internationalization in the two conflicts. Still, it is important to emphasize that the international involvements in the peace processes have been based on the consent from both primary conflicting parties, who have accordingly determined the features of the efforts to a large extent. This has had implications on the type of actors involved, their mandates and the possibilities for them to exert influence.

Common features for the actors who have been involved as the main third parties in the peace attempts in the 2000s (i.e., the two NGOs and the state of Norway) are that they are located geographically far away from the conflict zones and are generally associated with notions of impartiality. Furthermore, they can be categorized as a type of actor known for using a facilitative and low-profile approach in peacemaking rather than exerting power to influence the parties of a conflict. In this regard, there has not been any obvious reason for the conflicting parties to suspect these actors of having an interest of their own in the region, or of having the power to pose a threat. Because these peace processes in Aceh and Sri Lanka, notwithstanding the new dimensions of internationalization, have essentially been internally driven and based on the consent and ownership of the process by the warring parties, these types of third party actors have been perceived as an acceptable alternative that both parties in conflict could agree upon. Furthermore, while these more low-profile actors have been appointed to leading roles in the peace attempts and in the mediation of agreements, it is also important to notice that several other actors have backed the publicly well-known mediators by playing supportive roles 'behind the scenes'. These engagements have most notably been the funding of the peace processes, the deployment of monitoring missions to observe ceasefires, and the provision of development assistance in reconstruction projects. Thus, these activities have all been part of an overarching strategy in which the more resource-strong external actors with the capacity to provide financial support have been engaged alongside the more 'modest' actors involved as third party mediators. As a common feature to both the Aceh and Sri Lankan peace processes, donor conferences were held simultaneously with peace talks in order to create incentives for the warring parties to make progress towards a settlement. In this regard, the US,

Japan and the EU played central roles in both peace processes. Still, while some common features can be discerned from this overview, it can also be suggested that the case of Aceh demonstrates to a larger extent an ability to bring about changes, with new attempts being initiated that differ from earlier efforts. For example, the degree of international involvement increased with the establishment of the 'wise men' team of international diplomats, and furthermore, the mediation approach by Ahtisaari in the last process was characterized by the use of more leverage than in the former. This can be contrasted with the Sri Lankan process with its continuous mediation effort and ceasefire agreement that remained (on paper) for several years before being officially abandoned.

In many ways the structure of the peace processes in Aceh and Sri Lanka corresponds with the general trends in international peacemaking and peacebuilding efforts that are characterized by multidimensional approaches, where third party mediated peace talks are combined with security arrangements and development assistance. However, with regard to the ownership of the processes by the conflicting parties, the mandates for the external involvements have been comparatively limited. For example, the importance of facilitation rather than mediation has been stressed, and the observation teams set up to monitor ceasefires have had quite moderate mandates in comparison to the often more extensive peacekeeping missions. While it is beyond the scope of this paper to make an assessment of the impact of these strategies, the review of peace processes in Aceh and Sri Lanka suggests that to some extent the security arrangements and the development assistance at least temporarily improved the situation in conflict-affected areas. Furthermore, in the earlier stages of the negotiation processes these efforts seem to have stimulated some steps forward in the talks. Still, as Uyangoda (2005, 17) argues, donors' threats of stopping foreign aid was not enough to keep the parties in the process in Sri Lanka, which highlights the limitations of the role of international actors to impact the warring parties. Furthermore, the Sri Lankan case illustrates how actions taken by external actors can easily get caught up in the dynamics of the conflict. For instance, there were many debates during the peace process regarding Norway's involvement and accusations of them being biased towards the LTTE. Also, the pledges and delivery of aid essentially became matters of conflict. While there is a need to emphasize both linkages between underdevelopment and uneven development as part of the causes and consequences of war (Mac Ginty and Williams 2009, 2), the effect of uneven development has perhaps become most apparent during peace processes. Unevenness, or perceived unevenness, in the distribution of aid risks fueling already polarized relationships, and perhaps particularly so in territorial intra-state conflicts where the parties (at least to some extent) have control over different territories. This problem became particularly evident in the distribution of tsunami aid in Sri Lanka during the ongoing conflict, and to some extent also occurred in Aceh where the different conditions between aid for tsunami reconstruction and aid for post conflict reconstruction caused discontent. Since development assistance risks triggering and sustaining conflicts, the way in which it is managed in a particular context is essential. Thus, while the last decade's peace processes in Aceh and Sri Lanka made possible for the first time direct talks between the warring parties, (periods of) reduced violence, and improvements of the living conditions in war-affected areas, they also demonstrate the limits of external actors' roles in peace processes significantly owned by the conflicting parties. As Goodhand and Klem (2005, 75) put it: 'To an extent, the story is less about how international peacemakers influence domestic actors, than how the latter use the former to pursue their particular political projects'.

As Dayton (2009, 61) reminds us, intermediaries can thus be a 'useful and sometimes necessary component' in managing peace processes but are 'rarely a sufficient one'. While it is important to recognize the various structural factors that came together and enabled peace attempts in these long-lasting conflicts, the internal political dynamics and the role of leadership transitions deserves some special attention. The overview of peace processes in Aceh and Sri Lanka presented in this chapter suggests that the initiation of peace attempts has coincided with political-societal changes which have opened up a window of opportunity for transformative leadership; a new leader that has been pushing for an altered political approach to conflict management, or a present leader that has started to speak about the conflict in a different way and through various gestures expressed a new approach towards the conflict. For example, changes in Indonesia's political environment after the fall of Suharto's regime illustrate a number of such cases. Nevertheless, how the process eventually unfolds depends on the leadership's interactions with the conflict counterpart, internal factions and constituencies, as well as on the evolving circumstances in which such interplay takes place.

Notes

1 This chapter is partly derived from a paper presented at the 2009 Conference of the Swedish Network of Peace, Conflict and Development Research in Stockholm on 6–7 November 2009. Part of the chapter is adapted from Åkebo (2011).
2 Concepts such as 'external actors', 'outside actors', 'third parties' and 'intermediaries' are used interchangeably in this chapter.
3 While the geographical boundaries that the authors use in their study to define the Southeast Asian region do not include Sri Lanka, the Sri Lankan conflict is nevertheless mentioned in the analysis as sharing central characteristics with other civil wars in southern Asia. See Möller et al. (2007, 378).

4 Due to the complexity of contemporary intra-state conflicts a levels-of-analysis framework is often used in these kinds of studies (see, for example, Ramsbotham, Woodhouse and Miall, 2005, 163–4).

5 In Aceh the organization is commonly known by the acronym HDC. The organization itself, however, uses HD Centre in publications and on its website which will accordingly also be used in this chapter.

6 However, Huber (2004, 60) stresses that while the UN did not engaged in public diplomacy in Aceh, there was a regular exchange of information with the HD Centre on how the process was proceeding.

7 The review focuses on peace negotiation processes, not on political reforms.

8 These reasons were expressed in interviews conducted by the author in Sri Lanka in 2006.

9 Interviews by the author in Sri Lanka in 2006.

10 There have, however, been debates in Sri Lanka about the drafting procedure.

References

Aggestam, Karin and Annika Björkdahl. 2009. 'Introduction: War and Peace in Transition'. In K. Aggestam and A. Björkdahl (eds), *War and Peace in Transition: Changing Roles of External Actors*, 15–31. Lund: Nordic Academic Press.

Ahtisaari, Martti. 2008a. 'Lessons of Aceh Peace Talks'. *Asia Europe Journal* 6(1), 9–14.

_____. 2008b. 'Delivering Peace for Aceh: An Interview with President Martti Ahtisaari'. In Aguswandi and Judith Large (eds), *Reconfiguring Politics: The Indonesia–Aceh Peace Process*, 22–4. London: Conciliation Resources.

Aspinall, Edward. 2005. *The Helsinki Agreement: A More Promising Basis for Peace in Aceh?* Policy Studies 20. Washington DC: East-West Center Washington.

Aspinall, Edward and Harold Crouch. 2003. *The Aceh Peace Process: Why it Failed*. Policy Studies 1. Washington DC: East-West Center Washington.

Azar, Edward. 1990. *The Management of Protracted Social Conflict: Theory and Cases*. Aldershot: Dartmouth.

Balasingham, Anton. 2004. *War and Peace: Armed Struggle and Peace Efforts of Liberation Tigers*. Mitcham: Fairmax.

Barron, Patrick. 2008. 'Managing the Resources for Peace: Reconstruction and Peacebuilding in Aceh'. In Aguswandi and Judith Large (eds), *Reconfiguring Politics: the Indonesia–Aceh Peace Process*, 58–61. London: Conciliation Resources.

BBC. 2009. 'Norway "No Longer Peace Facilitator"'. Online news article at BBCSinhala.com, published 13 April. Online: http://www.bbc.co.uk/sinhala/news/story/2009/04/090413_norway_embassy.shtml (accessed 1 June 2009).

_____. 2011. 'Thousands Protest in Sri Lanka against UN Report'. Online news article at BBC News South Asia, published 1 May 2011. Online: http://www.bbc.co.uk/news/world-south-asia-13256015 (accessed 22 June 2011).

Ceasefire Agreement. 2002. 'Agreement on a Ceasefire Between the Government of the Democratic Socialist Republic of Sri Lanka and the Liberation Tigers of Tamil Eelam'. United States Institute of Peace: Peace Agreements Digital Collection. Online: http://www.usip.org/files/file/resources/collections/peace_agreements/pa_sri_lanka_02222002.pdf (accessed 18 October 2011).

CoHA. 2002. 'Cessation of Hostilities Framework Agreement between Government of the Republic of Indonesia and the Free Aceh Movement'. United States Institute of Peace: Peace Agreements Digital Collection. Online: http://www.usip.org/files/file/ resources/collections/peace_agreements/aceh_12092002.pdf (accessed 18 October 2011).

Crisis Management Initiative. 2011. 'Aceh Negotiations in 2005'. Crisis Management Initiative web page. Online: http://www.cmi.fi/activities/aceh.html (accessed 18 October 2011).

Crocker, Chester A., Fen Osler Hampson and Pamela Aall (eds). 2005. *Grasping the Nettle: Analyzing Cases of Intractable Conflict*. Washington DC: US Institute of Peace Press.

Darby, John and Roger Mac Ginty (eds). 2003. *Contemporary Peacemaking: Conflict, Violence and Peace Processes*. London: Palgrave, Macmillan.

————. 2008. *Contemporary Peacemaking: Conflict, Peace Processes and Post-War Reconstruction*, 2nd edition. London: Palgrave, Macmillan.

Dayton, Bruce W. 2009. 'Useful but Insufficient: Intermediaries in Peacebuilding'. In Dayton, Bruce W. and Louis Kriesberg (eds), *Conflict Transformation and Peacebuilding: Moving from Violence to Sustainable Peace*, 61–73. London and New York: Routledge.

de Silva, K. M. 1998. *Reaping the Whirlwind: Ethnic Conflict, Ethnic Politics in Sri Lanka*. India: Penguin Books.

Frydenlund, Iselin. 2005. *The Sangha and Its Relation to the Peace Process in Sri Lanka: PRIO Report 2/2005*. Oslo: International Peace Research Institute (PRIO) Online: http://www.prio.no/files/file46330_binder1.pdf (accessed 19 September 2005).

Frödin, Lina. 2008. 'The Challenges of Reintegration in Aceh'. In Aguswandi and Judith Large (eds), *Reconfiguring Politics: the Indonesia–Aceh Peace Process*, 54–7. London: Conciliation Resources.

Ganguly, Rajat. 2004. 'Sri Lanka's Ethnic Conflict: At a Crossroad between Peace and War'. *Third World Quarterly* 25(5): 903–18.

Goodhand, Jonathan and Bart Klem. 2005. *Aid, Conflict, and Peacebuilding in Sri Lanka 2000–2005*. Colombo: Asia Foundation.

HD Centre. 2009. 'About the HD Centre'. Centre for Humanitarian Dialogue. Online: http://www.hdcentre.org/about (accessed 28 October 2009).

Huber, Konrad. 2004. *The HDC in Aceh: Promises and Pitfalls of NGO Mediation and Implementation*. Policy Studies 9. Washington DC: East-West Center Washington.

————. 2008. 'Aceh's Arduous Journey to Peace'. In Aguswandi and Judith Large (eds), *Reconfiguring Politics: the Indonesia–Aceh Peace Process*, 16–21. London: Conciliation Resources.

Humanitarian Pause. 2000. 'Joint Understanding on Humanitarian Pause for Aceh'. Online: http://www.aceh-eye.org/data_files/english_format/peace_process/peace_process_hp/hp_agreement/hp_agreement.asp (accessed 3 April 2009).

Höglund, Kristine. 2004. *Violence in the Midst of Peace Negotiations: Cases from Guatemala, Northern Ireland, South Africa and Sri Lanka*. Report No. 69. Uppsala: Department of Peace and Conflict Research, Uppsala University.

Höglund, Kristine and Camilla Orjuela. 2011. 'Winning the Peace: Conflict Prevention after a Victor's Peace in Sri Lanka'. *Contemporary Social Science* 6(1): 19–37.

Höglund, Kristine and Isak Svensson. 2003. 'The Peace Process in Sri Lanka'. *Civil Wars* 5(4): 103–18.

————. 2009. 'Mediating between Tigers and Lions: Norwegian Peace Diplomacy in Sri Lanka's Civil War'. In Karin Aggestam and Annika Björkdahl (eds), *War and Peace in Transition: Changing Roles of External Actors*, 147–69. Lund: Nordic Acedemic Press.

International Crisis Group. 2009. 'Reports by Region: Sri Lanka'. International Crisis Group. Online: http://www.crisisgroup.org/home/index.cfm?id=4459&l=1 (accessed 2 November 2009; site now discontinued).

Lanka Academic Network. 2006. 'Joint Statement by the Government and the LTTE'. 23 February 2006. *The Lanka Academic*. Online: http://archive.lacnet.org/2006/2006_02_23/ (accessed 24 February 2006).

Large, Judith and Aguswandi. 2008 *Reconfiguring Politics: the Indonesia–Aceh Peace Process*. London: Conciliation Resources.

MacGinty, Roger and Andrew Williams. 2009. *Conflict and Development*. London and New York: Routledge.

Mack, Andrew. 2006. *Human Security Brief 2006*. Human Security Centre: University of British Columbia, Canada. Online: http://www.hsrgroup.org/docs/Publications/HSB2006/2006HumanSecurityBrief-FullText.pdf (accessed 7 January 2009).

Miller, Michelle Ann. 2008. 'The Conflict in Aceh: Context, Precursors and Catalysts'. In Aguswandi and Judith Large (eds), *Reconfiguring Politics: the Indonesia–Aceh Peace Process*, 12–15. London: Conciliation Resources.

Mitchell, Christopher. 2008. 'Mediation and the Ending of Conflicts'. In John Darby and Roger Mac Ginty (eds), *Contemporary Peacemaking: Conflict, Peace Processes and Post-War Reconstruction*, 94–104. 2nd edition. London: Palgrave, Macmillan.

Moolakkattu, John Stephen. 2005. 'Peace Facilitation by Small States: Norway in Sri Lanka'. *Cooperation and Conflict* 40(4): 385–402.

MoU. 2005. 'Memorandum of Understanding between the Government of the Republic of Indonesia and the Free Aceh Movement'. Online: http://www.consilium.europa.eu/uedocs/cmsUpload/MoU_Aceh.pdf (accessed 16 December 2010).

Möller, Frida, Karl DeRouen Jr., Jacob Bercovitch and Peter Wallensteen. 2007. 'The Limits of Peace: Third Parties in Civil Wars in Southeast Asia, 1993–2004'. *Negotiation Journal*. October: 373–91.

Nadarajah, V. S. 2003. 'Obstacles to the Peace Process'. In Jayadeva Uyangoda and Morina Perera (eds), *Sri Lanka's Peace Process 2002 Critical Perspectives*, 25–7. Colombo: Social Scientists' Association.

Nissan, Elizabeth. 1998. 'Historical Context'. In Liz Philipson (ed.), *Accord: Demanding Sacrifice: War and Negotiation in Sri Lanka*, 10–19. London: Conciliation Resources.

Noyahr, Keith. 2006. 'The Role of the International Community'. In Kumar Rupesinghe (ed.), *Negotiating Peace in Sri Lanka: Efforts, Failures and Lessons*, 355–404. Vol. 2. Sri Lanka: Foundation for Co-Existence.

Orjuela, Camilla. 2004. *Civil Society in Civil War: Peace Work and Identity Politics in Sri Lanka*. Gothenburg: Department of Peace and Development Research, Gothenburg University.

———. 2007. 'Biståndsfällor som motverkar fred' [Foreign Aid Traps That Work Against Peace]. In Sofia Wennerstrand and Malin Söderlund (eds), *Verktyg för fred: Exempel från Liberia och Sri Lanka* [Tools for Peace: Examples from Liberia and Sri Lanka], 127–32. Stockholm: Atlas.

———. 2009. 'Domesticating Tigers: the LTTE and Peacemaking in Sri Lanka'. In Bruce W. Dayton and Louis Kriesberg (eds), *Conflict Transformation and Peacebuilding: Moving from Violence to Sustainable Peace*, 252–69. London and New York: Routledge.

Provisional Understanding. 2001. 'Provisional Understanding between the Government of the Republic of Indonesia and the Leadership of the Free Aceh Movement'. Online: http://www.hdcentre.org/files/Provisional%20understanding.pdf (accessed 30 January 2010).

Ramsbotham, Oliver, Tom Woodhouse and Hugh Miall. 2005. *Contemporary Conflict Resolution: The Prevention, Management and Transformation of Deadly Conflicts*. 2nd edition. Oxford: Polity Press.

Rupesinghe, Kumar (ed.) 2006a. *Negotiating Peace in Sri Lanka: Efforts, Failures and Lessons.* Vol. 2. Sri Lanka: Foundation for Co-Existence.

————. 2006b. 'Interview with Erik Solheim, Minister of International Development'. In Rupesinghe, Kumar (ed.), *Negotiating Peace in Sri Lanka: Efforts, Failures and Lessons,* 339–54. Vol. 2. Sri Lanka: Foundation for Co-Existence.

Samuel, Kumudini. 1998. 'Straining Consensus: Government Strategies for War and Peace in Sri Lanka 1994–98'. In Liz Philipson (ed.), *Accord: Demanding Sacrifice: War and Negotiation in Sri Lanka,* 20–7. London: Conciliation Resources.

Schulze, Kirsten E. 2006. 'Insurgency and Counter-insurgency: Strategy and the Aceh Conflict, October 1976–May 2004'. In Anthony Ried (ed.), *Verandah of Violence: the Background to the Aceh Problem,* 225–71. Singapore: NUS Press.

SLMM. 2006. '21/08/06(a): Sri Lanka Monitoring Mission to Regroup in Colombo Temporarily'. Sri Lanka Monitoring Mission archive: Operational statements. Online: http://slmm-history.info/SLMM_Archive/Operational_statements/2006/21%2F08 %2F06+%28a%29+-+Sri+Lanka+Monitoring+Mission+to+regroup+in+Colombo+ temporarily.9UFRnO1O.ips (accessed 29 October 2010).

Social Scientists' Association. 2004. 'Hurting Negotiation Stalemate'. *Polity* 2(2).

Uppsala Conflict Data Program (UCDP). 2011. 'Indonesia'. *UCDP Conflict Encyclopedia.* Online: http://www.ucdp.uu.se/gpdatabase/gpcountry.php?id=75&regionSelect=11-Oceania# (accessed 18 October 2011).

Uyangoda, Jayadeva. 2005. Transition from civil war to peace: Challenges of peace building in Sri Lanka. Working Paper, November. Colombo: Social Scientists' Association.

————. 2007. *Ethnic Conflict in Sri Lanka: Changing Dynamics.* Policy Studies 32. Washington DC: East-West Centre Washington.

Wallensteen, Peter. 2007. *Understanding Conflict Resolution: War, Peace and the Global System.* 2nd edition. London, Thousand Oaks, New Delhi sand Singapore: Sage.

Wallensteen, Peter, Karl DeRouen Jr., Jacob Bercovitch and Frida Möller. 2009. 'Democracy and Mediation in Territorial Civil Wars in Southeast Asia and the South Pacific'. *Asia Europe Journal* 16 April: 241–64.

Wiratmadinata. 2009. *An Evolving Model for Conflict Transformation and Peacebuilding in Aceh: Analysis of the Aceh Peace Process from an Acehnese Perspective.* Banda Aceh: Aceh Justice Resource Centre.

Åkebo, Malin. 2011. 'The Role of External Actors in Managing Peace Processes in Asia: An Overview of Attempts in Aceh, Mindanao and Sri Lanka'. In Ramses Amer and Zou Keyuan (eds), *Conflict Management and Dispute Settlement in East Asia,* 83–106. Farnham and Burlington: Ashgate.

Chapter 7

THE CHALLENGES OF HUMAN SECURITY AND DEVELOPMENT IN CENTRAL ASIA

Marlène Laruelle and Sébastien Peyrouse

Introduction

For almost two decades, academic and expert milieus have developed a broad definition of security, one that is distinct from the traditional, state-centric view that focuses on military issues. This definition encompasses so-called non-traditional security issues: weak states and economies, unresolved conflicts, growing poverty, migration, organized crime, drug trafficking, and corruption, as well as terrorism, insurrectionist movements, energy security, nuclear proliferation and nuclear terrorism, chemical and biological weapons, maritime security, cyber crime, environmental degradation, health (pandemics), and food security – all of which reveal forms of low-intensity conflict and failures in governance (Preventing the Next Wave of Conflict 2003).

Research is now moving beyond the study of isolated and specific elements of security studies in order to provide a greater theoretical understanding of the complex interaction between security issues and, rather than simply point to local variables, examine their causal mechanisms (King and Murray 2001–2). Human security challenges are indeed interconnected and transnational in scope, defying unilateral remedies and requiring comprehensive – political, economic and social – responses (Tadjbakhsh and Chenoy 2006). As a result, they cannot be separately studied, nor individually resolved. The need to shift from a *state-based* to a *people-based* approach is still being debated (Paris 2001; Thomas 2001). The importance of human factors in these various issues has indeed to be taken into account, especially when it comes to finding resolutions, but the state remains the principle framework for regulating individuals (Richmond 2007). Human security challenges also invite a discussion of the concept of 'glocalization' that allows the local, regional and global levels (or micro, meso and macro) to be articulated as a single dimension by studying how global phenomena take root in very localized societal and historical realities.

This chapter examines the intersection of certain human security challenges – narcotics trafficking and the criminalization of the economy, societal risks, pauperization, and large migration flows – using the example of the Central Asian region (Kazakhstan, Kyrgyzstan, Uzbekistan, Tajikistan and Turkmenistan). These countries became independent in 1991 after the fall of the Soviet Union. Unlike many poor countries in Africa or Asia, Soviet Central Asia had relatively high human development indicators, which fell somewhat in the 1990s. The sense of a decline in living standards and reduced prospects over the near, medium and long terms play a major role in the perception by the population of the human security challenges it faces. The multiplicity and overlapping nature of these challenges make for a particularly tense social and political situation, as demonstrated by the violent events in Kyrgyzstan in June 2010.

The Central Asian Region, Two Decades after Independence

Nearly two decades after their independence, the five Central Asian states have each taken distinct social and political paths, with Kazakhstan as the only country to experience significant economic development. The economies of Central Asia are marked by two key elements. First, the question of land privatization is a particularly crucial one in the three states (Uzbekistan, Turkmenistan and Tajikistan) with mostly rural populations (Trevisani 2008); the second issue is an economic system that almost exclusively depends on state revenues from primary resources, especially hydrocarbons, precious metals and cotton. The Central Asian states therefore only have narrow room to maneuver. Their official discourses may point to the geographical centrality of the region, but given realities like border closures, weak regional cooperation and massive corruption, this is not likely to work in their economic favour over the next decade. The local populations have implemented schemes to get around these economic difficulties by appropriating the resources available to them – mainly petty trade and labour migration (Laruelle 2010).

Several elements underlying the economic development of the Central Asian states can be explained by geography and history. A relatively unfavourable climate, low population density, and economic specialization in raw materials instead of in value-added industries are old characteristics that have been rooted in the region's history for many centuries. Though these traits were accentuated by Russo-Soviet domination, they cannot be modified by political will alone. Added to these structural difficulties – for which oil, gas and mineral riches barely compensate – are particularly complex domestic and international political environments (Laruelle and Peyrouse 2012).

The five Central Asian states were thrust onto the international stage in 1991 with feelings of having been abandoned by Moscow and the 'Slavic republics' (Russia, Ukraine and Belarus). The initial conditions for independence proved challenging in many respects. Local elites were ill-prepared, economies interdependent, industries highly subsidized and borders complex; the populations, who were demanding autonomy, did not necessarily want independence (Fierman 1991). Nonetheless, for over almost two decades, the Central Asian states, with the exception of Tajikistan until 1997,[1] have managed to prevent their societies from sliding into civil war or violent inter-ethnic clashes like those seen in the Caucasus. However, the events in Kyrgyzstan in 2010 have served to confirm the deterioration of the situation (Melvin 2011).

The short-term challenges of independence have been overcome with relative success, but those of long-term development remain problematic. The Central Asian states have managed to secure identities as nation-states, develop their own political agendas, and forge distinct social and economic paths for themselves (Kavalski 2010). Each of them has contributed its specific solution to the problems affecting the whole region in accordance with its economic wealth and domestic situation. In the 1990s, numerous signs gave cause for optimism concerning the region's potential development. Kazakhstan, Turkmenistan, and Uzbekistan had a vast wealth of raw materials, gas and oil in particular, but also strategic minerals such as uranium (Rumer 2005). Many international investors, looking for complementary energy resources to reduce their dependence on the politically unstable Middle East, became very interested in Caspian Sea resources (Najman, Raballand and Pomfret 2007). Moreover, the disappearance of the bipolar world allowed a revival of geopolitical analysis on the strategic importance of this 'heartland' (Edwards 2003), which lies at the junction of several countries that are destined to play major international roles: China, India, Iran, Pakistan, and a still potentially powerful Russia.

In addition to this geopolitical situation, Central Asia had inherited many assets from the Soviet regime. Each state was equipped with a relatively developed industrial and/or agricultural sector, despite the fact that the breaking of links between the republics and the end of Moscow's subsidies for unprofitable factories put local economies in very difficult positions (Gleason 2003). A country such as Uzbekistan was also in a situation to take advantage of its significant agricultural potential in cotton. Central Asia enjoyed literacy rates close to one hundred percent, as well as relatively high levels of education, particularly in the technical sector. The health system was also well developed, and endemic diseases had been wiped out during the Soviet period. It was taken for granted that women were in the workforce, and child labour remained minimal. Hence, the situation of Central Asia immediately after independence was incomparable to that of third world countries (Fierman 1991). This is no longer the case today, especially in the education and health sectors.

Though each Central Asian state has contrasting economic possibilities open to it, they are all marked by the increasing confinement of their exports to primary resources. This situation is leading to the disappearance of the last of their transformation industries that survived the collapse of the Soviet Union. The Central Asian economies can indeed be classified as rent economies: Kazakhstan for its oil, Turkmenistan for its gas and cotton, and Uzbekistan for its cotton and gold (Pomfret 2006).

The two poorest states, Kyrgyzstan and Tajikistan, have neither hydrocarbon reserves nor exportable agricultural products, and have to make do with a few isolated extractions of precious metals. As a result, Kyrgyzstan's main source of revenue in hard currency is the Kumtor gold mine, which alone represents 40 per cent of Kyrgyz exports and 13 per cent of its GDP, and the taxes on re-exporting Chinese goods (Raballand and Kaminski 2009); while in Tajikistan, the Tursunzade aluminum smelter accounts for more than 60 per cent of exports. The region's development is thus subject to the ups and downs of world prices of oil, gas, metals and cotton (Pomfret 2006). What has come to bear in Central Asia is no different from the situation in other rent economies: an inability to distribute wealth; a widening of social inequalities and weak administrative structures; and an absence of real legal constraints and of institutional mechanisms to ensure that economic decisions are made in the public interest.

The political trajectories of the five states have many features in common. All have deteriorating political situations where opposition parties are either placed in very difficult situations (the case in Kazakhstan and Tajikistan) or are unable to exist (Uzbekistan and Turkmenistan). In this regard, Kyrgyzstan is unique in the region; however, its higher degree of political freedom has become synonymous with chronic destabilizations, which serve as negative examples to neighbouring regimes. The media has also had limits placed on its freedom of expression, to say nothing of the human rights situation (EUCAM 2010). All the first heads of state, many of whom were the former first secretaries of the Communist Party of their republics, have used and abused the principle of the referendum in their own interest throughout the 1990s and 2000s. They have done this either to extend their presidential mandate from five to seven years, or to seek several mandates in a row. The extreme presidentialization of power has led the heads of state to conduct multiple constitutional and legislative revisions, and to prevent the emergence of any political alternative. In such a context, elections are largely devoid of the democratic meaning that they are supposed to embody (Laruelle and Peyrouse 2006).[2]

Central Asian heads of state have also succeeded in maintaining power within their own families. This phenomenon is accompanied by the appropriation of the country's resources, and has led to the endemic corruption of the state edifice, from top to bottom (Kupatadze 2008). Indeed, all the Central Asian presidents have personally misappropriated some of the oil and gas revenues and demand high rents from foreign investors who want to establish themselves in the country, whatever their field of activity. This patronage-based system, deeply rooted in the daily reality of Central Asia, contributes to the development of widespread corruption at all levels of society (Ilkhamov 2007a).

The corruption of state employees is an endemic problem. All administrative posts must be bought, not only in key fields such as justice and the police, but also in public services, education, agriculture and industry (Engvall 2011). The population can be charged for even the smallest administrative procedure; the financial demands of the police are particularly feared. The privatization of the countries' wealth and the nepotism of the presidential clans deeply infiltrate the entire region. The process of 'catching the state' and placing the mafia and criminal groups under state supervision (Marat 2006) have further impoverished already weakened societies, for which the 'democratization' and 'market economy' established during the last years of the Soviet Union are often synonymous with the collapse of living standards.

Political stability has not been attained and, with the exception of Kazakhstan, which is the only state in the region that provides prospects of development to its population, the Central Asian states are at risk of internal political destabilization. The presence of clandestine Islamist movements was confirmed in the 1990s (Naumkin 2005),[3] and since spring 2009, renewed outbreaks of Islamic activism have been noted in areas where militants are historically rooted: the Uzbek–Kyrgyz border, the Batken region in Kyrgyzstan and the Karategin valley in Tajikistan. This can probably be attributed in part to the changing situation in Afghanistan and Pakistan but is mainly due to a revival of domestic tensions in the regions (Heathershaw and Roche 2011).

Though a large part of Central Asia's population remains in favour of a secular state that respects the right of the majority population to practice Islam freely and of the minorities to administer their churches (Khalid 2007), political and social tensions have sparked the emergence of Islamist movements (Rasanayagam 2010). Today the dominant movement is the Hizb ut-Tahrir, which officially endorses non-violent methods of acceding to power and recruits by spreading educational and moral precepts, as well as through charity to underprivileged circles (Collins 2007). Although it is much closer to the model of 'Islamo-nationalism' than to jihadism, the Hizb ut-Tahrir appears to be encountering competition due to a revival of more internationalized violent groups.

Criminalization of the Economy and State Apparatus

The main non-traditional threat menacing the region is linked to its proximity to Afghanistan and drug trafficking. Until the end of the 1990s, Central Asia's role in world drug trafficking was as a transit space. This situation has gradually evolved, and today the five states have also become sites for production, processing and consumption. The disappearance of the Soviet Union has enabled the development of commercial rationales, stimulating the commercialization of production, which until then was limited to traditional usage. The region's entry into the drug trafficking scene was accelerated by the civil war in Tajikistan, as the Islamic opposition used it for much of its financing (Cornell and Swanström 2006). The war permitted organized criminal structures to take over sets of integrated activities: transport networks, chemical and pharmaceutical products, money laundering companies, and banking structures. The UNODC (United Nations Office on Drugs and Crime) has estimated that Central Asia ranks as the third-largest opium export zone after Iran and Pakistan, with close to one-third of these flows. In 2008, 121 tonnes of heroin and 293 tonnes of opium had passed through the region (UNODC 2008). In 2009 the UN calculation decreased to 90 and 200 tonnes, respectively (UNODC 2011, 28). The principal regions of production are still situated in the south of Afghanistan, but the provinces bordering the former Soviet Union such as Badakhshan, Balkh and Badghis have seen a rapid increase in production.

Very many points of passage, hidden high in the mountains and difficult to control, make it possible to skirt each of the three main border posts with Afghanistan, namely Nizhnii-Piandzh in Tajikistan (route Kabul-Dushanbe), Kushka in Turkmenistan (route Herat-Ashgabat), and Termez in Uzbekistan (route Mazâr i-Sharif-Karshi) (Chouvy 2010).

Similar to the tribal zones of Pakistan, Central Asia is witnessing a rapid development of transformation laboratories, enabling the amassing of enormous profits locally before stocks are freighted to Russia and Europe (UNODC n.d.). The region is also becoming a production area. A 2007 UNODC mission to the Chui Valley in southern Kazakhstan indicates that wild cannabis growth can be well above 100,000ha (UNODC 2009, 26). Kyrgyzstan, experts have reported, yields close to 5 million tonnes of cannabis, able to produce close to

6,000 tonnes of hashish, and more than 2,000 hectares of opium poppies that can yield 30 tonnes of opium per year (Hohmann 2006). The other states have also seen mafia networks set up in the modest production of hashish and opium poppies, principally for the domestic market.

The drug traffic that passes through Central Asia is principally headed for Russia and Western Europe, but it also appears increasingly to seek the Chinese market (UNODC 2011). According to some OSCE intelligence officers, about one-third of the drugs trafficked in Central Asia is supposedly destined for domestic usage (anonymous interviews, Dushanbe, June 2010). Central Asia officially counts 358,000 drug users (UNOCD 2011), but the real number is probably higher: the World Health Organization calculate about 200,000 injecting drug users for Kazakhstan alone (WHO 2005), and the cases of drug addiction are rising quickly, in particular among youth. The social problems associated with drug addiction are considerable in some abandoned industrial areas, for instance Temirtau, near Karaganda, which had been plagued by unemployment and was considerably affected by the industrial collapse that followed the disappearance of the Soviet Union.

In the other republics, in particular in Tajikistan, the local populations are hostage to drug traffic. They produce the drugs in their raw state, the least financially profitable form, and serve above all as couriers, an activity that, again, is poorly paid, very dangerous, and often undertaken by women and children (interview with the director of the Dushanbe-based Panorama Center, Tatiana Bozrikova, 26 March 2008). These drug trafficking operations are in fact embedded in the social structure of these countries. They make use of populations with no other economic alternatives, and also incite the development of injection drug use in vulnerable populations that have come to constitute veritable 'risk groups'. The low cost of heroin in Central Asia (less than ten US dollars per gram in Tashkent, for example) greatly facilitates this spread (Hohmann 2010).

The actors involved in drug trafficking fit into two categories, local actors and international actors. The local actors are often established on a national basis and are supported by patronage networks; thus ethnicized mafia groups (Uzbek, Kyrgyz, Tajik, etc.) operate by taking Afghan networks as a model (Paoli and Rabkov 2007). This points to the formation of zones of influence where each group is specialized in a part of the trafficking. These local mafias establish connections with high-level state employees, in particular with the customs officers. However, the large-scale distribution is the preserve of much better organized transnational organizations, which often involve several types of criminality.

The Islamist movements also profit from this revenue source; the Islamic Movement of Uzbekistan (IMU), for example, attracted attention after moving great quantities of raw opium from Tajikistan to its border bastions in Kyrgyzstan. The implication seems to be that opium refinement and its transformation into heroin have become financial activities in themselves and are no longer simply supplements to trafficking revenues. Several observers note that the incursions of the IMU in the Batken region in 1999 and 2000 were a response to the Kyrgyz government's relative success in monitoring more closely the major drug trafficking route from Khorog to Osh. These operations reportedly also served as a cover for other simultaneously undertaken missions, in particular transfers of large quantities of opiates via other routes (Cornell 2005, 2006).

Border securitization thus proves crucial but complex since the region has 2,400 km of shared borders with Afghanistan (Tajikistan alone has close to 1,400 km), principally in mountainous areas. It is supposed that less than 4 per cent of the stocks are seized by Central Asian customs services (UNODC 2008, 9). In addition, the shadow economy, essentially drug trafficking, reaps important revenue and finances sections of the ruling circles. A number of state representatives, at each administrative level, from directors of kolkhozes (collective farms) to regional authorities and the highest ranking state officials (sometimes the presidential families), are directly involved in the drug trade. It has corrupted the entire state apparatus, in particular the customs officers and the police corps (De Danieli 2011). The fact that both the political leadership and Islamist circles – ostensibly wholly opposed to each other – receive considerable revenues from similar sources and markets reveals the real problem of waging an effective struggle, since in reality, both milieus are totally interdependent. The international community will have difficulties in proposing effective measures against the drug trade so long as the authorities responsible for implementing them form part of the trade itself.

The Diversity of Societal Risks in Central Asia

With the exception of Kazakhstan, the arrival of a market economy has meant for Central Asia the impoverishment of a still largely rural population that subsists through agriculture. Pressure on the land is strong; birth rates remain high, especially in the countryside, where more than half of the population of the four southern republics resides.[4] From 2000 on, all the Central Asian states have enjoyed positive rates of growth. Nevertheless, Kyrgyzstan and Tajikistan are still classified among the poorest countries in the world, with a GDP of about $2,200 per capita, while Uzbekistan has a little higher GDP of $3,100 (CIA World Factbook 2010). In 2009, more than half of Tajikistan's population lived below the poverty line on less than two dollars per day. In Kyrgyzstan and Turkmenistan, where this figure is

43 and 30 per cent, respectively, several rural zones still remain on the edge of economic strangulation (UNDP 2010). These difficult situations contribute to the strengthening of traditional domestic economies: patriarchal social functioning, withdrawal into the family (a growth of endogamy), subsistence production centred on working a plot of land, and partially demonetarized economies. The only cash resources available come from the sale of products in the markets, and remittances from labour migrants, with the rest of the economy operating on systems of subsistence and barter.

The energy situation continues to paralyze the two poorest states, Kyrgyzstan and Tajikistan. The explanations for this situation are many. Some are structural – natural aridity, mountainous areas, difficulty in irrigation and limited natural resources other than water – while others are contingent – the Soviet heritage of water sharing and the focus on the cultivation of cotton, the need to rebuild hydroelectric infrastructure that dates from the Soviet era, the absence of regional cooperation between states, large-scale corruption, and the need to train populations on responsible water usage. With the fall of the Soviet Union and the rupture in relations between the republics, electricity production in Central Asia fell dramatically. Although they were theoretically compatible with three gas and oil producing states (Kazakhstan, Uzbekistan and Turkmenistan) and two hydroelectric producing ones (Kyrgyzstan and Tajikistan), cooperation on energy issues between Central Asian states has proved more than difficult. Negotiations to exchange water for oil and gas regularly break down, with each of the participants undermining the terms of engagement (Wegerich 2009). The two 'water castles' of the region, Kyrgyzstan and Tajikistan, both upstream of the main rivers, want to take advantage of their multiple possible sites for hydroelectric stations, as the already existing dams which were constructed during Soviet times were designed to irrigate downstream agricultural zones, not to produce electricity. The largest projects, namely Rogun in Tajikistan and Kambarata in Kyrgyzstan, are at once extremely costly and geopolitically complex (Asian Development Bank 2005), and have therefore been delayed for several years.

While the winter of 2007–8 was very difficult in terms of harsh weather, the winter of 2008–9, despite its milder temperatures, was accompanied by a worsening of the dire energy situation. The water levels in the reservoirs of Toktogul in Kyrgyzstan and of Nurek in Tajikistan fell drastically (Juraev, 2009). The hydroelectric plants were heavily affected, and some Kyrgyz and Tajik industries were hampered in their production. In Tajikistan, the electricity went off throughout the country for months, and even the capital had only two hours of electricity per day during the winter and failed heating. The impact on agriculture was particularly visible: 30 per cent less water, even irregularly, caused 40 per cent less crops. Both countries now have their backs

against the proverbial wall, forced to see their economy almost stopped by
lack of electricity; they must now rethink their development or, perhaps more
importantly, to successfully negotiate with their neighbors in the short and
long term (Linn 2008a).

The questions of water management and electricity are intrinsically linked
to that of food security (Fumagalli 2008). The UN food program stated that
for 2009, 2.2 million Tajik citizens were in a situation of food insecurity –
34 per cent of the rural population, 37 per cent of the urban population, and
800,000 directly threatened by famine (Linn 2008b). The Tajik regions most
affected are those that are traditionally the poorest (Khatlon in the south and
Pamir) as well as Sogd, in the north, which paradoxically are historically the
richest regions in the country (UN WFP Emergency 2008). In Kyrgyzstan,
the number of people subject to food insecurity in 2010 was reportedly
1.38 million (Dhur 2010). While food self-sufficiency has become a key
element of public policy, the agricultural capacity of Central Asian states
remains modest. In the country with the most agriculture, Uzbekistan, only
10 per cent of land is arable; in Kyrgyzstan and Tajikistan this is about
6.5 per cent, and in Turkmenistan, less than 5 per cent (CIA World Factbook
2010). Lands that have been rendered fertile were done so more by the
irrigation system that was constructed than by surface water (that is, rivers).
The stress on the soil is therefore increasing. In the mountainous states of
Kyrgyzstan and Tajikistan, farmers are trying to occupy any spaces still
available on plains or hillsides, while Kazakhstan continues to work the lands
extensively cultivated during the virgin lands campaign launched by Nikita
Khrushchev in the 1950s. Uzbekistan and Turkmenistan are straining their
rural populations and agricultural lands by promoting the sole cultivation of
cotton (Kandiyoti 2007).

Rural populations suffer very high unemployment rates given the
scarcity of land. Marked on the whole by low population density,[5] Central
Asia is experiencing severe overcrowding in its agricultural zones. In
Turkmenistan like Uzbekistan, a process of ruralization set in during the
1990s, although it was already visible since the 1970s, as a consequence
of the difficulties of urban life in the absence of work opportunities.
The most difficult situation is in the Ferghana Valley, where more than
10 million inhabitants, or nearly 20 per cent of the entire population of
Central Asia, live and where the population density reached 559 people
per square km near Andijan (Chislennost 2005). Except Kazakhstan, all
the Central Asian countries are increasingly affected by unemployment,
and deliberate de-mechanization ensures the use of the largest possible
number of individuals, thus reducing risks of social tension. Rising fuel
prices, a lack of spare parts and difficulty repairing Soviet tools do not foster

technological development. Moreover, liberalization of input prices makes the use of machines more expensive, which encourages harvesting by hand. Manual harvesting therefore remains largely favoured. In Uzbekistan, the share of mechanized harvest fell to 57 per cent in 1990, 35 per cent in 1993, and is probably less than 20 per cent today (Leroi 2002).

The work of children and adolescents in the cotton fields, especially during the harvest, is one of the biggest controversies in the Central Asian agricultural sector, especially in Uzbekistan, Tajikistan and Turkmenistan (Ilkhamov 2007a). Each year in Uzbekistan, about 450,000 children are forced to leave school and participate in the cotton harvest (Illkhamov 2007b). Recruitment is compulsory for children between the ages of 10 and 15 years; they are employed in the fields between 51 and 63 days per year without weekend breaks (Kandiyoti 2008). The testimonies of several farmers denounced the use of very young children. A child is supposed to pick up to 80 kg of cotton per day, but many of them cannot harvest even 40 kg. About three cents is paid per harvested kilogram, thus those who manage to collect the 80 kg earn the equivalent of between $2.50 and $3.00 a day (Ferghana.ru 2008). Officially, the Uzbek regime explicitly prohibited child labour in 2008. However, it is unlikely that this law is enforced since without the virtually free work of children and adolescents, the harvest could not be completed and the state would not be able to pocket the profits.

Finally, Central Asian agriculture poses many environmental problems. Issues include the poor condition of irrigation structures, which have particularly high loss rates; overuse of water by farmers; difficulty in demanding payment for its use, given the low rural standard of living; high salinity (according to the World Bank, over 60 per cent of irrigated cropland in Central Asia is affected by the problem of salinization (Bucknall et al. 2003)); and the degradation of soil quality and its impact on public health (Peyrouse 2009).

Land reform would be a priority for the growth of investment, increased productivity, and, consequently, the reduction of rural unemployment and poverty. However, pressed by the choice of cotton versus self-sufficiency in food production, the Central Asian states remain hesitant (Deshpande 2006). They can give preference to cotton, which guarantees substantial foreign exchange earnings for the state, or choose to develop vegetable and grain production for the sake of food self-sufficiency. It is therefore necessary to strike a balance between cotton acreage and space devoted to feeding people. According to the FAO (Food and Agriculture Organization), Tajikistan needs 1.6 million tonnes of grain per year but, in the best-case scenario, produces just over half this and is therefore largely dependent on humanitarian aid and grain imports (Chorshanbiyev 2011).

The question then becomes whether cotton should be considered a major contributor to the food crisis affecting Central Asia. A Mercy Corps study shows that malnutrition is mainly concentrated in cotton growing areas (International Crisis Group 2005). As an essential source of foreign exchange, cotton is at the heart of the corruption of the state apparatus and the lack of wealth redistribution to the people. The ruling circles are enriched much faster through their control of cotton exports than by the profits obtained from vegetable or grain production, which are minimal and difficult to privately control (Peyrouse 2009).

Some international organizations and NGOs like the International Crisis Group thus argue for the reduction in cotton production in favour of producing more grain and vegetables (International Crisis Group 2005). To some experts, this position is excessive; more should be done to reform the agricultural sector, upstream and downstream, so that the rural population has access to the riches of cotton, rather than replacing it with other products that would continue to finance the system of coercion imposed by states on their rural populations (Spoor 2007).

Other non-traditional threats endanger the countries of the region, in particular from an ecological and pandemic viewpoint. The Soviet legacy, accentuated by the difficulties of altering the economy, has contributed to a general deterioration of the ecological situation (as for example in the Aral Sea catastrophe) but also to the retention of polluting chemical industries with detrimental effects for public health, the deterioration of access to potable water and of water quality, and poor upkeep of irrigation structures and of major hydroelectric dams. Though Central Asia has not yet experienced great waves of ecological refugees, parts of its population may well soon find the living situation in some regions increasingly impossible, a danger to which the present governments are impotent to respond given the current state of affairs. The dismantling of the health system they inherited from the Soviet Union and widespread pauperization have also heightened the physical fragility of the populations. In the 1990s, the steady decline in the share of GDP spent on public health combined with the dismantling of the Soviet system of care makes the reforms being pursued ineffective (McKee, Healy and Falkingham 2002). The system of care is officially free, but in reality payment is required for good doctors, medications, and the items necessary for operations, like syringes (Falkingham, Akkazieva and Baschieri 2010).

In Kazakhstan, the mortality rate between 1987 and 1995 more than doubled for men and aged 30 to 44 years, and increased 75 per cent for 45 to 54 age group (Becker and Urzhumova 2005). As in Russia, the incidence of alcoholism contributed to higher morbidity, but this is less true in other Central Asian states, where the predominance of Islam reduced the use of alcohol without banning it. The increased incidence of cardiovascular, endocrine and chronic diseases (goiter, anemia and diabetes) demonstrates the process of decline that pushes people to self-medicate. In two decades of independence, the results in public health terms have been negative: lower life expectancy, lower epidemiological supervision (in particular concerning vaccinations), growing cases of malnutrition in rural areas (in particular among children), a rise in at-risk pregnancies among women, renewed outbreaks of pathologies that had supposedly disappeared such as tuberculosis, cholera and black plague, an upsurge of cases of sexually transmitted diseases, and a possible epidemic of HIV/AIDS (McKee, Healy and Falkingham 2002).

Serious Threats to Literacy

Exact literacy figures are difficult to obtain because the governments have blocked the dissemination of this information. Education spending as a percentage of GDP has declined from 8 to 9 per cent at the end of the Soviet Union to about 3 per cent in Kazakhstan and Tajikistan, and 6 per cent in Kyrgyzstan.[6] Officially, the Central Asian states continue to have the same literacy rates as under the Soviet regime, which is about 99 per cent of the population. The reality of the situation is altogether different. Numbers provided by UNICEF reveal a drop of between 10 and 15 per cent in enrollment in primary schools in over little more than a decade; the level of enrollment is reported to be 84 per cent in Tajikistan, 88 per cent in Uzbekistan, and 89 per cent in Kyrgyzstan (Childinfo 2008). These statistics are contested, however, since they are based on official figures provided by local administrations and do not take into account the hours of instruction actually provided (Baschieri and Falkingham 2009).

The main problems are concentrated in rural areas (Central Asia Human Development 2005). Numerous factors prevent the primary and secondary school system from functioning: increased use of child labour, absence of transport to get to school, shortage of teachers, lack of heating during winter months, and buildings that are too dangerous. Officially, the public school system is still free, but in reality parents must pay several related fees. Some of these are official, such as building restoration, lunch, and the purchase of textbooks and notebooks, while others depend on the level of corruption among teachers and the administration. Rural families cannot pay even a few dollars per month for these fees, and so take their children, mainly girls, out of public schooling (field work observations). Faced with a shortage of teachers, the states have reduced their weekly workloads so that they can perform two or three services a day. In rural zones, it has become common to send school-aged children to school for two or three hours per day. In some primary schools of the Tajik capital Dushanbe, daily programs are only two hours long. During school hours in secondary schools, teachers often work without textbooks; certain subjects like foreign language and science have disappeared owing to the lack of teachers. Girls leaving school prematurely has become a growing phenomenon in Tajikistan, and to a lesser extent in Uzbekistan and Kyrgyzstan. For poor families, there can be no question of investing in their daughters' education, and young girls leave the educational system on a large scale at 16 years of age (field work observations).

At higher levels, technical teaching has collapsed. In Kazakhstan, Kyrgyzstan and Tajikistan, the entry rates of youths into technical and professional institutions of higher education have halved; in Turkmenistan they have dropped to one-fifth of the previous levels. Only Uzbekistan, in the 2000s, has managed to regain rates similar to those during Soviet years (Central Asia Human Development 2005). Although economic reasons can partly explain this situation in Kyrgyzstan and Tajikistan, in the two most authoritarian republics, Uzbekistan and Turkmenistan, increasing illiteracy must also be attributed to political will; their population pays a high cultural price for the break with the Soviet past by the change of alphabet from Cyrillic to Latin. In all five states, the authorities have shown no great foresight in educational matters for their rural populations and have deliberately slashed public education spending. The private system, which is still in its infancy, enables only the upper classes to make up for these deficiencies by offering the possibility of an alternative education, either locally or abroad (Heyneman and De Young 2004).

In all the Central Asian states, the medium-term consequences of the collapse of the school system have probably not yet been fully accounted for. These repercussions will weigh heavily on the future of Central Asia and will compel it to mortgage part of its future in a world in which the mastery of knowledge is one of the drivers of economic development. This situation has become especially dire, particularly considering that the Soviet regime had bequeathed education to an almost completely literate population. There is a direct relation between the degree of female education, the possibility for women to work, issues of public health, and the rates of human development. This question is crucial since Central Asian societies are particularly young. Persons under 15 years of age represent 29.3 per cent of the population in Kyrgyzstan and 39 per cent in Tajikistan (CIA World Factbook 2010).

Migration Flows

The sudden introduction of market reforms and the collapse of public services seem to have succeeded in one area where the Soviet Union had failed.

Central Asian societies, once reluctant to see their respective populations move to other republics, move to urban areas and learn the Russian language, have now become mobile populations, frequently crossing the borders of their states. All of Central Asia is experiencing strong migratory dynamics, which involve at least three million Tajiks, Uzbeks and Kyrgyz working abroad either permanently or seasonally. The migration flows are mainly bound for Russia, but also for Kazakhstan, which hosts many Uzbeks and Kyrgyz in agriculture and construction. These massive migrations entail a thorough transformation of the Central Asian social fabric, in particular in Tajikistan and Kyrgyzstan, where depending on the region, migrants reportedly represent between 25 and 45 per cent of the male working-aged population (Olimova and Bosc 2003). Remittances comprise a regular source of revenue, which helps to combat poverty and increase the domestic demand for goods, but accentuate workforce shortages, small entrepreneurship in rural areas and the 'brain drain' of qualified urban elites.

Such migration does not occur in geographically stable societies. Even before the internationalization of migration, domestic situations weighed heavily. The Tajik civil war and its massive population displacement undoubtedly triggered an initial dynamic. Migration flows are also internal for states; population movements within the same region, between regions, and especially towards cities became key elements of spatial reconfigurations at the turn of 1980s–90s. Repatriation programs for 'co-ethnics abroad', especially in Kazakhstan, have emphasized the sense that states themselves have sought to change the ethnic compositions and urban–rural ratios of their populations. The phenomena may seem contradictory. The Central Asian societies have undergone a process of de-urbanization due to the mass exodus of Russian speakers, but the social advancement offered by independence (in particular in civil service hiring) and the expansion of tertiary services encourage those in rural areas to escape extreme poverty by going to cities. Migration is therefore a part of a complex reconfiguration of the Central Asian urban landscape, all the more rapidly in Kyrgyzstan and Tajikistan, where unlike in Uzbekistan, the registration system (*propiska*) has been relaxed or abolished, accelerating the influx of newcomers.

Rural areas are most active in these migratory flows. The breakdown of the social fabric that resulted from the disappearance of the Soviet Union creates fertile ground for the search for work away from home. However, migration does not only affect rural areas; growing unemployment among recent university graduates is equally if not more disturbing. The technical courses in colleges and the proliferation of universities in small towns (former training colleges for secondary school teachers have often been promoted to university status) offer the emerging middle classes a sense of a possible social progress through higher education. For them, the lack of opportunities is even more poorly experienced and can potentially generate political mobilization. Given the attraction of the Russian and Kazakhstani labour markets, where working conditions are better, wages more competitive and the atmosphere more dynamic, Uzbekistan, Kyrgyzstan and Tajikistan are not able to compete. But the brain drain reduces the prospects for these sending states. They gain social stability through migration, which serves as a safety valve to relieve the pressure of a sclerotic labour market, but at the cost of a lost future from the disappearance of their small pools of qualified urban elites (Laruelle 2010).

Meanwhile, Uzbekistan continues to reject the significance of migration in order to deny the deteriorating socio-economic situation. In expressing support for migration, the Tajik and Kyrgyz governments employ a different strategy. The weakening of state control over citizens, its inability to operate with closed borders, and weak political influence over the formation of both intra-national and supra-national groups is more accepted in these countries that are aware of their intrinsic weaknesses than in those where the conventional standards of power are still valued, as in Uzbekistan. In the two smallest countries, the message the authorities send is very clear: the state cannot meet the needs of its citizens, who are invited to accept greater autonomy. As a social mechanism that works to circumvent the state, those involved in migration do not experience it as a victorious struggle for independence, but as a battle for survival (Dolotkeldieva 2010). The disappearance of the Soviet welfare state often makes the Central Asian populations nostalgic for the comforting and stabilizing character of the old regime, where everyone's future was predictable. This discourse arises in opposition to contemporary unpredictability and to the sentiments of states that are now reluctant to play the role of providing social assistance.

Mass migration changes the relationship between individuals, the state and development. One can question whether the remittances sent by migrants would replace state aid and help to counter the failure of public institutions. The idea that individual financial self-sufficiency is adequate to regulate the market and streamline supply and demand is a neo-liberal principle that implies the futility of the state as the manager of the public good. For now, migration appears similar to a survival rather than market capturing strategy. It does not include any macroeconomic investment. The money sent home by migrants satisfies immediate needs (like food, medicine, clothing and debt repayment) or the strengthening of social bonds. It does not help to create new ways of life (opening a small business, improving a piece of land or purchasing cattle, for example). Furthermore, such an outpouring of working-aged men and women hinders the work on the land and the creation of small enterprises. However, remittances make up part of the present, standard economic cycle

(Marat 2009). Mobility as a way of life is viewed as normal, and is generally coupled with the distant goal of returning home to a sedentary life in one's country of origin around the age of fifty, when the family is established and autonomous.

Migration can potentially become a driving force for the democratization of Central Asian societies. Migrants in essence constitute a new social force with real financial power, capable of competing with the state; in Tajikistan, remittances bring in about $2 billion, or about 40 per cent of the country's GDP: $5.6 billion in 2010 (Migration Policy Institute 2011). While, for the moment, the few attempts at the politicization of migrant communities in Kyrgyzstan have not really born any fruit, one can assume that social and political legitimacies will evolve. Migrants are indeed carriers of change. They can disseminate knowledge of Russia to their home village through memories, talks, objects and standards of living, whereas the Soviet Union failed to export perceptions of the colonial metropole to daily life. By constructing migratory narratives, migrants transform their societies of origin and create new dynamics. Analysing the reciprocal influences between internal political orders and external ones will therefore be on the agenda over the coming years, encouraging a reconsideration of the interactions between Russia and Central Asia (Laruelle 2010).

Conclusions

Despite their subsoil wealth, and with the exception of Kazakhstan, the Central Asian states have a limited capacity to find a model of economic development capable of lifting them out of their post-Soviet pauperization by facilitating international investment. The Central Asian states are particularly lacking in transport infrastructure and are some of the most isolated areas of the world, making transport costs exorbitant. The agricultural sector happens to be caught in a complex logic, since the cotton-producing states (essentially Uzbekistan and Turkmenistan) tend to intensify cotton production and refuse to wager on market produce. The question of water distribution, crucial in a region in which the risk of 'water wars' has become real in recent years, blocks the development of inter-regional cooperation in a domain that is nonetheless growing, namely hydroelectricity. Lastly, the process of de-industrialization is continuing and these Central Asian states do not for the moment have the means to invest in innovative technology or in the service industries, again with the exception of Kazakhstan. The deterioration of the regional situation linked to Afghanistan, and the recurrent inability of some of these states to offer their population opportunities to escape from poverty are working to weaken the region's development, as well as its global and regional integration.

Human security challenges are therefore not only numerous, but overlapping. The example of Kyrgyzstan confirms the need for a comprehensive approach to security. A labyrinth of security issues mainly explains the violent riots in Osh in June 2010. After the 7 April 'revolution,' the central government was weak and had no control over police forces and secret services, especially in the south, where they remained loyal to former President Kurmbanbek Bakiyev. The family of the former president was directly involved in trafficking drugs from Afghanistan, as a brother of the president was the head of secret services and oversaw the criminal underworld in the south of the country. The Uzbek community leaders were themselves engaged in shadow economy. The recurrent weakness of the state strengthened nationalist sentiments in both the Kyrgyz majority and the Uzbek minority, and criminal groups associated with state organs easily reactivated latent ethnic tensions. The impoverishment of rural areas facilitated the enlistment of idle youth, responsible for the violence committed in Uzbek neighbourhoods. These all serve to demonstrate the importance of a holistic approach at the micro, meso and macro levels, combining historical, sociological, political and economic analyses, in order to articulate these human security issues, find ways to prevent new conflicts, and solve more global security challenges.

Notes

1 The Tajik civil war, which lasted from 1992 to 1997, was presented as an opposition between two camps, with communists on one side, and democrats and Islamists on the other. In reality, it involved a series of conflicts and collusions of interest between regional groups: the Khudjand region (formerly Leninabad), which was for a long time associated with Kurgan-Tiube, was opposed to the southern regions of Garm and of Pamir. Since the 1997 peace agreement, there has been a strict distribution of posts in the state service, designed to maintain the republic's fragile balance by giving each region access to power and economic resources. But due to the monopolization of power by President Rakhmon and his clan in the Khatlon region, this balance is in the process of disappearing.
2 See also Freedom House reports by country, online: http://www.freedomhouse.org/ (last accessed 15 November 2011).
3 Assassinations of local political figures at Namangan in 1997 and 1998; bomb attacks in the capital, Tashkent, on 16 February 1999 (whose attribution to Islamists has never been confirmed); incursions of the Islamic Movement of Uzbekistan into Tajikistan and Kyrgyzstan during the summers of 1999 and 2000; suicide bombings in Tashkent and Bukhara against institutions of power in March and April 2004; and attacks against the US and Israeli embassies in July 2004.
4 According to the 2010 Human Development Report (UNDP 2010, 161–2), this is 43.1 per cent in Kyrgyzstan in 2004, and 30 per cent in Turkmenistan, 27.2 per cent in Uzbekistan and 15.4 per cent in Kazakhstan in 2009 and 53.5 per cent in Tajikistan.
5 There are 5.5 people per square km in Kazakhstan, 10 in Turkmenistan, 28 in Kyrgyzstan, 49 in Tajikistan, and 64 in Uzbekistan; detailed annual figures are available

online through the University of Sherbrook at http://perspective.usherbrooke.ca./bilan/ stats/0/2006/fr/1/carte/EN.POP.DNST/x.html (last accessed 15 November 2011).
6 See the UNData online database, online: http://data.un.org/ (last accessed 15 November 2011).

References

Asian Development Bank. 2005. *Electricity Sectors in CAREC Countries. A Diagnostic Review of Regulatory Approaches and Challenges*. Asian Development Bank. Online: http://www.adb. org/Documents/Studies/Electricity-CAREC/drrac.pdf (accessed 15 July 15 2010).

Baschieri A. and J. Falkingham. 2009. 'Staying in School: Assessing the Role of Access, Availability, and Economic Opportunities – the Case of Tajikistan'. *Population, Space and Place* 15(3): 205–24.

Becker, C. M. and D. D. Urzhumova. 2005. 'Mortality Recovery and Stabilization in Kazakhstan, 1995–2001'. *Economics and Human Biology* 2: 97–122.

Bransten, Jeremy. 2003. 'Central Asia: As World Marks Literacy Day, What of USSR's Legacy?' EurasiaNet.org. Online: http://www.eurasianet.org/departments/insight/ articles/eav090703a.shtml (accessed 15 July 2010).

Bucknall, Julia, Irina Klytchnikova, Julian Lampietti, Mark Lundell, Monica Scatasta and Mike Thurman. 2003. *Irrigation in Central Asia: Social, Economic and Environmental Considerations*. The World Bank.

Central Asia Human Development. 2005. *Central Asia Human Development Report: Regional Cooperation for Human Development and Human Security*. Washington DC: UNDP. Online: http:// europeandcis.undp.org/home/show/301A44C5-F203-1EE9-B2E001AFF98B054B (accessed 15 July 2010).

Childinfo. 2008. 'Statistics by Area/Education'. Online database. Unicef. Online: http:// www.childinfo.org/education_499.htm (accessed 15 November 2011).

Chislennost. 2005. *Chislennost' Naseleniia Respubliki Uzbekistan na 1.1.2005*. Tashkent: Goskomstat.

Chorshanbiyev, Payrav. 2011. 'FAO Expects Global Wheat Production to Increase in 2011'. *Asia-Plus*, 24 March. Online: http://news.tj/en/news/fao-expects-global-wheat-production-increase-2011 (accessed 22 October 2011).

Chouvy, Pierre-Arnaud. 2010. *Opium: Uncovering the Politics of the Poppy*. Cambridge, MA: Harvard University Press.

CIA World Factbook. 2010. CIA World Factbook. Online: https://www.cia.gov/library/ publications/the-world-factbook (accessed 15 July 2010).

Collins, K. 2007. 'Ideas, Networks, and Islamist Movements: Evidence from Central Asia and the Caucasus'. *World Politics* 60(1): 64–96.

Cornell, Svante E. 2005. 'Narcotics, Radicalism and Armed Conflict in Central Asia: The Islamic Movement of Uzbekistan'. *Terrorism and Political Violence* 17(4): 577–97.

_____. 2006. 'The Narcotics Threat in Greater Central Asia: From Crime-Terror Nexus to State Infiltration'. *China and Eurasia Quarterly* 4(1): 37–67.

Cornell, Svante E. and Niklas L. P.Swanström. 2006. 'The Eurasian Drug Trade: A Challenge to Regional Security'. *Problems of Post-Communism* 53(4): 10–28.

De Danieli, F. 2011. 'Counter-narcotics Policies in Tajikistan and their Impact on State Building'. *Central Asian Survey* 30(1): 129–45.

Deshpande, R. 2006. 'Land Reform and Farm Restructuring in Central Asia: Progress and Challenges Ahead'. in S. C. Babu and S. Djalalov (eds), *Policy Reforms and Agriculture Development in Central Asia*, 131–70. New York: Springer.

Dhur, Agnès. 2010. *Emergency Food Security Assessment in the Kyrgyz Republic*. World Food Program.

Dolotkeldieva, Asel. 2010. 'Les migrants kirghizes à Moscou: politiques publiques, stratégies migratoires et réseaux associatifs' [Kyrgyz Migrants in Moscow: Public Policies, Migratory Strategies, and Associative Networks]. In Marlène Laruelle (ed.), *Dynamiques migratoires et changements sociétaux en Asie centrale* [Migratory Dynamics and Societal Changes in Central Asia], 123–45. Paris: Petra.

Edwards, M. 2003. 'The New Great Game and the New Great Gamers: Disciples of Kipling and Mackinder'. *Central Asian Survey* 22(1): 82–102.

Engvall, J. 2011. *The State as Investment Market: An Analytical Framework for Interpreting Politics and Bureaucracy in Kyrgyzstan*. Uppsala: Uppsala University Press.

EUCAM. 2010. 'Into Eurasia: Monitoring the EU's Central Asia Strategy, Executive Summary and Recommendations'. EUCAM Policy brief 13, February 2010. M. Emerson and J. Boonstra (rapporteurs) with N. Hasanova, M. Laruelle and S. Peyrouse. EU-Central Asia Monitoring. Online: http://www.eucentralasia.eu/fileadmin/user_upload/PDF/Policy_Briefs/PB13.pdf (accessed 15 July 2010).

Falkingham, J., G. Akkazieva and A. Baschieri. 2010. 'Trends in Out-of-Pocket Payments for Health Care in Kyrgyzstan, 2001–2007'. *Health Policy and Planning* 25(5): 427–36.

Ferghana.ru. 2008. 'Uzbekistan: Children Continue to Work on Cotton Fields despite Official Ban'. Ferghana.ru Information Agency, 16 September. Online: http://enews.fergananews.com/article.php?id=2466 (accessed 22 October 2011).

Fierman, W. (ed.) 1991. *Soviet Central Asia: The Failed Transformation*. Boulder, CO: Westview.

Fumagalli, Matteo. 2008. 'The "Food-Energy-Water" Nexus in Central Asia: Regional Implications of and the International Response to the Crises in Tajikistan'. EUCAM Policy brief 2, October 2008. EU-Central Asia Monitoring.

Gleason, Gregory. 2003. *Markets and Politics in Central Asia: Structural Reform and Political Change*. London: Routledge Press.

Heathershaw, J. and S. Roche. 2011. 'Islam and Political Violence in Tajikistan: An Ethnographic Perspective on the Causes and Consequences of the 2010 Armed Conflict in the Kamarob Gorge'. *Ethopolitics Papers* 8.

Heyneman, S. P. and A. J. De Young (eds). 2004. *The Challenge of Education in Central Asia*. Greewich: Inormation Age Publishing.

Hohmann, Sophie. 2006–7. 'Le narcotrafic en Asie centrale: enjeux géopolitiques et répercussions sociales' [Narcotraffic in Central Asia: Geopolitical Stakes and Social Impact]. *La Revue internationale et stratégique* 64: 110–19.

———. 2010. 'L'infection par VIH/SIDA en Ouzbékistan: réactions à l'inconnu des mutations post-soviétiques ?' [Infection by HIV/AIDS in Uzbekistan: Reacting to the Unknown Part of Post-Soviet Changes?]. *Revue d'Études Comparatives Est–Ouest* 41(1): 95–116.

Ilkhamov, Alisher. 2007a. 'Neopatrimonialism, Interest Groups and Patronage Networks: the Impasses of the Governance System in Uzbekistan'. *Central Asian Survey* 1: 65–84.

———. 2007b. Use of child labour in the cotton sector of Uzbekistan: Agenda for human rights advocacy. Presentation to the EJF Roundtable on Sustainable and Ethical Cotton, 25 April 2007.

International Crisis Group. 2005. 'The Curse of Cotton: Central Asia's Destructive Monoculture'. Asia Report 93. International Crisis Group.

Juraev, Shairbek. 2009. 'Energy Emergency in Kyrgyzstan: Causes and Consequences'. EUCAM Policy brief 5. EU-Central Asia Monitoring.

Kandiyoti, Deniz (ed.) 2007. *The Cotton Sector in Central Asia: Economic Policy and Development Challenges*. London: School of Oriental and African Studies.

_____. 2008. *Invisible to the World? The Dynamics of Forced Child Labour in the Cotton Sector of Uzbekistan*. London: Centre of Contemporary Central Asia and the Caucasus.

Kavalski, Emilian (ed.) 2010. *Stable Outside, Fragile Inside? Post-Soviet Statehood in Central Asia*. Surrey: Ashgate.

Khalid, A. 2007. *Islam after Communism: Religion and Politics in Central Asia*. Berkeley: University of California Press.

King, Gary and Christopher Murray. 2001–2. 'Rethinking Human Security'. *Political Science Quarterly* 116(4): 585–610.

Kupatadze, Alexander. 2008. 'Organized Crime before and after the Tulip Revolution: the Changing Dynamics of Upperworld–Underworld Networks'. *Central Asian Survey* 3–4: 279–99.

Laruelle, Marlène. 2007. 'Central Asian Labor Migrants in Russia: The "Diasporization" of the Central Asian States?' *The China and Eurasia Forum Quaterly* 5(3): 101–19.

_____. 2010. 'Introduction'. In Marlène Laruelle (ed.), *Dynamiques migratoires et changements sociétaux en Asie centrale* [Migratory Dynamics and Societal Changes in Central Asia], 9–18. Paris: Petra.

Laruelle, Marlène and Sébastien Peyrouse. 2006. *Asie centrale, la dérive autoritaire* [Central Asia, the Drift towards Authoritarianism]. Paris: CERI-Autrement.

_____. 2012. *Central Asia in an Era of Globalization*. New York: M. E. Sharpe.

Leroi, Richard. 2002. 'La filière du coton en Asie centrale. Le poids de l'héritage'. *Le Courrier des Pays de l'Est* 1027, 40–51.

Linn, Johannes F. 2008a. 'The Impending Water Crisis in Central Asia: An Immediate Threat'. Brookings Institution. 19 June 2008. Online: http://www.brookings.edu/opinions/2008/0619_central_asia_linn.aspx (accessed 15 November 2011).

_____. 2008b. 'The Compound Water-Energy-Food Crisis Risks in Central Asia: Update on an International Response'. Brookings Institution Commentary. 12 August 2008. Online: http://www.brookings.edu/opinions/2008/0812_central_asia_linn.aspx (accessed 15 July 2010).

Marat, Erica. 2006. *The State-Crime Nexus in Central Asia: Silk Road Paper*. Washington DC: The Central Asia-Caucasus Institute.

_____. 2009. *Labor Migrations in Central Asia. Implications of the Global Economic Crisis: Silk Road Paper*. Washington DC: The Central Asia and Caucasus Institute.

McKee, Martin, Judith Healy and Jane Falkingham (eds). 2002. 'Part Two: Health Systems and Services'. In Martin McKee, Judith Healy and Jane Falkingham (eds), *Health Care in Central Asia*, 77–194. Berkshire: Open University Press.

Melvin, N. 2011. 'Promoting a Stable and Multiethnic Kyrgyzstan: Overcoming the Causes and Legacies of Violence'. *Central Eurasia Project Occasional Paper Series* 3.

Migration Policy Institute. 2011. 'Remittances Profile: Tajikistan'. Migration Policy Institute Data Hub. Online: http://www.migrationinformation.org/datahub/remittances/Tajikistan.pdf (accessed 15 November 2011).

Najman, B., G. Raballand and R. Pomfret (eds). 2007. *The Economics and Politics of Oil in the Caspian Basin: The Redistribution of Oil Revenues in Azerbaijan and Kazakhstan*. London: Routledge.

Naumkin, Vitali V. 2005. *Radical Islam in Central Asia. Between Pen and Rifle*. Lanham: Rowman & Littlefield.

Olimova, Saodat and Igor Bosc. 2003. *Trudovaia migratsiia iz Tadzhikistana* [Labor Migration from Tajikistan]. Dushanbe: International Organization for Migrations.

Paoli, L., I. Rabkov, V. Greenfield and P. Reuter. 2007. 'Tajikistan: The Rise of a Narco-State'. *Journal of Drug Issues* 37(4): 951–79.

Paris, Roland. 2001. 'Human Security. Paradigm Shift or Hot Air?' *International Security* 26(2): 87–102.

Peyrouse, Sébastien. 2009. 'The Multiple Paradoxes of the Agriculture Issue in Central Asia'. *EUCAM Policy Papers* 6. Online: http://www.eucentralasia.eu/fileadmin/user_upload/PDF/Working_Papers/WP6-EN.pdf (accessed 15 November 2011).

Pomfret, Richard. 2006. *The Central Asian Economies since Independence*. Princeton: Princeton University Press.

Preventing the Next Wave of Conflict. 2003. *Preventing the Next Wave of Conflict: Understanding Non-Traditional Threats to Global Stability*. Washington DC: The Woodrow Wilson Center for International Scholars. Online. (Content no longer available; accessed 15 July 2010).

Raballand, G. and F. Esen. 2007. 'Economics and Politics of Cross-border Oil Pipelines: The Case of the Caspian Basin'. *Asia Europe Journal* 5(1): 133–46.

Raballand, G. and B. Kaminski. 2009. 'Entrepôt for Chinese Consumer Goods in Central Asia: The Puzzle of Re-exports through Kyrgyz Bazaars'. *Eurasian Geography and Economics* 50(5): 581–90.

Rasanayagam, J. 2010. *Islam in Post-Soviet Uzbekistan: The Morality of Experience*. Cambridge: Cambridge University Press.

Rumer, Boris Z. 2005. 'Central Asia at the End of the Transition'. In Boris Z. Rumer (ed.), *Central Asia at the End of the Transition*, 3–71. Armonk: M. E. Sharpe.

Spoor, Max. 2007. 'Cotton in Central Asia: "Curse" or "Foundation for Development"'. In Deniz Kandiyoti (ed.), *The Cotton Sector in Central Asia: Economic Policy and Development Challenges*, 54–74. London: School of Oriental and African Studies.

Richmond, Olivier. 2007. 'The Problem of Peace. Understanding the "Liberal Peace"'. In Ashok Swain, Ramses Amer and Joakim Öjendal (eds), *Globalization and Challenges to Building Peace*, 17–37. London: Anthem Press.

Tadjbakhsh, Shahrbanou and Anuradha Chenoy. 2006. *Human Security: Concepts and Implications*. London: Routledge.

Thomas, Caroline. 2001. 'Global Governance, Development and Human Security: Exploring the Links'. *Third World Quarterly* 22(2):159–75.

Trevisani, T. 2008. *Land and Power in Khorezm: Farmers, Communities and the State in Uzbekistan's Decollectivization*. Halle: Mack Planck Institute.

UN WFP. 2008a. 'Emergency Food Security Assessment in Urban Areas of Tajikistan'. United Nations World Food Program and the Government of Tajikistan. Online: http://documents.wfp.org/stellent/groups/public/documents/ena/wfp188192.pdf (accessed 9 December 2011).

UN WFP. 2008b. 'Emergency Food Security Assessment in Rural Areas of Tajikistan'. United Nations World Food Program, the Food and Agriculture Organization of the United Nations, UNICEF and the Government of Tajikistan. Online: http://home.wfp.org/stellent/groups/public/documents/ena/wfp187141.pdf (accessed 9 December 2011).

UNDP. 2010. *The Real Wealth of Nations*. Human Development Report 2010. United Nations Development Program.

UNODC. 2007. Securing Central Asia's borders with Afghanistan. Outline action plan September 2007 – work in progress. UN Office on Drugs and Crime. Online: http://www.unodc.org/documents/regional/central-asia/Microsoft%20Word%20-%20yellow_paper__no%20maps_16.09.17.pdf (accessed 15 July 2010).

———. 2008. *Illicit Drug Trends in Central Asia*. UN Office on Drugs and Crime. Online: http://www.unodc.org/documents/regional/central-asia/Illicit%20Drug%20Trends_Central%20Asia-final.pdf (accessed 15 November 2011).

_____. 2009. *Compendium: Drug Related Statistics*. UN Office on Drugs and Crime. Online: http://dbroca.uz/pubs/Compendium_2009.pdf (accessed 23 October 2011).

_____. 2011. *The Global Afghan Opium Trade. A Threat Assessment*. UN Office on Drugs and Crime. Online: http://www.unodc.org/documents/data-and-analysis/Studies/Global_Afghan_Opium_Trade_2011-web.pdf (accessed 15 November 2011).

_____. n.d. 'Precursor Control on Central Asia's Borders with China'. UN Office on Drugs and Crime, Regional Office for Central Asia. Online: http://www.unodc.org/pdf/uzbekistan/PrecursorRep.pdf (accessed 15 July 2010).

Wegerich, Kai. 2009. 'Politics of Water in Post-Soviet Central Asia'. In Dominic Heaney (ed.), *Eastern Europe, Russia and Central Asia 2010*, 27–31. 10th edition. London: Routledge.

WHO. 2005. 'Kazakhstan: Summary Country Profile for HIV/AIDS Treatment Scale-up'. World Health Organization. Online: www.who.int/hiv/HIVCP_KAZ.pdf (accessed 15 November 2011).

.

Chapter 8

DIASPORAS' ROLE IN PEACEBUILDING: THE CASE OF THE VIETNAMESE-SWEDISH DIASPORA

Ashok Swain and Nhi Phan

Introduction

The main purpose of the study is to investigate how the linkages between some key dimensions of current globalization trends involving advances in aviation and global telecommunication systems have enhanced international travel and facilitated migrations, thereby making it easier for people to stay connected with family and friends all over the world. Diasporas are transnational communities formed when people migrate from their country of origin to live in one or more host countries, but maintain identity with the ancestral homeland. There are various circumstances, such as violent conflicts, natural disasters, poverty at home and economic opportunity abroad, under which people leave their homeland in search of a new place to settle (Hall, Kostić and Swain 2007, 9).

The role of diasporas in peacebuilding or conflict promotion in their homeland has been a subject of debate among scholars. Case studies of the Armenian, Kurdish, Sikh and Tamil diasporas have been presented as clear examples to illustrate their roles in supporting conflicts in their respective homelands (Cochrane, Baser and Swain 2009; Singh 2007; Hoffman et al. 2007). On the contrary, Ghanaian, Jewish and Irish diasporas have been cited as examples diasporas promoting peace in their country of origin.[1] However, diasporas have very complex allegiances and may choose whether to promote peace or conflict in the homeland, depending on the prevailing circumstances. Moreover, there are even disagreements within members of the same diaspora group on whether to promote peace or engage in conflict. For instance, within the Vietnamese diaspora itself there are noticeable differences between the older and larger communities in North America, Australia, France and Germany, and the younger and smaller Vietnamese diaspora in Nordic countries. The former constitute groups which are regarded as 'extremely anticommunist' by the Vietnamese government, while the latter are characterized as peaceful and moderate (Carruthers 2008). Incidentally, very little is discussed about the Vietnamese diaspora in Nordic countries, which comprises of one of the youngest and smallest communities in Europe (Tranguyen 2007). The varying circumstances under which the Vietnamese refugee diaspora arrived in Nordic countries, the size of the community, and its different political climates render this group an ideal case for investigation.

Recently, the importance of remittances has become more apparent as a double-edged sword by which most diasporic groups assist peacebuilding or conflict creation in their homelands. Remittances are transfers of funds from diasporas to support development and reconstruction in the homeland (World Bank 2008b). They may also be used as an incentive to encourage conflict resolution or in some cases fuel existing conflicts. The growing importance of remittances is evident in their use during an economic downturn, natural disaster or political conflict, especially because unlike private capital flows, such transfers to the receiving country increase during times of crisis when they are most needed. Remittances to Vietnam have increased significantly since the 'Renovation' process in 1986. Given the importance of remittances to the local economy, the Vietnamese government has taken several measures to streamline their efficient transfer. This chapter aims to examine *the Vietnamese-Swedish diaspora's contribution to peacebuilding and reconstruction in Vietnam.*

Diaspora in the Era of Globalization

Diaspora is an elusive term that can be interpreted in many ways. Simply stated, a diaspora is, as Jacob Bercovitch (2007, 18–19) describes, 'a community of people embedded, through psychological and physical links, in a larger context or environment'. What all diasporic communities have in common is that 'they settled outside their original or imagined territories, and acknowledge that the old country has some claims on their loyalty, emotions and level of possible support' (ibid.). In other words, 'diasporas' are transnational communities, which arise when people move from their homeland to live in one or more host countries, where they organize on the basis of solidarity, shared ideas, collective identity and loyalty to their country of origin.

Although several definitions are associated with 'diasporas', a key ingredient is the maintenance of identity with the country of origin, even after living in a host country for several years. Despite the heterogeneous nature of diaspora members, they share one thing in common: an attachment to the same country of origin by a group which is no longer permanently resident in that country (Bush 2007, 17). Clifford (1994, 256) portrays this relationship by asserting that each individual is 'part of an on-going transnational network that includes the homeland, not as something simply left behind, but as a place of attachment in a contrapuntal modernity'. He envisions the relationship, as one involving coexistence between the homeland and hostland, in both the psychological and lived experiences of individuals.

Diasporas are not homogeneous, and therefore differ in their identities and patterns of relations, as well as their associations with the host country and homeland. Moreover, generational, ideological and social differences are apparent in relations between diasporas, their host countries and homelands. Diasporic communities always attempt to maintain multiple levels of identity. As Bercovitch (2007, 18–19) points out, this is usually accomplished through the establishment of 'intricate support organizations' in the host country. He also mentions that they maintain continuous contacts and exchanges (financial, political, cultural and even military) with their homeland and fellow diasporic groups in other host countries. However, these relationships are complex and often involve different problems and issues.

Diasporas and Globalization

The United Nation's Population Division (UN 2006) estimates that the number of persons living outside their country of birth increased from 76 million in 1960 to 175 million in 2000 and 190.6 million in 2006 (which accounts for 3 per cent of the world's population). However, these data only represent a small percentage of people involved in the movements and transnationalism. An increased mobility of people, fuelled by better transportation and communications systems, has contributed to the erosion of state boundaries and promoted globalized diasporas.

As a consequence of globalization, diasporas have built vast transnational networks, with a potential to contribute to peace, reconciliation and development. Improved communications, transport and finance have allowed diasporas to act internationally without the consent of their host states. This new-found freedom strengthens the influence of diasporas as political agents in several ways. A positive outcome is an improved ability to promote peace, resolve conflicts and create economic opportunities at home. Policy-makers in the host states are, however, also rightfully concerned about their diminished ability to pressure immigrants and their descendants to sever ties with their homelands and become fully acculturated in their new environment. Diasporas dispersed throughout the world are able to maintain ties through publications, websites and chat groups on the Internet.

Diasporas: Peacebuilders or Conflict Creators?

Diasporas' involvement in conflicts is not a new phenomenon, a fact substantiated by existing studies on the activities of militant and hard-line diasporas (Hall and Swain 2007, 9). Diasporic remittances are an invaluable form of economic support for the homeland. While the incoming funds may be used for economic development, there is substantial evidence to suggest that finances have been channelled through charitable organizations for the sole purpose of supporting insurgent or terrorist groups in the homeland. In these instances, remittances are used to escalate rather than resolve conflicts.

Financial support during the conflict escalation phase may encourage more bellicosity and create further instability, as observed with the Palestinian, Jewish, Tamil, Lebanese, Kurdish, Armenian and several other diasporic groups (Bercovitch 2007, 31). Besides economic support, diasporas also offer military assistance, thereby undermining the peace process. Many diaspora communities have provided weapons, training or even personnel. The Irish, Tamil, Sikh and Kurdish diasporas present the most obvious examples of conflict promoters. There is mounting evidence to suggest that the Irish Republican Army (IRA) had regularly received significant financial support from the Irish diasporas during its violent conflict in the 1980s and 1990s (Cochrane, Baser and Swain 2009).

Similarly, the Kurdish diaspora in Europe also substantially contributes to conflicts in its homeland by providing financial and military support, as well as fighters, to rebel groups. India in particular, suffered bitterly from the violence perpetrated by the Sikhs in the 1980s and 1990s, when the Sikh diaspora offered considerable support to armed Sikh guerrilla organizations (Singh 2007). Meanwhile, violent eruptions between the government and the Liberation Tigers of Tamil Elam (LTTE) have existed for decades in Sri Lanka. The guerrillas used cultural and political events to instil a common cause among the Tamil diaspora and ensure their radicalization and support (Hoffman 2007; Cochrane, Baser and Swain 2009).

However, despite their blemished record as conflict promoters, some recent evidence suggests that diasporas are not only conflict enthusiasts but have also become crucial peacebuilders, through their work in peace development and democracy in their homelands. They can also contribute to conflict resolution in their homelands by encouraging negotiations, or acting as mediators rather than resorting to military force as a way to solve conflicts. Diaspora groups have assisted the international community in their efforts to establish contacts with leaders of warring factions, as a prelude to negotiating ceasefires or peace processes during conflicts. A thorough understanding of the local issues, historical complexities and personalities of the groups leaders, makes diasporas well suited to offer international mediators the insight necessary to effectively manage negotiations (Baser and Swain 2008).

Consequently, some have argued that the direction a diaspora takes in either supporting or resolving conflicts depends on the different opportunity costs that such action would entail. Diasporas are complex and sometimes face dilemmas, whereby some members within the same group may support and promote conflicts, while others work for peace, development and democracy in their homelands. Moreover, the roles of peacemaker or conflict creator can be swapped in different circumstances as well. Especially in conflict situations, diasporas can secure tangible and intangible resources to fuel armed conflicts, and they can provide opaque institutional and network structures that enable the transfer of arms and money to terrorist groups (Bercovitch 2007, 17–38).

Furthermore, diasporas are not only considerably involved in the conflict or post-conflict phase, but also help to prevent conflicts in their homelands by contributing to the development process. While it is admittedly difficult to capture the widespread impacts diasporas can have on the development of their homelands, the role of diasporas on their homeland's development has been characterized as the 'four T's': money transfer, transportation, telecommunication and nostalgic trade (Orozco 2005). Diaspora relations with their countries of origin are based on remittances, direct and indirect political support, investment in economic activities, integration into international networks, education and training, and the exchange of experiences.

Homeland and hostland governments are important actors that can influence the behaviour of diasporas groups, with implications for political decision-making processes, affecting both countries. It may be that maintaining a keen interest in issues affecting their country of origin is a way for diasporic communities to reinforce their core values and beliefs, as well as to preserve their identity in the shadow of globalization. Diasporas aim to create opportunities and foster cooperation between their homeland and host country. In other words, 'diasporas are in fact increasingly building bridges between their home and host societies', or 'often play a role as a distinct third level between interstate and domestic peacemaking' (Baser and Swain 2008, 12).

The Growing Importance of Remittances

Remittances, generally considered the flow of funds from migrant workers, especially diaspora communities, back to their home countries, have been sent in the billions of dollars over the decades. Recent World Bank (2008a, 2008b) reports claim that they are not only an important source of income in many developing economies, but also a critical element for development, with an increasingly enormous aggregate cash flow and number of participants.

Moreover, remittances sent by many diaspora communities have contributed significantly to the peacebuilding processes in their homelands. Although these huge international flows of remittances have significantly increased in recent years, their impact is 'only beginning to be understood' (Terry and Wilson 2005).

According to the World Bank's estimation, officially recorded remittance flows to developing countries totalled $283 billion in 2008 (Rath, Mohapatra and Xu 2008). Remittances are an important source of both family and national income in many developing countries, representing in some cases up to a third of GDP for recipient countries and accounting for about a third of the total global external finance. Moreover, surveys indicate that the flow of remittances constitutes a higher percentage of national income in poorer countries (36.2 per cent of GDP in Tajikistan and Moldova, 32.3 per cent in Tonga and nearly 20 per cent in Armenia in 2006 (World Bank 2008b)), and is more stable than other forms of external finance; for instance, developing countries in total receive one-and-a-half times more money in the form of registered remittances than they do in official development assistance (World Bank 2004).

Monetary remittances are sent in different ways, depending on cost, speed and convenience. A variety of flows, from the migrants themselves or their descendants, are sent by individuals, mostly either as small or regular financial transfers, to support their relatives or friends in their country of origin or to finance economic investment. Moreover, remittance flows are transferred by individuals or as collective philanthropic support to development projects. However, remittances can also be considered to encompass in-kind gifts, value transfers or domestic financial transfers (in case of internal migration), as well as financial flows to developed economies. They are typically transmitted within the global financial system, in the form of cheques or money transfers by banks or other financial service providers such as Western Union, MoneyGram and Vigo (IFAD 2006, 14).

Remittances and Peacebuiding

The presence of millions of diaspora community members who are regularly connected to their homelands, as well as the impact that those connections have on local economies, communities and various dynamics, including peace development, are not negligible. Interestingly, diasporas interact in complex global networks with mixed identities and loyalties in relation to their country of origin, while also adapting and identifying to varying degrees with the host country. Remittances are considered the tool of choice by which most diasporas assist the peace process in their homelands. Some have argued that 'migrants and especially migrant diasporas are the motor forces driving remittances'

(Fagen and Bump 2006, 6). The effectiveness of remittances as a tool in peacebuilding is due in part to the fact that they are stable, countercyclical, and they augment the recipients' incomes more directly than official aid could.

Despite the fact that diasporas have transferred remittances to their homelands for several generations, their contributions have largely been ignored by donors and international finance agencies until the last decade. Evidence showing the role of remittances in stimulating economies of developing countries has catapulted their relevance to the forefront and caught the attention of the international community. Fragile democracies susceptible to conflict situations and crisis management are especially dependent on remittances as a tool to resolve conflicts, build infrastructure, reduce poverty and promote broad-based economic development. In countries emerging from or still experiencing conflicts (e.g., Bosnia and Herzegovina, Sri Lanka, Afghanistan, Somali, Liberia and others), remittances can be seen as a *sine qua non* for peacebuilding and reconstruction (Fagen and Bump 2006, 1).

During the post-conflict phase, diasporas (especially those in rich countries) can play a major economic role in the reconstruction by offering financial support to undo the effects of a conflict and to help bring about a process of disarmament and demobilization. Remittances from diasporas can help to promote economic recovery and thus consolidate the foundations of durable peace. Private sector investments through remittances have particularly made serious contributions to building the kinds of institutional mechanisms and services needed for sustainable post-conflict rebuilding and for the reintegration of the war-affected populations (Ibid., 8).

The Vietnamese Diaspora

Profile-Collective History

The Vietnamese diaspora (commonly known as 'Overseas Vietnamese') has a particularly distinct profile from most others originating elsewhere in the world. Vietnam's turbulent history offers a glimpse into the forces that have shaped this unique diaspora in transition. Over the past fifteen centuries, the external influences of wars and conflicts with China and other neighbors, followed by recent periods of colonialism and imperialism, as well as internal forces such as nationalism and communism, have all exerted a toll on this small country. Yet the Vietnamese diaspora is mostly associated with recent historic events since the 1960s. As Nguyen and Cunningham (1991, 73) describe:

It is a small diaspora but one which has had a very high profile internationally because of the implication of major western countries in the conditions which led to the creation of the group: the US and

French involvements in Vietnam, together with the crucial nature of the Vietnam War for the course of international relations and ideological alignments in the 1960s and the 1970s.

As such, most overseas Vietnamese often recall this period of war, conflict and division with heartbreak and immense sadness.

As Chuyen, Small and Vuong (2008, 252) observe, Vietnamese migrations abroad have existed long before the Vietnam War, hence their inclusion by contemporary Vietnamese historiography in a continuous narrative highlighting contributions to the homeland. The early Vietnamese migrants are known to have arrived in Europe during the French colonial period (1897–1954), with notable increases during World War I, when the French government aggressively recruited young men from Indochina, particularly Vietnam, to meet their battlefield demands in Europe. The French sent 183,928 strong young Vietnamese men to fight alongside their soldiers during combat in various European battles; most of them perished, with only a few returning home or attempting to integrate into a new life in Europe (Vietnamese History 2008).

French colonialism also impacted the migration trend in such a way that, because of the harsh rules imposed by the colonial masters on the Vietnamese, many of them became convinced that the attainment of knowledge and skills abroad was the best hope for eventually overcoming French authority (McConnell 1989). Arguably, the most celebrated example of this era is Ho Chi Minh, the first President of Vietnam, who roamed Europe and Asia before returning home in the 1940s to lead a nation and inspire a people. The 1940s and 1950s were especially chaotic for Vietnam, with the French colonial demise, Japanese occupation, and anticipated American involvement (Tranguyen 2004, 15). Numerous students and expatriates left the country and opted for France or Japan, where they build up some of the oldest Vietnamese diaspora groups today.

Vietnamese diasporas have only existed in significant numbers since the period surrounding 1975 and the end of the Vietnam War, a time with which the diasporic community is largely associated and well-known for all over the world. Three major waves of post-war Vietnamese refugees are usually classified as follows.

The first wave consisted of about 132,000 South Vietnamese who fled the country or were airlifted by the Americans following the end of the Vietnam War (Rutledge 1992, 3). At 12 noon on 30 April 1975, General Duong Van Minh (the last president of the Republic of Vietnam) surrendered to the North Vietnamese communist troops at Independence Palace in Saigon, thereby signalling the fall of the Republic of Vietnam to the communist North and ending the war. A massive refugee exodus actually began weeks before the final fall, comprising mostly government elites and military officials in the South Vietnamese society (Chuyen, Small and Vuong 2008, 251–83). Their abrupt departure in 1975 was a traumatic experience that left most people in shock, even long after the evacuation. Thiennu Vu[2] narrates as follows: 'My family left on the 23rd of April, 1975. At the time, my Dad worked for Bank of America who told us to ready ourselves to leave the country any minute' (Tranguyen 2004, 17).

During the post-war period (1977–85), a second wave of refugees fled the country to escape persecution, socio-political oppression, dire economic conditions, as well as the forced re-education camps imposed on former military officials and senior civil servants from the South Vietnam. Several thousands of Vietnamese attempted to escape the country by small boats to seek asylum in neighbouring Hong Kong, Malaysia, Thailand and the Philippines, while others opted for the US, Australia and Canada. The journey taken by these refugees was often dangerous; half of all 'boat people' are believed to have drowned at sea, while thousands of young men, women and children died of starvation and dehydration along the way. Even the surviving refugees were often attacked and robbed, and the women raped and held captive by pirates, prompting the phrase 'disappeared members' of the Vietnamese diaspora used by Tranguyen (2004, 17), Chuyen, Small and Vuong (2008, 253) and Carruthers (2008, 70). Other refugees that travelled on foot to the neighbouring countries of Laos, Thailand, Cambodia and China, also faced problems similar to those of the 'boat people'. They died along the way, were robbed and often subjected to military attacks. This group comprised a broader cross-section of the population, including senior civil servants, peasants, workers, the petite bourgeoisie, the urban middle class, and a disproportionately high number of ethnic Chinese Vietnamese as well as Catholics (Carruthers 2008, 70). The plight of the suffering Vietnamese refugees caught the attention of the international community, which responded by enthusiastically opening their borders to the new migrants.

A notable group of refugees that fled Vietnam for China and Southeast Asia during 1978–9, was the ethnic Chinese (Hoa). Most of them had been successful entrepreneurs and amassed a disproportionate amount of wealth and property, but became victims of a changing Vietnamese policy during the escalation of the Sino-Vietnamese conflict. Previous communist governments had discouraged anti-Chinese sentiments and promoted amiable relations between Hoa and Vietnamese as a symbol for cooperation between China and Vietnam. Nevertheless, ethnic Vietnamese harboured some resentment for the ethnic Chinese, whom they viewed as an unassimilated and privileged minority. Although the South Vietnam had imposed Vietnamese nationality on the Hoa with only partial success, the Vietnamese authorities and the Hoa minority maintained cordial relations until the beginning of the Hoa exodus in the spring of 1978. The Vietnamese government interpreted the development as an effort by the People's Republic of China (PRC) to destabilize and undermine the Vietnamese economy and society before launching the inevitable military confrontation with Vietnam. Consequently a new Vietnamese policy towards the Hoa was introduced to address perceived security threats as the Hanoi government prepared for an anticipated war with China (Porter 1980, 55–60). According to the US Committee for Refugees and Immigrants 2004 world refugee survey country report, an estimated three hundred thousand Vietnamese refugees (mostly ethnic Chinese) remain in China, including about one thousand in Hong Kong (USCRI 2004). Although most of those refugees in mainland China have successfully integrated into the local society, they have not been granted Chinese citizenship and remain without status in China.[3]

In the mid-1980s and early 1990s a third wave of refugees left the country, comprising mostly less-educated, rural people; Chinese-Vietnamese; Amerasians; and former South Vietnamese officials released from re-education camps and their family members (Chuyen, Small and Vuong 2008, 253–4). This exodus was organized under two programmes: the Orderly Departure Program (ODP) and Comprehensive Plan of Action (CPA). The former involved a heterogeneous group of migrants, including family reunion migrants, Ameriasians, and former political prisoners, whereas the latter included a high proportion of 'economic refugees' mainly from the provinces of the northern seaboard (Rutledge 1992, 65; Hitchcox 1994). These programmes allowed for the direct departure of qualifying Vietnamese refugees to camps in third countries, such as the Philippines and Malaysia, where they would stay for a period of time before moving on to permanent resettlement (Chuyen, Small and Vuong 2008, 253–4).

Nevertheless, Vietnamese diasporic communities worldwide are not made up only of refugees; current migration flows include expatriates, overseas students, temporary migrant workers and spouses. The number of Vietnamese refugees has declined largely due to the 'Renovation' (Doi Moi) policies instituted by the Vietnamese government in 1986, which have permitted structured legal emigration since 1989 (Nguyen and Cunningham 1991, 74), and secondly as a consequence of the United Nations High Commission for Refugees (UNHCR) directive to halt refugee programmes in Southeast Asia in 1996 (Tranguyen 2004, 18). A significant proportion of Vietnamese workers migrated to the former Soviet Union and Soviet Bloc countries in Eastern Europe, to former East Germany, and to the

Middle East. Meanwhile, the number of female Vietnamese migrating to Asian countries such as Taiwan, Korea and China as brides has increased rapidly in recent years. According to 2005 statistics, about 32,000 Vietnamese women were married to foreigners during the years 2003–5; recent estimates suggest that 180,000 Vietnamese have been married to foreigners, mostly Korean, Taiwanese and Chinese, with 15–17,000 Vietnamese brides migrating to Korea each year.[4]

Constructing/Reconstructing Identity

According to official Vietnamese government statistics, there are currently about three million overseas Vietnamese in different parts of the world. Regardless of the timing or circumstances of their migration and differences in generations, they currently reside in more than ninety countries, with 80 per cent located in developed nations (Committee for Overseas Vietnamese 2005). Most overseas Vietnamese reside in the US, France, Australia and Canada. The Vietnamese diaspora in these countries represents a majority of those who left under conditions of the post-1975 refugee exodus and are a part of today's permanent settled Vietnamese diaspora (Chuyen, Small and Vuong 2008, 255).

Most Vietnamese diasporas with the exception of the ethnic Chinese (whose circumstances of departure were different) share a 'culture core' which is in part still unified by 'a collective memory and myth about the homeland, including its location, history and achievements' (Cohen 1997, 26); they still trace their common identity, language, cultural and religious beliefs and practices to a common ancestry. The Vietnamese have always had a very strong sense of community, so it is not surprising that even in the hostland they maintain relationships with one another. The diasporas founded in the post-war era mostly share similar backgrounds of war, conflicts, survival and heartbreak.

However, significant differences exist within the global Vietnamese diaspora, depending on the timing and circumstances of their departure, and also on their subsequent country of residence. While political contradictions between Vietnamese diaspora communities in the former Eastern Bloc countries and their neighbouring countries do indeed exist, they are not regarded as significant and these groups are typically considered by the Vietnamese state to constitute a loyal diaspora (Carruthers 2008, 70). In the case of diaspora in the West, however, considerable ideological differences remain. As such, communities in Australia, America and Canada have been ranked as 'extremely anticommunist'.[5] However, the diaspora groups in Western Europe are considered by Hanoi to be moderate.

Remittances: Opportunities and Challenges

According to a World Bank report, remittances in 2003 were enough to finance about 62 per cent of Vietnam's trade deficit and equalled 7.4 per cent of GDP and 160 per cent of foreign direct investment.[6] Even though the actual amount of received remittance is unknown, due to the nature of undocumented informal transfers sent through a network of underground financial institutions, directly carried home by diasporas, or through other unofficial sources, it is clear that remittances have significantly increased over the years. In 2006, according to the Vietnamese official statistics, the remittances to Vietnam had reached $6.8 billion, just behind India ($24.5 billion), China ($21.07 billion) and the Philippines ($14.8 billion) in the Asian region.[7] The State Bank of Vietnam has estimated remittances for 2008 at above $8 billion, a 60 per cent increase over 2007.[8]

In addition to family remittances, transfers from overseas Vietnamese have recently included investment capital in real estate, business and securities, and the like. From 1988 to 2004, according to the Vietnamese Ministry of Foreign Affairs, business activity reached 1630 projects in total worth $630 million. In 2007, the investment reached $89 million . The Committee on Overseas Vietnamese estimates that remittances sent by diasporas to support the country during natural disasters such as floods or storms have increased in recent years (for instance $4.7 billion was cited for 2007).[9] Besides investment and empathy remittances, since 1989 overseas scientists, business leaders and other expatriates' talents have constituted the so-called *social remittances*, a transfer of knowledge, ideas and technical skills from the developed countries to Vietnam, through the TOKTEN programme (Transfer of Knowledge Through Expatriate Nationals).

Nevertheless, the return of diaspora members to the homeland presents risks as well as rewards, due to the trauma and historical circumstances under which Vietnamese refugees were forced to flee their homeland. The contributions of overseas Vietnamese to the homeland are well documented, but resentment and distrust for the current ruling party cannot be ignored even after several decades with enormous changes enacted by the government. Memories from the past still loom large and sometimes make it difficult for overseas Vietnamese to speak with a common voice or support government policies. In today's global village, improved telecommunication systems make engagement in political discourse especially effective, even from a host country thousands of miles away.

In addition to the impact of its death toll, the Vietnam War still affects life in Vietnam, where numerous mines remain buried in rural areas and often explode and kill civilians. The carcinogen dioxin (or 'Agent Orange') was also widely used by the American forces during the war, and its effects on health are still visible in the people born with missing limbs or other physical deformations. Beyond the physical destruction and loss of life associated with the Vietnam War, the psychological impact on ordinary Vietnamese is very traumatic. Divisions occurred between the North and South, and some families and communities were torn apart when members fled the country. It is no surprise that some overseas Vietnamese still maintain a distorted view of life in the homeland, and internationally Vietnam is largely associated with war and conflict.

Anti-communist sentiments amongst the diaspora remain a great challenge to the precarious political situation in Vietnam, and to some extent negatively impact the amount and purpose of remittances from overseas Vietnamese. Some diasporic communities use extremist tactics and target members who send remittances or invest in Vietnam as a way to sanction the current leadership in Vietnam. As Andrew Lam (2008) points out, there is a practice within some extremist Vietnamese communities in the US, called 'putting the communist hat on someone', whereby those who maintain any dealings with Vietnam become automatically suspect and any deviation from the prevalent anti-communist sentiment may cause one to be labelled 'pro-communist'. Although over the past three decades it has become common for the American Vietnamese diasporic communities to hold rallies and denounce the Vietnamese government, their actions have not thus far translated into effective political action or coherent foreign policy.

Some other extremist overseas Vietnamese have used remittances as a tool to create conflicts in the homeland and thereby destabilize the government. There are a few examples of conflict promotion with support from the diaspora and remittance. The Western Highlands of Vietnam, a strategic enclave where Vietnam borders both Laos and Cambodia, was in 2004 the scene of an uprising involving several minor ethnic groups. The region encompasses four provinces, the majority of which is populated by several minor ethnic groups, and was also one of the most important bases of the American army during the Vietnam War. Therefore, many of the anti-government Vietnamese abroad who used to be soldiers serving the American army during the 1960s and mid-1970s were located in this region. On 11 April 2004, Kok[10] and other leaders of the group 'Catholics De Gar' incited an uprising involving several youth from many minor ethnic groups in the region who rushed out to the streets and destroyed government offices, houses, schools and also blocked the National Highway 19. The violent riots which were put down a few days later signalled the unresolved grievances between the government and the anti-communist Vietnamese diaspora.

The conflict between the Vietnamese government and a group, or 'bloc', named '8046' has existed for several decades. In the group's press release of 22 August 2006, it boasts of 1,951 members living in Vietnam and claims to have 3,881 official members who are overseas Vietnamese, 139 of whom are international politicians representing various democratic groups and organizations all over the world. The bloc rules, assigned by former Vietnam People's Army officer Tran Anh Kim and a Catholic priest Nguyen Van Ly, demand a complete change in politics and regime, as well as transparency in its democratic institutions. The Vietnamese government has accused the group of attempting to overthrow the government and therefore being a threat to national security. The bloc countered with support from some Vietnamese diaspora members and a letter of support signed by 50 US congressmen on 9 May 2006, as well as other international groups including religious and democratic associations, affirming the group's important work to promote democracy in Vietnam. On 30 March 2007, the People's Court of Thua Thien-Hue rendered a decision charging the priest Nguyen and other leaders of the bloc with promoting conflicts, riots and destruction of the nation's solidarity and government, sending him and the others to prison for eight years.[11] Internationally, the court's decision was met with widespread objection, especially within the overseas Catholic community and other international associations which supported the bloc.

In December 2007, the Vietnamese government claimed that Viet Tan (New Viet), an organization supported by the anti-communist Vietnamese diaspora, was a 'terrorist group' that has been trying to destroy the country and create conflict in Vietnam. The group was established in 1980 by former military officials allied to the Americans during the Vietnam War. The group's objective is to overthrow the current Vietnamese government, reform the country's entire political and governing system and democratic institutions. Viet Tan has received considerable support from several extremist Vietnamese diasporas worldwide. On 4 April 2007, the Vietnam Agency for Anti-Terrorism informed the US that they considered Viet Tan a dangerous terrorist organization and requested America's cooperation in dealing with it.

Above all, as Andrew Lam (2008) argues, 'the question here is whether the Vietnamese Diaspora can be an effective agent of change and find new ways to influence the future of the country. To do so, it needs to ask tough questions regarding freedom and democracy.' That is a reasonable way to look at the complicated situation of Vietnam, especially with regard to 'democracy' which, although complex and understood in different ways by each side, is a basis for most conflicts. The reality is that even though some extremist Vietnamese diasporas have intentionally promoted conflicts in the homeland, many others have supported democracy, reconstruction, peace and development in

Vietnam. Sometimes situations are complex, as for instance when diasporas contribute money for the purpose of promoting development in the homeland and their transfers are channelled to support conflicts instead. In such cases, the good will of diasporas is misused to create conflicts in the homeland, and thereby promote the agendas of groups whose views they oppose.

The Vietnamese-Swedish Diaspora and the Bilateral Relations between Home and Host Country

Vietnamese Diaspora in Sweden

The first Vietnamese came to Sweden as refugees, with about 631 asylum seekers in 1979 (four years after the end of the Vietnam War). Today, Sweden's Vietnamese community consists of 13,184 people,[12] with a small number adding to the community in recent years comprising: Vietnamese students, experts coming to pursue study or training programmes and subsequently settling, and Vietnamese brides. Vietnamese refugees came to Sweden involuntarily, after the loss of family and source of livelihood caused by war and conflict. Unlike the Vietnamese diaspora in North America, France, Australia or Germany, whose destinations were by choice, those in Sweden were 'boat people', mainly peasants, fishermen and Chinese-Vietnamese. They were refugees who had fled the country at the end of the 1970s and through the 1980s, but stayed in camps for a transit period before being transferred to a third country. During the transit period, most resettlement countries selected refugees partly by establishing monthly or annual quotas or occasionally responding to appeals launched by the UNHCR; Sweden fit the latter profile (Mignot 1995, 453).

In comparison to the diaspora in the US, Canada, Australia, etc., the population in Sweden is very small. By 2005, the number of Vietnamese immigrants in the US had quintupled to 1.3 million, making them the fifth-largest immigrant group in the US, whereas there were 250,000, 245,000 and 200,000 in France, Australia and Canada, respectively. Moreover, the Vietnamese-Swedish community differs significantly from the other Vietnamese diaspora groups. In Sweden, this community is scattered and is described by Tranguyen (2007), as one of the younger and smaller communities in Europe. She also observes that there are fewer Vietnamese cultural activities within the community in Sweden. This is quite different from the Vietnamese diaspora groups in Canada, France, Australia, and especially in the US, where they are considered a 'model minority' (Kosonen 2008, 15) which easily integrates into society, as measured by school achievements and workforce participation.

Another issue influencing the differences between the Vietnamese group in Sweden and the ones in other countries such as the US, Germany, France,

Australia or Canada has to do with the character of the waves in which the community's members came. Compared to the Vietnamese diaspora in the US, whose members immigrated in big groups and mostly comprised elites (highly educated personnel and high-ranking military officials), the Vietnamese in Sweden arrived in smaller numbers and from less privileged circumstances. This partly explains why the Vietnamese diaspora in Sweden is not as strongly coordinated as their counterparts in larger Western countries.

Language and cultural differences also cannot be ignored as a hindrance to the integration process of the Vietnamese diaspora group in Sweden. During the French colonial period that lasted over half a century and then the American presence in the South of Vietnam, a majority of Vietnamese could speak French and English. Moreover, there was also an influence on the education system, lifestyles and cultural activities, making French and American culture quite familiar to the Vietnamese. As such, the Vietnamese that immigrated to North America, Australia or France were comfortable and familiar with the language and culture of their host countries. In contrast, the Vietnamese group in Sweden experienced language and culture barriers, which hampered their full integration into society.

Unlike the Vietnamese diaspora groups in Australia, the US, or Canada, which are political, those in Sweden, Denmark and Finland are apolitical (Dorais 1998; Kosonen 2008). Dorais (1998, 120) argues that the diaspora in Sweden has no political agenda and therefore is not involved in organizing political activities to influence particular events in the homeland. Besides, diasporic behaviour has a certain hostland dimension as well; as Baser and Swain (2008, 24) point out, activities of diasporas towards their homelands are influenced by the respective government policies in the hostlands. Despite having initial language and cultural barriers, as well as smaller networks, Vietnamese diaspora members in Sweden are relatively comfortable with their new life. Swedish policies in promoting the integration of immigrants have had some sort of a positive impact on their assimilation.

The Diaspora and Bilateral Relations

The foundation for the close ties between Sweden and Vietnam was laid during the Vietnam War, with the strong solidarity movement in Sweden for the Vietnamese people. Sweden and Vietnam established diplomatic relations on 11 January 1969, making the former the first Western country to take such a step. Sweden's bilateral development cooperation with Vietnam, which includes support for reconstruction and socio-economic development projects, dates back to that time. Although in earlier years Sweden mostly funded humanitarian and infrastructure related projects, it has since shifted emphasis to the Doi Moi reforms and supports projects supporting human rights and democracy in Vietnam. Decades of diplomatic relations between the two countries have created a bilateral environment of mutual trust and respect.

Furthermore, the total Official Development Assistance (ODA) from Sweden to Vietnam has already exceeded $3 billion. The main areas for Swedish support include: poverty alleviation, public administration reform, economic reform, public financial management, health care, legal reform, natural resources and environment, rural energy, research cooperation, culture and media.[13] Recently, Sweden strongly supported Vietnam's efforts to join the WTO in 2006 and influenced EU member states to resolve anti-dumping measures affecting the Vietnamese shoe industry. Sweden's cooperation with Vietnam has not only positively contributed to overall development in Vietnam, but has also strengthened ties between the two states.

After thirty years since the first Vietnamese refugees arrived in Sweden, the first generation have settled down and tried to integrate successfully into the new society. It is noteworthy that although the majority of them fled the country as political refugees, they no longer regard themselves as exiles. The host country and its policies play critically important roles in shaping diaspora's attitudes towards the homeland. This may either depend on the degree of relations between the host and home country, or how far the host countries' policies help diaspora to economically and socially assimilate, thereby limiting their interest in political issues affecting the homeland. There is no doubt that for last several decades, Sweden and Vietnam have maintained warm and positive bilateral relations.

There are no official figures on remittance transfers by the Vietnamese-Swedish diaspora to Vietnam. Even EU statistics are not able to determine the extent of the transfers, on the grounds that informal remittance systems are the dominant channel for remittances to Vietnam (ECDGEFA 2004, 6). Many European countries report the existence of unregistered transfers but are unable to provide any estimate on the amounts involved. Determining remittance estimates from Sweden to Vietnam is especially complicated. A study by Luong and Kristesson (2008), reasons that price, speed, convenience, mutual cultural sharing and recommendations from friends are the main reasons why diasporas choose informal money transfers. As our informal interviews confirm, remittances carried directly by hand are still the most popular and preferred amongst the Vietnamese diaspora community in Sweden.

Besides the remittances sent back to support their relatives and families in Vietnam, philanthropy is also another significant contribution of this diaspora group to the homeland in recent years. The economic condition of the Vietnamese diaspora in Sweden has improved significantly over the previous decades, as they have resettled and economically integrated in the host society.

Increasingly, they are contributing financially and making concerted efforts to remain connected to their country. Even though the amount of their financial contribution is less than that from other Vietnamese groups in North America or France, for instance, they have most importantly always actively participated in various philanthropic activities ranging from supporting victims of flood or storm disasters to aiding victims of 'Agent Orange' dioxin in Vietnam. Particularly during the flood disaster of 2007 in central Vietnam, the philanthropy channel of the Vietnamese Embassy in Sweden received considerable financial contribution from the diaspora group.

Moreover, the Vietnamese-Swedish community has contributed to the economic development of Vietnam and its cooperation with Sweden on other issues involving education or cultural promotion. Several projects are aimed at contributing to economic growth in Vietnam, by supporting and strengthening the bilateral economic relationship between host and home countries. Vietnamese diaspora members in Sweden are increasingly working as mediators and their competencies are being mobilized to forge relationships between Swedish enterprises and companies in their homeland.

In terms of cultural contribution, the Suphu Academy, a Vietnamese traditional martial arts academy and medical centre, has been established at Linkoping. Besides providing training in martial arts and providing medical treatment, the centre holds courses on Vietnamese language, history and gastronomy. The Vietnamese community here has also played an important role in establishing three big pagodas in different cities of Sweden, which have attracted many Swedish followers and interest in Vietnamese religion. Moreover, the diaspora community, through the Vietnam-Sweden Cultural Fund, has sponsored about 2,000 cultural projects in Vietnam over the past 15 years, the most effective of which is to receive ten water puppetry villages in the Red River Delta Region. Other projects serve diverse purposes ranging from helping to preserve southern folk opera and music to familiarizing local people with democracy and quintessential works of Vietnamese, French or American culture. Presently, the Vietnam-Sweden Cultural Fund is trying to preserve historical honour-conferring documents at 500 localities nationwide.

Although as a measure of contributions from remittances and philanthropy, the Vietnamese-Swedish diaspora still lags behind its counterparts in North America, Germany, France or Australia, it has contributed to the development of their homeland in other intangible ways. Their contribution and involvement in the homeland has also been less controversial. Vietnamese-Swedes are apolitical and are therefore regarded as less hostile to the government in Vietnam, which potentially strengthens their influence in promoting peace in the homeland. They have also promoted cooperation between Vietnam and Sweden on various projects, ranging from technological skill transfer to agriculture and sustainable development. Their contributions quietly promote democracy and market economy policies, while supporting the respect for human rights.

Concluding Observations

In today's world, diasporas are an increasingly active and potentially crucial link between their often war-torn countries of origin and the migrant receiving countries. As such, studies on the role of diasporas in either peacebuilding or conflict escalation have been catapulted to the forefront, in the hope of finding long-lasting solutions to crisis situations. Diasporas may either benefit or challenge their homelands, depending on whether they use remittances to aid in sustainable peacebuilding or fuel pre-existing conflicts. The complex nature of diasporas is such that in some cases they promote peace while in others supporting conflicts, depending on the various opportunity costs involved (Swain and Hall 2007, 110–11). Consequently, both home and host countries have a vested interest in understanding how diasporas may be encouraged to support peacebuilding efforts rather than foment ethnic nationalism and war.

Relationships among diasporas, homeland, and hostland countries are quite complex and depend on different contexts and specific situations. The case of the Vietnamese-Swedish diaspora is especially unique, because of the circumstances of their departure from Vietnam and arrival in Sweden. Unlike other Vietnamese diaspora groups in other parts of the world, the Vietnamese-Swedish community has a different history of exile, includes a diversity of socio-economic classes and lives in a hostland that has maintained strong and positive diplomatic relations with the government in Hanoi for several decades. The role of the Vietnamese diaspora community in Sweden confirms that diasporic behaviour has a certain hostland dimension, in which the nature of the hostland regime determines the way the diaspora community organizes itself and interacts with its homeland. Despite limited remittances by the Vietnamese diaspora in Sweden, their intangible contributions are a promising aspect of the peace development process in Vietnam.

Notes

1 The Jewish diaspora has contributed to the debate on conflict resolution for many years, and the evolution of the Irish-American diaspora, and its use of 'soft-power' strategies played a pivotal role in the development of Irish republicanism during the peace process (Cochrane 2007, 16). The peace-contributing role of the Ghanaian diaspora can be found in Samuel (2004).
2 Professor of medicine at the University of California, San Francisco.
3 For more information, see USCRI (2004).

4 International Organization for Migration and the Embassies of Vietnamese Abroad (VietNamNet 2007).
5 Many in these communities continue to identify themselves with the former South Vietnam (Carruthers 2008, 71).
6 *New York Times*, 18 March 2005.
7 Official website of Vietnam's Ministry of Foreign Affairs. Online: www.mofa.gov.vn (accessed 2 October 2008).
8 *Vietnam Economy Times*, 5 August 2008.
9 Official website of Vietnam's Ministry of Foreign Affairs. Online: www.mofa.gov.vn (accessed 2 October 2008).
10 The leader of the uprising (Kok) was a soldier on the American side during the Vietnam War, who had fled to America and joined the group 'Fulro', an anti-government diaspora group, and then founded the 'Minor Ethnic People' in South Carolina and the 'Catholics De Gar' in Vietnam. It is believed that Kok and his supporters used remittances to leverage support from minority ethnic communities in the Western Highlands of Vietnam. They used propaganda, religion and promises of wealth and a happy life in America for those who joined their cause. Another sub-group, the 'Independent State of De Gar' in Vietnam, is alleged to have sent people several times for training in Cambodia before the uprisings.
11 *Tuoitre*, 26 February 2007.
12 Statistics Sweden online statistics database. Online: http://www.scb.se/ (accessed October 2008).
13 Official website of Vietnam's Ministry of Foreign Affairs. Online: www.mofa.gov.vn (accessed 2 October 2008).

References

Baser, Bahar and Ashok Swain. 2008. 'Diasporas as Peacemakers: Promoting and Supporting Third Party Mediation in Homeland Conflicts'. *International Journal on World Peace* 7(7): 7–28.

Bercovitch, Jacob. 2007. 'A Neglected Relationship: Diasporas and Conflict Resolution'. In Hazel Smith and Paul Stares (eds), *Diasporas in Conflict: Peace-Makers or Peace-Wreckers?*, 17–38. Hong Kong: United Nations University Press.

Bush, Kenneth. 2007. 'Diaspora as Peacebuilders: Considerations for Analysis, Policy, and Practice'. In Ashok Swain (ed.), *Diasporas, Armed Conflicts and Peacebuilding in Their Homeland*. Report 79. Sweden: Uppsala University.

Carruthers, Ashley. 2008. 'Saigon from the Diaspora'. *Singapore Journal of Tropical Geography* (29): 68–86.

Chuyen, Truong Thi Kim, Ivan Small and Diep Vuong. 2008. Diaspora giving: An agent of change in Asia Pacific communities? Paper for the 'Conference on Diaspora Giving: An Agent of Change in Asia Pacific Communities?', 251–83. Vietnam: Hanoi.

Clifford, J. 1994. 'Diasporas'. *Cultural Anthropology* 9(3): 302–38.

Cochrane, Feargal. 2007. 'Irish-America, the End of the IRA's Armed Struggle and the Utility of "Soft Power"'. *Journal of Peace Research* 44(2): 215–31.

Cochrane, Feargal, Ashok Swain and Bahar Baser. 2009. 'Home Thoughts from Abroad: Diasporas and Peace-Building in Northern Ireland and Sri Lanka'. *Studies in Conflict and Terrorism* 32(8): 681–704.

Cohen, Robin. 1997. *Global Diasporas: An Introduction*. London: UCL Press.

Committee for Overseas Vietnamese. 2005. *Overseas Community: Questions and Answers*. Committee for Overseas Vietnamese. Hanoi: Gioi Publishing House.

Dang, Nguyen Anh. 2005. 'Enhancing the Development Impact of Migrant Remittances and Diaspora: The Case of Vietnam'. *Asia-Pacific Population Journal* 20(3): 111–22.

Dorais, Louis-Jacques. 1998. 'Vietnamese Communities in Canada, France and Denmark'. *Journal of Refugee Studies* 11(2): 108–25.

ECDGEFA. 2004. 'EU Survey on Workers' Remittances from the EU to Third Countries'. *ECFIN/235/04-EN (rev 1)*. 28 April. Brussels: European Commission Directorate General Economic and Financial Affairs.

Fagen, Patricia Weiss and Micah N. Bump. 2006. 'Remittances in Conflict and Crisis: How Remittances Sustain Livelihood in War, Crises, and Transitions to Peace'. *The Security-Development Nexus Program Policy Paper*. International Peace Academy and Georgetown University, February.

Hall, Jonathan and Ashok Swain. 2007. 'Catapulting Conflicts or Propelling Peace: Diasporas and Civil War'. In Ashok Swain, Ramses Amer and Joakim Öjendal (eds), *Globalization and Challenges to Building Peace*. London: Anthem Press.

Hall, Jonathan, Roland Kostić and Ashok Swain. 2007. 'Diasporas and Peace Building: A Multifaceted Association'. In Ashok Swain (ed.), *Diaspora, Armed Conflicts and Peacebuilding in their Homelands*, 9–16. Report 79. Sweden: Uppsala University.

Hitchcox, Linda. 1994. 'Relocation in Vietnam and Outmigration: The Ideological and Economic Context'. In Judith M. Brown and Rosemary Foot (eds), *Migration: The Asian Experience*, 202–20. Oxford: St. Martin's Press.

Hoffman, B. et al. (eds). 2007. *The Radicalization of Diasporas and Terrorism: A Joint Conference by the RAND Corporation and the Center for Security Studies, ETH Zurich*. RAND.

IFAD. 2006. 'Remittances: Strategies and Operational Considerations'. *Annex to IFAD Tools for Rural Finance*. IFAD.

Kosonen, Liisa. 2008. 'Growing Up Vietnamese in Finland: Looking Back 12 Years Later'. *The Well-Being and Sociocultural Adaptation of Vietnamese as Children or Adolescents and as Young Adults*. Helsinki: University of Helsinki.

Lam, Andrew. 2008. 'New Year, Old Unresolved Passion: Vietnam and its Diaspora'. *New America Media*. News Analysis, 7 February.

Luong, Quang and Yulia Kristensson. 2008. 'Bank's Money Transfer Service in Sweden: Qualitative study of Swedbank, Nordea and Handelsbanken'. Sweden: Högskolan i Jönköping, IHH, EMM.

McConnell, Scott and Leftward Journey. 1989. *The Education of Vietnamese Students in France, 1919–1939*. New Brunswick: Transaction Publishers.

Mignot, Michel. 1995. 'Refugees from Cambodia, Laos and Vietnam, 1975–1993'. In Robin Cohen (ed.), *The Cambridge Survey of World Migration*, 452–6. Cambridge: Cambridge University Press.

Nguyen, Tina and Stuart Cunningham. 1991. 'Population Media of The Vietnamese Diaspora'. *The Public* 6(1): 71–92.

Orozco, Manuel. 2005. 'Transnationalism and Development: Trends and Opportunities in Latin America'. In Munzele Maimbo S. and Ratha Dilip (eds), *Remittances: Development Impact and Future Prospects*, 307–29. The International Bank for Reconstruction and Development. Washington DC: World Bank.

Porter, Gareth. 1980. 'Vietnam's Ethnic Chinese and the Sino-Vietnamese Conflict'. *Bulletin of Concerned Asian Scholars* 12(4): 55–60.

Rath, Dilio, Mohapatra Sanket and Xu Zhimei. 2008. 'Outlook for Remittance Flows 2008–2010: Growth Expected to Moderate Significantly, but Flows to Remain Resilient'.

Migration and Development Brief. Migration and Remittances Team, Development Prospects Group. World Bank, 11 November.

Rutledge, P. J. 1992. *The Vietnamese Experience in America.* Bloomington: Indiana University Press.

Samuel, Zan. 2004. One nation, one people, one destiny? The Ghanaian diaspora's contribution to national development using diverse channels. Report prepared as part of the programme 'Hello Africa: Shifting power, tackling poverty by connecting Africa and the African diaspora'. SEND Foundation of West Africa.

Singh, Pritam. 2007. 'The Political Economy of the Cycles of Violence and Non-violence in the Sikh Struggle for Identity and Political Power: Implications for Indian Federalism'. *Third World Quarterly* 28(3): 555–70.

Terry, Donald F. and Steven R. Wilson. 2005. *Beyond Small Change: Making Migrant Remittances Count.* Inter-American Development Bank.

Tranguyen, Trangdai. 2004. 'Orange County, Yellow History: An Intimate Encounter with Vietnamese American Lives'. *Journal of Archival Organization* 2(4): 5–28.

UN. 2006. 'World Population Monitoring, Focusing on International Migration and Development'. *Commission on Population and Development.* Report of the Secretary-General, Population Division, Department of Economic and Social Affairs (39th Session 3–7 April). United Nations.

USCRI. 2004. 'U.S. Committee for Refugees World Refugee Survey 2004 – Vietnam'. United States Committee for Refugees and Immigrants. Online: http://www.unhcr.org/refworld/docid/40b4594b4.html (accessed 23 September 2011).

Vietnamese History. 2008. Vietnamese history homepage [in Vietnamese]. Online: http://www.lichsuvietnam.vn/home.php?option=com_content&task=view&Itemid=357i (accessed 10 September 2008).

VietNamNet. 2007. Published 30 August 2007 [in Vietnamese]. Online: http://tintuc.timnhanh.com/kieu_bao/20070830/35A65319/ (accessed 15 September 2007).

World Bank. 2004. *Global Development Finance 2004.* Washington DC: World Bank.

World Bank. 2008a. *Financial and Private Sector Development, Payment Systems and Remittances-Remittances.* Washington DC: World Bank.

World Bank. 2008b. *Migration and Remittances Factbook 2008.* Development Prospects Group, World Bank. Washington DC: World Bank.

Chapter 9

TRACING MINERALS, CREATING PEACE: THE SECURITY-DEVELOPMENT NEXUS IN THE DRC

Ruben de Koning

Introduction

Since the early 1990s, resource conflict, state failure and criminal violence have dominated the security agenda of many African countries. These emerging threats challenge the traditional notion of security as the protection of territorial integrity, stability and vital interests, mostly through military means. Rather than originating from other states, the above security threats come from within the state. They involve state and non-state (security) actors as main perpetrators of violence, and tend to emerge from adverse socio-economic conditions and national political crises (IPA 2006). The 'developmental' underpinnings of emerging security threats are increasingly understood and integrated in multilateral peacekeeping missions and peacebuilding activities that are spearheaded by the United Nations and other western donors. For instance, there has been much attention paid to the role transparent and formalized resource governance can play in preventing conflict and promoting post-conflict recovery, notably through generating official state revenues (EITI 2010; UNEP 2009). Yet there has been relatively little analysis of (1) how resource governance can be improved to enhance security and development for communities at the production level and (2) how post-conflict resource governance, as a development priority, relates to and depends on more conventional security sector governance.

This chapter considers the mutual interaction, or nexus, between security and development through the lens of resource conflict and post-conflict resource governance in the Democratic Republic of the Congo (DRC). The DRC is probably the longest-lasting resource-driven conflict in Africa since the end of the Cold War, starting in 1996 and continuing to this date. Violent conflict in the DRC has often been explained as a way for belligerents to make economic profits through the exploitation of natural resources (Ndikuma and Emizet 2003; Nest 2006). This understanding has been much fostered by investigations of UN Groups of Experts (GoE), and fits the model of post–Cold War civil war proposed by Collier and Hoeffler (2001) that features economic greed as the underestimated but often overriding motive for insurgents to mobilize rebellion. Following this perception of war in the (eastern) DRC, the international community explores and implements a number of mechanisms to block the 'dirty' trade of minerals from which armed groups benefit, and formalize and facilitate 'clean' trade from which they presumably do not benefit. The UN explores the case for selective commodity sanctions and can already sanction individuals and entities that support illegal armed groups through the illicit trade of natural resources (UN GoE 2007; UNSC 2008). Meanwhile, the DRC government, metals industries and international donors explore opportunities to certify the trade of precious metals from 'legitimate' mines and block or interrupt exports of non-certified resource products.[1]

The dominant policy response of cracking down on (illegal) mineral trade has been criticized for overemphasizing the economic rationale of war and the centrality of minerals therein. Garrett and Mitchell (2009), for example, argue that the militarization of resource sectors is a consequence rather than a cause of insecurity and declining state institutions, and that armed groups infiltrate mineral resource sectors in the east as much as any other economic sector. Blocking rebel access to minerals could therefore lead to intensified military involvement in other sectors, such as cattle farming, or it could even intensify looting. Another important point of criticism is that by uniquely banning illicit trade benefiting illegal armed groups, trade interventions fail to address economic profiteering by regular armed forces that are often involved in and profit from 'legitimate' mining activities. Following these points of criticism, this chapter argues that trade interventions will have limited impact in terms of ending violence and enhancing security and development for mining communities if no simultaneous efforts are made to remove military actors from mineral trade and production. Accordingly, this chapter suggest that security sector reform (SSR) and resource governance innovations, such as the formalization and certification of mineral trade, are ideally implemented jointly, in a coordinated and mutually supportive manner, reaching down all the way to the production level. At the same time, this chapter is conscious of the concern that, as security and development in general, SSR and resource management are likely to remain separated domains in institutions designed to provide development and ensure security, and in the implementation of security and development in particular and localized sites (Öjendal and Lilja 2009).

The chapter introduces two case studies in Katanga province in the southeast corner of the DRC that demonstrate the challenges and opportunities for demilitarizing mines and for improving (resource) governance at the production level. The first is a militarized coltan mining area in the north of the province; the second is a non-militarized copper mining area in the south. The author visited both sites in June–July 2009. In the south, formalization processes are further advanced, including formal recognition of artisanal miners' rights of access to resources and the formation of cooperative associations. These improvements in local resource governance could be replicated in the north, and may have positive spin-offs for security in the mining areas. However, exploitative structures and the implication of security actors in artisanal mining appear difficult to put to a stop in both areas. Before moving to case studies in the third and fourth part of the paper, the first part of this chapter provides a conceptual framework for analyzing resource-related conflict in the DRC. The second part discusses the importance of the artisanal mining sector in Katanga. After the case studies, the final part of the chapter provides general conclusions and a set of policy recommendations on how developmental engagement and security sector reform can work towards the common objective of the demilitarization of mines.

Natural Resources and Conflict in the DRC

In recent years three broad concepts have emerged in the literature to explain the relationship between natural resources and armed conflict. The 'resource curse' refers to the negative effects of resource dependency on the quality of governance and economic performance through phenomena such as 'Dutch disease' and the 'rentier state' (de Soysa 2000).[2] The term 'resource wars' refers to conflicts that revolve to a significant degree around the pursuit and possession of critical resources, confronting actors with seemingly incompatible claims to these resources (Klare 2001). Resource wars comprise livelihood conflicts related mostly to renewable resources like land, water and forest, as well as inter-state or intra-state competition over non-renewable resources like oil and gas (Le Billon 2008). 'Conflict resources' are generally understood as resources used by rebel groups to finance their armed struggles against the government.[3]

While describing distinctively different dynamics, the above three relationships between natural resources and conflict may coincide, reinforce or follow up on each other. In the DRC one can see a certain evolution. The resource curse describes the dynamics prior to the conflict that erupted in 1996. It came about as a result of Mobutu's 'Zairisation' policy of the 1980s, by which the state nationalized foreign-controlled mining and agricultural companies, and put influential people in control as a means to buy political loyalty and so ensure regime survival (de Koning 2008). Economic mismanagement of and corruption within state companies, in combination with dropping commodity prices, reduced agricultural and mineral outputs, destroyed the formal economy and slashed state revenues and public spending. In turn, the reduced coercive power and moral credibility of the state paved the way for Laurent Kabila to mobilize forces in the east of the country to remove Mobutu from power during the first Congolese war (1996–7).

The second Congolese war (1998–2003) is often characterized as the real 'resource war', in that it involved foreign parties whose principal objective was to exert territorial control over parts of the eastern DRC in order to extract and trade precious resources such as coltan, gold and diamonds (e.g., Samset 2002). The trade and production of these resources had, because of years of economic mismanagement, become almost completely informal and was rerouted from Kinshasa in the west of the country to Rwanda, Uganda, Burundi and Tanzania. During the second Congolese war, Uganda and Rwanda switched their support from the Kabila government to a new rebel movement, the *Rassemblement Congolais pour la Démocratie* (RCD), mainly to be better able to capture and profit from these trading chains. Competition between the two over areas of influence even led to their forces clashing in Kisangani in 2001, the main diamond-trading centre in the eastern DRC. This confrontation clearly demonstrated the importance of mineral wealth as military objective.

In the current war dynamics in the eastern DRC – that is, since the RCD and its local opponents accepted peace and military and political integration at the end of 2002 – military access to resources ceases to be a main driver of conflict. However, the trade in 'conflict resources' prolongs conflict and makes it harder to resolve. For example, Rwandan rebels hide out in remote areas, surviving largely through the exploitation and trade of minerals. Intensified military campaigns in the course of 2009 removed these rebels from some main trading centres, only to draw them deeper into the forest, close to small deposits of gold and other precious metals. Particularly the gold trade provides good opportunities for Rwandan rebels to finance war efforts because it is easily smuggled across the border compared to bulkier cassiterite and coltan ores.

In the above characterization of resource–conflict linkages, several discontinuities appear that need to be nuanced, namely between formal and informal, peaceful and violent, and state and rebel control. First of all, contemporary resource-linked conflicts in Africa, like the one in the DRC, are rooted in the violent colonial and post-colonial history of resource extraction. This involved a high degree of physical and structural violence, such as resource appropriation, price manipulation, forced labour, or population displacement, as well as a degree of military control of legal and illegal exploitation schemes (Le Billon 2005). One can imagine that long-standing societal grievances associated with resource extraction and trade have not only fed into the war, but have also intensified during the war as a result of shifting patterns of control. Indeed, the capture of mineral resource exploitation and trading links during the war by 'foreign' military elements and Congolese rebel proxies, set off the mobilization of local self-defence militia, grouped under the term Mai-Mai to defend 'indigenous' territories. Despite regional and national peacemaking, there are concerns that simmering local conflicts over land – including mines, forests and grazing areas – between competing ethnic alliances will set off new rounds of violence and insurgent mobilization (Autesserre 2008).

Secondly, the rebel networks of resource control established during war are often no different from pre-war networks of control. Rather than new politico-military players overtaking exploitation and trade, controlling state actors turn into rebels, detaching themselves from the state. During the second insurgency of 1998, rebel leaders of the RCD were almost all members of the political establishment either in Kinshasa or in the eastern provinces, controlling significant sources of patronage in the pre-war state (Tull 2007). Likewise, in transition and post-conflict contexts, politico-military systems of resources control established during the war often persist, despite the fact that military players (re)align with the state and trade (re)enters the formal legal sphere. For example, in the beginning of 2009, Laurent Nkunda's rebel group – a Tutsi dominated RCD battalion – accepted integration into central state institutions, but continues to operate a parallel administration, with rebel-appointed agents working in administrative offices and posted along roads to collect taxes, thereby generating income independent from the state (UN GoE 2009).

Thirdly, military dominated resource exploitation areas and trade networks are not necessarily beyond governance or even security. In many areas in Africa, particularly where insurgencies take place, a variety of non-state actors provide security with varying degrees of competency and legitimacy. The concept of 'security governance' describes a situation whereby the military actor invests in the establishing a monopoly on violence, and, once achieved, focuses its capacity to provide security for a certain social group either by imposition – e.g., in case of the inhabitants of the territory under control – or by its being selectively chosen by a group of ethnic affiliates or simply those willing to pay for security provision (Garret et al. 2009). In DRC the common scenario is that security provision is forced upon miners and traders, but there are exceptions where there is a more voluntary type of cooperation. For example Nande gold traders in Butembo actively invested in militia formation in order to protect their particular economic interests and defend their home territory, thereby generating an island of relative peace and prosperity amidst wartime chaos (Kabamba 2007).

Rather than signifying a rupture or breakdown of social and political order, war represents a transformation of institutions governing access to resources and revenues. War and the parallel military-dominated resource governance arrangements that emerge can, according to David Keen (2000), 'offer alternative systems of profit, power and protection for significant groups in society'. At the same time, it must be recognized that the persistence of such systems undermines the Congolese reconstruction process by diverting potential revenues for mining communities, as well as the state that could constitute significant 'peace dividends'.[4] In addition, Vlassenroot and Raeymaekers (2009) observe a process of commodification of public security and argue that this 'gradually transformed Congolese statehood into a very weak centre of power that had to rely on strategies of mediation and accommodation in order to maintain even a semblance of authority'. In summary, the parallel resource governance cum profiteering structures erected by state and non-state security actors during the conflict put off economic reconstruction as well as state consolidation in the post-conflict period. Before moving to case studies relating to local (security) governance arrangements in Katanga, the next section first highlights the economic significance of artisanal mining in the province in general.

The Artisanal Mining Sector of the DRC and Katanga

The DRC holds large proportions of global reserves of many mineral substances, and Katanga province is particularly well endowed. In the south copper and cobalt production are most important, the trade of which is oriented to southern Africa. In 2007 artisanal copper and cobalt production (an estimated 80 per cent of the total) was estimated to represent a value of $325 million at the export level (Berke et al. 2007). In the centre, cassiterite mining is developing, while in the north coltan exploitation is most important (both are 100 per cent artisanal). Trade from the centre and north of the province is oriented to Bukavu in South Kivu from where it is exported to countries in East Africa. In comparison, export values of these minerals are modest: an estimated $2.6 million per year for cassiterite in 2008,[5] and $9.5 million per year in 2009 for coltan.[6] The value of recorded exports of cassiterite and coltan for 2009 for the DRC as a whole is about $90 million and $12 million respectively (CEEC 2009).[7] In total the artisanal mining sector of Katanga employs between 150,000 and 200,000 people (Pact Inc. 2009).

The proliferation of artisanal mining in Katanga and the DRC as a whole followed the decline of the industrial mining sector in the 1980s.

In south Katanga this affected the state copper and cobalt mining company Gécamines most of all. In the mid 1990s the company was forced to transfer or lease its most important rights and assets to private companies. Through joint ventures it retains between 15 and 25 per cent interest in new industrial operations. While the company retained some concessions, it has proven unable to generate enough capital to revive industrial mining on its own. In contrast, newly created joint ventures are moving towards industrial exploitation or are already exploiting, this despite some severe recent cuts in investment in the beginning of 2009. As in the south, smaller scale industrial cassiterite mining operations in the centre of the province closed down in the mid 1990s. While some international companies have expressed interest in obtaining rights over newly discovered deposits, there have to date been no serious investments for large scale industrial mining.

The artisanal mining sector in the DRC is similarly organized. Small teams of diggers (*creuseurs*) supply middlemen (*négociants*) who, in turn, supply trading houses (*comptoirs*). *Négociants* often pre-finance mining operations, supplying miners with food, tools and other necessities, in return for a share of production and/or the first right to buy minerals. Most of the *comptoirs* have official licences but *négociants*, particularly those buying at the mines, often do not. Some *comptoirs* have processing facilities (*fondeurs*). Others export their ores unprocessed to international trading or processing companies. As a result of a 2007 ban imposed by the provincial governor to export raw material, Katanga witnessed the construction of a large number of processing companies in the south, thereby increasing metal production and state fiscal revenues. On the other hand, *comptoirs* systematically undervalue exported volumes with complicity of customs official in order to lower tax payment due, and some are involved in outright illegal smuggling activities. These practices are rampant particularly in the coltan and cassiterite trade, for which export taxes are high compared to Rwanda and Uganda.

Box 9.1. Coltan production and commodity chain from Kisengo

Kisengo is the principal coltan mining area of Katanga, generating about a third of quantity officially exported from DRC.[8] *Creuseurs* come from all over the DRC. Some are able to finance their operations, and sell their minerals to whomever they want. However, most depend on so-called *managers* who lend money and/or provide foods and tools. Miners that are pre-financed repay their debt in the form of coltan but with a 30–50 per cent interest. This leaves them very little, if any, minerals to commercialize independently. Some miners are continuously indebted, and loose all potential income generation ($15–30 per person, per week). Besides reimbursement of loans, miners face illicit taxes from soldiers (in quantities unknown and haphazard) and the traditional chief (one tin of coltan worth $6 per person, per week).

Managers are permanently based in the mines and sell to *négociants* who mainly come from South Kivu. *Négociants* pay the truck owners who evacuate the purchased minerals (ranging between 200–500 kg per *négociant*, per month, paying $1 per kilo for transport). Among *négociants* some work independently, while others operate as agents who are pre-financed by Bukavu-based *comptoirs*, such as Panju and Muyeye. The *comptoirs* sell to international trading companies that transport ores directly from the DRC or from neighbouring Uganda, Rwanda and Tanzania to processing facilities overseas.

China is the primary consumer of DRC coltan exports, with the majority of imports destined for the state-owned Non-Ferrous Metals Smeltery (Ma 2009). Coltan ore is not sold centrally at the London Metal Exchange and therefore has no world market price. There is no open marked for coltan elsewhere. Instead, *comptoirs* sell to those international traders with whom they have made prior agreements about quantity and price. Processors in Asia make tantalum powder or wires that they sell to capacitor producers, whose products are turned into circuit boards for high-tech industries.

The formalization of the mineral sector in the DRC mainly concerns the trade level. About 100 *comptoirs* and several hundred *négociants* are licensed to trade and export minerals (World Bank 2008). At the production level, most artisanal mining activities are technically illegal because they take place on concessions that are supposed to be industrially exploited, or because they take place in an area not allocated for (artisanal) mineral exploitation. The 2002 mining code provides for the delimitation of Artisanal Mining Zones (AMZs) where miners that posses a diggers card (*carte de creuseur*) can legally mine. In Katanga, as in the rest of the country, very few such zones have been delimitated due to the fact that almost all mineral-rich land has been allocated for industrial mining. Where AMZs *have* been created, hardy any diggers have been able to obtain their diggers cards because these are only issued in the provincial capital. Garret (2008) qualifies the mining code as a 'parallel rule system', which is largely ignored by the majority of actors active in the artisanal mining sector.

Although illegal by law, artisanal mining activities are not beyond regulation. State-owned companies occasionally grant temporal permission to miners to access their concessions, usually in return for a share of their production. In South Katanga, the state governor has intervened on numerous occasions to convince the state mining company Gécamines to agree to such deals. In addition, provincial state officials, notably the governor and the Provincial Minister of Mines, also verbally declare that artisanal mining is allowed in some areas although no zones are officially delimitated. Upon such informal agreements or declarations, mining authorities are often deployed in artisanal mining sites. The Small-Scale Mining Technical Assistance and Training Service (*Service d'Assistance et d'Encadrement du Small-Scale Mining*, SAESSCAM) registers miners, allocates pits, and instructs on safety measures, while the state Mining Service (*Service des Mines*) registers and taxes production and transported volumes of minerals. The presence of state mining authorities is taken as a form of official state recognition of artisanal mining activities.

Rather than cracking down on illegal mining activities, provincial and local mining authorities try to regulate the sector with the intention of avoiding social unrest, but also of being able to generate official taxes from largely informal activities. In many areas mining authorities are resisted and challenged by local actors. Artisanal miners and traders circumvent legal requirements and official taxes. More importantly, mining authorities face competition by unauthorized state and non-state bodies present at mines, including other state security services, military elements and customary authorities. These all extort a share of the production and trade. In November 2008 a state governor's decree was communicated to ban unauthorized state actors from mines and to remove illegal roadblocks in order to help the sector cope with the economic crisis. The decree was widely ignored. Likewise a request by the provincial mining minister to the armed forces to vacate artisanal mines has not been acted upon.

So rather than deriving from mining laws and related policies, the stability of local artisanal mining operations results from negotiation between local government and non-government actors, both civil and military. While some understanding is usually reached about the relative power of stakeholders, confrontations do occur generating a climate of insecurity. More importantly, the negotiated aspect of access to resources, in combination with an uncontrolled security services, makes mines highly vulnerable to violent looting and unbridled rent-seeking. The next section will illustrate these problems by focusing in on one militarized coltan mine in northern Katanga.

Artisanal Coltan Mining and Security in the Nyunzu Territory

Nyunzu territory in northern Katanga is one of the main production areas for coltan in the eastern DRC. In addition there are a number of relatively small gold mines. Artisanal gold and coltan mining is a relatively recent phenomenon. The main coltan mine of Kisengo was discovered in 2007 and the main gold mine in Lunga was discovered in 2002. The production of mines is very unstable, and some have already been abandoned after just a few years of exploitation. New discoveries are made though, which generates a highly mobile mining community, and very limited state representation and service provision in the villages that have emerged around the mines. Since the start of artisanal mining, the territory experienced an influx of miners and traders. The Bashi ethnic group from South Kivu dominates the trade. The autochthonous population is mainly involved in mining and the supply of agricultural goods to mining communities. Traditional authorities that allocate land and levy taxes tend to exclude pygmy populations from taking part in mining operations. Unequal opportunities of ethnic groups to access mines and/or enter trade generate tensions and localized social conflicts, but these do not seem to degenerate into violence.

The main security risk associated with coltan mining is that of contested control between different armed factions. The main protagonists in the areas are the Mai Mai militia under the command of Kabeja Tango Fort[9]; integrated FARDC (Armed Forces of the DRC) soldiers based in the town of Kalemie and in Nyunzu; and non-integrated FARDC soldiers based in the town of Kongolo. On several occasions FARDC elements have engaged each other in violent confrontations, usually followed by the retreat of one party or the conclusion of some form of agreement over respective areas of influence. Since 2007 no major violent clashes have occurred. Instead of military showdown, competing forces tend to reach agreement, with each other as well as with traditional authorities and local elites, on the distribution of parcels of mineral-rich land. A good example of this is the recently discovered coltan mine near the village of Kayebe. According to the state Mining Inspector of Tanganika district, who recently visited the mine – but was eventually chased away by controlling FARDC officers – one section of the mine is controlled by soldiers of the Kongolo brigade. They allegedly mandated an unlicensed mining company by the name of SOCOMIN to manage the section on their behalf.[10] Another section is presumably divided in parcels that are attributed to Nyunzu-based security actors from the national police, military intelligence service, and FARDC.

Direct violent confrontation over mining areas may be rare, and seems to have reduced in recent months, but mineral resources influence conflict dynamics more indirectly. Access to mineral revenues seems to delay the proper integration of former rebel and Mai Mai militia units. The military reintegration process, or *brassage*, that started in 2003 intends to create new brigades composed of soldiers from different factions, who are trained and deployed away from previously controlled areas. Unwilling to give up their economic opportunities in the mines of Nyunzu, the non-integrated soldiers from Kongolo have repeatedly refused military orders from the provincial capital Lubumbashi to return to and reassemble at their army barracks, prior to moving to the *brassage* camp in Kamina in the southwest of the province. Likewise, the Mai Mai of Tango Fort did not leave for *brassage*, but negotiate with military authorities in Kalemie to form a new Border Guard Brigade (Spittaels and Hilgert 2008). This would keep the unit intact and in the position to control trans-border flows of goods, including minerals. While wearing FARDC uniforms, command structures of above-mentioned units are not broken down, as the *brassage* process intends. This precludes the creation of a unified and non-partisan professional army, and risks defection of non-integrated or poorly integrated units as soon as they see their economic interests threatened.

Apart from the effect on the wider conflict situation in northern Katanga, military control over mines has consequences for local economic and human rights. Military profiteering from mining takes many forms. Soldiers that are permanently posted at mining sites tend to 'own' mining pits. This means that they confiscate up to half of the production generated by a team of three to five miners.[11] In return they offer some supplies, mimicking the function of *managers*. In addition, military sponsors offer protection from harassment by other soldiers, as well as against tax levying by customary chiefs and formal state authorities, including authorized mining services as well as unauthorized state actors. In contrast, soldiers that are not posted at mining sites visit them to extort money or coltan from miners and traders under the threat of physical violence and captivity. These moving soldiers are considered to be the biggest threat to physical security of miners, while locally posted soldiers are considered to deploy lower levels of violence.[12] In summary, there seems to be a difference between locally posted, 'rent seeking' soldiers, who have long-term interests in the local production system, and 'loot seeking' soldiers who prey on local communities and move on after having extorted their share. Curiously, in Kisengo both belonged to the same brigade.

Higher military and political authorities do not seem to be very keen on challenging FARDC military control over mining areas in North Katanga. In public statements authorities do call units back to the barracks, but decisions are not backed up by force and refusal is not or limitedly sanctioned (*Radio Okapi* 2008a). For example in 2007 the military justice garrison tried to arrest a number of soldiers of the Kongolo brigade in Kisengo following complaints by the local population. Shortly after being arrested the soldiers were liberated by force by their commanding officer, a certain Captain Mamadou. His military superiors summoned him to Lubumbashi, but instead of being punished he received the grade of Major and was posted elsewhere.[13] No further action was taken against lower cadres. This level of inaction of the military hierarchy is characteristic for the entire eastern DRC. By turning a blind eye to military profiteering from natural resources the state makes up for its own inability to pay decent and regular wages. Furthermore, it assures itself a minimum level of loyalty from renegade – yet government – forces to the central command in an area that is still vulnerable to attacks by the Mai Mai and FDLR (Democratic Forces for the Liberation of Rwanda) operating from the provinces of Maniema and South Kivu.

Although higher military and political authorities insufficiently address militarized control over mines, a decline in troop intensity has been observed in some areas, like Kisengo. Here the number of soldiers reduced from 200 in the beginning of 2007 to about 25 in the middle of 2009. The reasons for this are not fully clear, but a significant withdrawal followed a flash deployment by UN peacekeepers after the skirmishes in 2007 described above , and the subsequent installation of a police force. To some degree soldiers fear negative reports of their behaviour coming from UN sources to higher military authorities as this could potentially lead to prosecution or translate into lower ranks upon integration into the national army. As a further illustration, the author's visit in Kisengo – along with a UNDP (UN Development Programme) officer, a mining official, a migration office official and a civil society organization representative – prompted one captain to release a prisoner that was arrested after having tried to intervene when soldiers extorted miners earlier that day. This shows that increasing the presence of the UN as well civil authorities could help to convince soldiers to move away or moderate their behaviour. Of course the risk exists that soldiers that move away from certain mines will occupy other mines where public scrutiny is less, adopt a more looting-centred mode of operation, or gain access to revenues through installing a front company. Due to the diverse ways by which soldiers are inserted in the commodity chain, the gradual demilitarization of mines does not imply a definite end to military profiteering.

Artisanal Mining and Security in Kambove Territory in Southern Katanga

The history of mining in the south of Katanga goes back a century. Dramatic transformations have taken place in recent years from industrial to artisanal mining, and back again. Some artisanal miners' camps have existed for more than a decade, permanently housing diggers and their families. Still there are usually no facilities like running water or electricity. The mining population consists of a pluriform mix of people, but is mostly of native Katangan origin. The long history of in-migration of Luba peoples from the Kasai provinces, and associated competition over land and artisanal mines, sparked widespread conflict in the beginning of the nineties and flares up occasionally, particularly around the town of Kolwezi. *Comptoir* owners and smelters are often of foreign origin (Indian, Chinese, Zambian), but this is not a factor of social conflict.

Mines in southern Katanga are not militarized as in the north of the province. There is one notable exception, and that is the uranium mine of Shinkolobwe. Artisanal cobalt mining from the same mine has been forbidden since 2004 by presidential decree. The site is supposed to be sealed off from artisanal miners by the FARDC as well as Presidential Guards. However, soldiers let miners pass after payment and artisanal mining continued at least until July 2009. Elsewhere in the region, soldiers also perform roadside controls in order to check transporters' required documentation and to levy illegal taxes (Spittaels and Hilgert 2008). On the artisanal mining sites military elements are seldom present but are substituted by a plethora of security services. These include: ordinary police forces; a special branch of mining police (*police minière*) that can be called in by local administrators; Gécamines' own security guards (*Garde Industrièlle*); and security services established by mining cooperatives. These security actors can be mobilized in cases of conflicting economic interests, as further elaborated in the conflict cases below.

The main source of conflicts in recent years has been the forced resettlement of artisanal miners from Gécamines concessions where mostly foreign investors have resumed industrial mining in partnership with the state mining company. A recent incident occurred in November 2009 at the Luiswishi concession. The concession is exploited by the *Compagnie Minière de Sud Katanga* (CMSK) – a joint venture involving Group Forrest International – but about 3,000 artisanal miners dig for minerals as well, causing landslides and damages to company assets. The company turned to the provincial authorities to find a solution, which responded by sending in the police to search houses in the adjacent village of Kawama for 'stolen' minerals from the concession. In response to local resistance to the search, the provincial Ministry of Interior sent in a demolition brigade the following day composed of anti-riot and mining police (ACIDH 2009). These proceeded with the demolition of at least 565 houses.[11] One human rights NGO claims that a large number of houses destroyed were located outside the concession area (ASADHO 2009), a claim a company spokesperson denies.[15] After protests in the provincial capital, provincial authorities decided to give financial compensation to the displaced miners.[16] According to a company spokesperson CMSK may have provided the money.[17] Meanwhile, villagers not involved in mining who claim their houses were destroyed have not been compensated. Official sources indicated that the provincial government intends to negotiate with the CMSK in order to provide compensation for the remaining claimants.

Miners displaced from active concessions in the region mostly move to Gécamines' inactive concessions. The conflict issues that arise here relate to the buying arrangements the company puts in place. After several years of failed attempts to set up a structure responsible for buying from artisanal miners and delivering to Gécamines, the company now tasks the artisanal miners' cooperative *Exploitants Miniers Artisanaux du Katanga* (EMAK) to manage affairs in the concessions. For example in Kamatanda EMAK was made responsible for training miners, commercializing local production and finding a private partner to better equip the site for artisanal production. In return, EMAK ensures that Gécamines receives 20 per cent of the local production, while the partner company takes another percentage depending on the size of its investment.[18] Miners and traders not associated with the cooperative, however, disagree with the suggested buying monopoly that was being created in favour of one company by the name of Venger, leading to protests (Mikombe 2009). However, due to the lack of legal status, and therefore risk of expulsion, miners are likely to comply with the buying structure imposed on the mine.

Box 9.2. Cooperatives in South Katanga

EMAK was created in 1999 to carry out similar functions as SAESSCAM today, but it soon also started to operate as intermediary trading agent that buys from artisanal miners and sells to trading and processing companies. In 2002 Gécamines and EMAK agreed on protocol related to the delivery of minerals to Gécamines.[19] In December 2008 the organization divided itself according to these two functions.[20] SEMAK carries out syndicalist functions (i.e., representing members interests) and EMAK-Federation functions as a cooperative of *négociants* with a profit-making objective. Besides EMAK, two other cooperative structures were legally recognized by 2007: CMKK (*Cooperative Minière Maadini Kiwa Kilimo*) and COMAKAT (*Cooperative Minière des Artisanaux du Katanga*) (RRN 2007). To avoid conflict over areas of operation, the cooperatives requested the provincial minister of mines to attribute each of the seven legal artisanal mining zones to only one of them, which he accepted as an experiment.[21] Cooperatives also operate in illegal artisanal sites, where EMAK and CMKK are at times both present. A fourth cooperative was legally established in 2009, MDS (Mining Systems Development), but the cooperative is not part of the agreement about distribution of AMZs.

Even legal Artisanal Mining Zones are not free of conflict. These face similar issues over who is entitled to buy from artisanal miners. For example in the AMZ of Shamitumba, physical confrontations occurred in May 2009 between the members of two rival mining cooperatives and their respective security services. The Katanga Provincial Ministry of Mines confined the management of the mine to the CMKK, obliging the members of the alternative cooperative Mining System Development (MDS) to leave the site.[22] The latter represents the interests of a Russian mining company (MIRUCO) while the former works together with a Zambian company (ATLANTIKA). CMKK called in the mining police to settle the matter, while MDS is supported by SAESSCAM, thus polarizing different state agents. CMKK accuses SAESSCAM of having hidden commercial interest in the Russian company. It seems that CMKK will prevail in Shamitumba, as it has the support of the Mining Police and the Mining Ministry. Because the law does not foresee any exclusive attribution of AMZs to one cooperative, settlement of the conflict in favour of one or the other party rests on their respective ability to mobilize political players and security services to act in their favour.

Conclusions and Recommendations

A narrow definition of 'conflict resources', as revenues derived from natural resources rebel groups use to wage war against the state, does not adequately describe the contemporary resource–conflict dynamics in Katanga province. In northern Katanga, as in many areas in the eastern DRC, resource revenues do not only fuel conflict by financing the struggle of rebel groups. Equally important is that resources provide the means and motive for FARDC forces to refuse full integration and break up parallel military command and administrative structures, thereby undermining or denying the power the central government intends to exercise over the national territory. Paradoxically, the government's intentional failure to break down parallel (resource) control structures can be perceived as a bid to assure minimal level of loyalty of the 'renegade' forces in question. This reminds us of pre-war systems of (resource) patronage, with the main difference that distribution of command over the economy to turn potential opponents into allies now concerns artisanal production areas and trade networks rather than functioning state enterprises. In southern Katanga, resources do not fuel any larger military conflict, but trade and extraction are associated with other kinds of security threats such as violent protests and subsequent repression. These conflicts can result in violations of human rights.

The formalization of production and trade is proposed and to a degree implemented to simultaneously tackle security and developmental problems associated with the artisanal mining sector. For the eastern DRC, including northern Katanga, the formalization agenda is one that is largely driven by external donors that wish to establish the traceability of mineral trade in order to reduce conflict financing. The fact that the militarization of mines continues and intensifies at the production level, jeopardizes this objective. Because mining authorities are resistant to enter mining areas and because their presence does not drive away controlling military units, resources that are registered and enter the legal trade may still derive from military-occupied mines. This puts into question the credibility of any future 'conflict free' certificate based on the legality of traded goods. In southern Katanga the formalization agenda is one that has emerged from within the mining population, mainly to enhance local livelihoods at the production level. This developmental objective is compromised as a result of commercial actors' attempts to monopolize buying rights in state-recognized artisanal mining sites.

Without neglecting the security risks associated with compromised development in southern Katanga, security problems are more severe in the north. The key question here is how demilitarization can be achieved through formalization. At the trade level there is no attempt to interrupt resources from FARDC-occupied mines. As a result, the incentive to demilitarize has to emerge from pressure at the production level. It was noticed in Kisengo that the presence of civil actors in general, including mining administrators, moderates soldiers' behaviour vis-à-vis the mining community and may even stimulate them moving away. This process could be given further impetus by installing AMZs in the area, as in the south of the province. This was shown to attract private investors, as well as potential development projects, for example in support of mining cooperatives. The increasing presence of development actors and civil society initiatives would, in turn, increase the public scrutiny of security actors.

The above presumption is, however, based on the premise that soldiers indeed try to avoid negative reports about their conduct to higher military authorities, like the military justice system or the to the military structure dealing with integration. The first has the capacity to take soldiers out of the bush to stand trial, while the second can reward good behaviour through providing senior posts in the new integrated regular army. Unfortunately both organs rarely show the capacity and political will to hold perpetrators to account, particularly when these concern powerful commanders, who lead highly mobile non-integrated units that could easily turn against the state. As shown, these units are inclined to loot rather than govern by coercion. Given the fact that these looting units pose the main security threat to mining communities, security sector governance may need to be pragmatic and use controlling units with a decent track record on human rights to formally provide protection against looting bands of soldiers. For instance, support programmes are imaginable that transform military units controlling mines into a special branch of Mining Police.

Resource governance alone cannot improve security in the mines or remove soldiers from the commodity chain. Security sector reform, including the army's restructuring, police deployment and military justice, must be particularly geared towards the demilitarization of mining areas. So far this has not been sufficiently attempted in donor-funded SSR programmes. UN- or other donor-supported army training programmes do not engage units that control important resource deposits. Also, externally supported police deployments in the east do not target mining areas. The only initiative that in some way harmonizes security sector governance and resource governance is a UN-funded project that erects five trading centres (*centres de négoce*) where UN peacekeepers and trained mining police are supposed to provide security, prevent military interference, and facilitate the registration and taxation of traded volumes. To really help to demilitarize important mines, it is recommended here that similar activities be brought down to the production level.

The importance of SSR in mining areas does not mean that development engagements must be put on hold until significant progress is achieved in this regard. Instead, aid organizations should engage more boldly in artisanal mining areas in the eastern DRC. Mining areas in areas like Kisengo are very much like refugee camps. They house thousands of war-displaced populations, are erected in remote areas with no basic services, and are of temporal nature. In order to attract development engagement targeting mining populations, the legalization of artisanal mining is important. To date, international development organizations like the UNDP and the German Technical Cooperation refrain from implementing support programmes in the eastern DRC, not only because of insecurity, but also because most mining activities are illegal.

In an attempt to illustrate the 'security-development nexus', this chapter used case studies from the DRC mining sector to discuss a set of analytical concepts, i.e., 'conflict resources' that describe the interplay between security and development, as well as regulatory initiatives that echo a plea for attention to the nexus, i.e., trade formalization and certification (development) to address conflict financing (security). It was argued that proposed development interventions, even if they reach down to the production level, can only do very little to resolve the security issue at stake. In this context, it is unfortunate that donors (over)emphasize the potential effect of trade formalization and traceability, and fail to see how security sector governance can contribute to the demilitarization of the mining sector in eastern DRC. The danger here is that attention to the nexus – quite comfortably – diverts donor attention away from addressing security issues associated with mining through security sector reform, which would seem most logical. Surely, efforts to dislodge or transform security actors on the ground are much riskier than controlling trade flows in a few trading centres and border posts. But unless comprehensive efforts are made to improve governance and civil protection at the production level, mineral certification – as an interpretation of the nexus in the policy realm – will function as a façade that hides the real challenges and responsibilities.

Notes

1 One notable industry-led initiative is that of the international tin industry body ITRI. With the Congolese government ITRI aims to set up a system that provides for registration and tracing of minerals from the mine up to the export level, so that its members can demonstrate they source from acceptable locations (see ITRI 2010). A notable donor-led initiative is one implemented by the German Federal Institute for Geosciences and Natural Resources (BGR), which aims to work with the Congolese government to improve conditions in selected mining areas and set up a system that traces mineral exports back to these mines by analyzing their unique physical characteristics.

2 Dutch disease is a concept that explains the relationship between the increase in exploitation of natural resources and a decline in the manufacturing sector. Rentier states gain a large proportion of their revenues from external sources, such as resource rents, which presumably reduces the necessity of state decision-makers to levy domestic taxes, in turn, causing leaders to be less accountable to individuals and groups within civil society.

3 See for instance a definition by the UN General Assembly (2001) for conflict diamonds as 'diamonds that originate from areas controlled by forces or factions opposed to legitimate and internationally recognized governments, and are used to fund military action in opposition to those governments'.

4 In this context the concept refers to an economic incentive for sustaining peace.

5 Quantity from *Radio Okapi* (2008b); export value from CEEC (2009).

6 Quantity from the mining inspector of the Mining and Geology Department of Tanganika District, Katanga, interview with the author, Kalemie, 3 July 2009; export value from CEEC (2009).

7 It must be noted though that a large share of cassiterite and coltan production is not recorded and taxed when exported.

8 Production data from the mining inspector of the Mining and Geology Department of Tanganika District, Katanga, interview with the author, Kalemie, 3 July 2009; official export data from CEEC (2009).

9 Kabeja Tango Fort should not be confused with FARDC chief commander of the land forces General Gabriel Amisi, whose *nom de guerre* is also Tango Fort.

10 Mining inspector of the Mining and Geology Department of Tanganika District, interview with the author, Kalemie, 3 July 2009.

11 Per week this comes down to about 5 kg (worth $86.50).

12 Interviews with artisanal miners in Kisengo, 6 July 2009.
13 Director of Progrès des Peuples Indigènes (PPI), interview with the author, Kalemie, 7 July 2009.
14 Representative of the UN Joint Human Rights Office, correspondence with the author, 22 March 2010.
15 Spokesperson of Group Forrest International, interview with the author, 1 March 2010.
16 Representative of SAESSCAM, interview with the author, 4 March 2010.
17 Spokesperson of Group Forrest International, interview with the author, 1 March 2010.
18 Administrative director of EMAK-C, interview with the author, Lubumbashi, 29 June 2009.
19 Protocole d'accord N° 410/6775/SG/GC relatif à la livraison des minerais cobaltifères à la Gécamines [Protocol agreement number 410/6775/SG/GC concerning the supply of cobalt-containing minerals to Gécamines]. Unpublished government source.
20 Letter to the provincial governor of Katanga entitled, 'Sortie officielle de L'EMAK-Federation et présentation de son document de base' [Official establishment of the EMAK-Federation and presentation of its founding document]. Number REF/EMAK-FEDERATION/DK/06/12/2008. Unpublished government source.
21 Letter from the provincial minister of mines to CMKK on the subject of 'Proposition de répartition des zones d'exploitation minière artisanale' [Proposal to repartition artisanal mining zones]. Number CAMIN/0773/CSM/019/MMM/KAT/2008. Unpublished government source.
22 Katanga Province Ministry of Mines, letter number CABIM/0165/MM/053/BMG/KAT/2009, 13 March 2009. Unpublished government source.

References

Action Contre l'Impunité pour les Droits Humains. 2009. La malédiction des richesses minières frappe les habitants du village Kawama [The curse of mineral richness hit the inhabitants of Kawama village]. Press release, 4 November 2009. Action Contre l'Impunité pour les Droits Humains.

Agence France-Presse. 2008. 'Katanga (RDC): violents heurts entre police et mineurs (ONU)' [Katanga (DRC): violent clashes between police and miners (UN)]. Agence France-Presse. 7 March 2008.

African Association for the Defence of Human Rights. 2009. Violation de droit des populations environnant les sites miniers [Violation of rights of people in the vicinity of mining sites]. Press release 2 December 2009. African Association for the Defence of Human Rights.

Autesserre, Séverine. 2008. 'The Trouble with Congo'. Foreign Affairs, May/June: 94–110.

Berke, Carla, Jens Pulkowski, Nicola Martin, Jurgen Vasters and Markus Wagner. 2007. Les ressources naturelles en République Démocratique du Congo: Un potentiel de développement [Natural resources in the Democratic Republic of the Congo: A potential for development?]. Frankfurt am Main: Entwicklungsbank. Online: http://www.congoforum.be/upldocs/Ressources%20naturelles%20rapport%20Allemand%20avril%202007.pdf (accessed 12 January 2010).

Centre d'Expertise et de Certification. 2009. Situation of exports from January 2009 to June 2009. Unpublished data.

Collier, Paul and Anke Hoeffler. 2000. Greed and grievance in civil war. World Bank Policy Research Working Paper No. 2355 Online: http://www.papers.ssrn.com/sol3/papers.cfm?abstract_id=630727 (accessed 12 December 2008).

de Koning, Ruben. 2008. 'Resource–Conflict Links in Sierra Leone and the Democratic Republic of Congo.' *SIPRI Insights on Peace and Security 2008/2*. Stockholm International Peace Research Institute. Online: http://books.sipri.org/files/insight/SIPRIInsight0802.pdf (accessed 16 November 2011).

_____. 2010. *Controlling Conflict Resources in the Democratic Republic of the Congo*. Stockholm International Peace Research Institute Policy Brief. Online: http://books.sipri.org/files/misc/SIPRIPB1007.pdf (accessed 16 November 2011).

de Soysa, Indira. 2000. 'The Resource Curse: Are Civil Wars Driven by Rapacity or Paucity?' In Mats Berdal and David M. Malone (eds), *Greed and Grievance: Economic Agendas in Civil War*, 113–36. Boulder, CO: Lynne Rienner.

EITI. 2010. *Impact of EITI in Africa: Stories from the Ground*. Extractive Industries Transparency Initiative, International Secretariat. Online: http://eiti.org/document/impact-africa (accessed 5 March 2010).

Garrett, Nicholas. 2008. '*Walikale: Artisanal Cassiterite* Mining and Trade in North Kivu'. Communities and Small-Scale Mining. Online: http://www.resourceglobal.co.uk/documents/CASM_WalikaleBooklet2.pdf (accessed 12 September 2009).

Garrett, Nicholas, Sylvia Sergiou and Koen Vlassenroot. 2009. 'Negotiated Peace for Extortion: The Case of Walikale Territory in Eastern DR Congo'. *Jounal of Eastern African Studies* 3(1): 1–21.

Garrett, Nicholas and Harrisson Mitchell. 2009. 'Beyond Conflict: Reconfiguring Approaches to the Regional Trade in Minerals from Eastern DRC'. Communities and Small-Scale Mining. Online: http://www.resourceglobal.co.uk/index.php?option=com_docman&task=doc_download&gid=90&Itemid=41 (accessed on 12 September 2009).

ITRI. 2010. Supply chains unite to start the iTSCi mineral traceability project in DRC. Press release 19 March 2010. ITRI. Online: http://www.itri.co.uk/pooled/articles/BF_NEWSART/view.asp?Q=BF_NEWSART_318425 (accessed 19 March 2010).

Inter Press Service. 2009. 'Congo-Kinshasa: Joblessness Rises as Global Crisis Hits Mining'. Inter Press Service. 12 February 2009. Online: http://allafrica.com/stories/200902120486.html (accessed 3 May 2009).

IPA. 2004. 'The Security-Development Nexus: Conflict, Peace and Development in the 21st Century'. International Peace Academy. Online: http://reliefweb.int/sites/reliefweb.int/files/resources/905AE30BAEE61FC38525742D005CACD3-IPA_Security-Development_Nexus_May04.pdf (accessed 23 January 2010).

Kabamba, Patience. 2007. Capital accumulation and emergence of new power elite in South Africa and the DRC. Presentation of a doctoral research project at the Woodrow Wilson International Center for Scholars, Washington DC, 22 August 2007. Online: http://www.wilsoncenter.org/index.cfm?fuseaction=events.event_summary&event_id=270422 (accessed 23 January 2010).

Keen, David. 2000. 'Incentives and Disincentives for Violence'. In Mats Berdal and David M. Malone (eds), *Greed and Grievance: Economic Agendas in Civil War*, 19–41. Boulder, CO: Lynne Rienner.

Klare, Michael. 2001. *Resource Wars: The New Landscape of Global Conflict*. New York: Henry Holt and Co.

Le Billion, Philippe. 2005. 'The Geography of "Resource Wars"'. In Colin Flint (ed.), *The Geography of War and Peace: from Death Camps to Diplomats*, 217–241. Oxford: Oxford University Press.

_____. 2008. 'Diamond Wars? Conflict Diamonds and Geographies of Resource Wars'. *Annals of the Association of American Geographers*. 98(2): 345–72.

Mikombe, M. 2009. 'Plainte des négociants Kamatanda' [Complaint of Kamatanda brokers]. *Gouvernance en Afrique*. 27 May. Online: http://www.afrique-gouvernance.net/fishes/dph/fishe-dph-1239.html (accessed 3 April 2010).

Ma, Tiffany. 2009. 'China and Congo's Coltan Connection'. Project 2049 Institute. Online: http://www.scribd.com/China-and-Congos-Coltan-Connection/d/17000907 (accessed 30 May 2010).

Ndikumana, Leonce and Kisangani Emizet. 2003. The economics of civil war: The case of the Democratic Republic of Congo. Peri Working Paper No. 63, July 1. Online: http://www.peri.umass.edu/fileadmin/pdf/working_papers/working_papers_51-100/WP63.pdf (accessed 12 January 2010).

Nest, Michael. 2006. *The Democratic Republic of Congo: Economic Dimensions of War and Peace*. Boulder, CO: Lynne Rienner.

Öjendal, Joakim and Mona Lilja (eds). 2009. *Beyond Democracy in Cambodia: Political Reconstruction in a Post-Conflict Society*. Copenhagen: Niaspress.

Pact Inc. 2007. 'Kolwezi: Economic Development and Governance Transition Strategy'. Final Report. Online: http://www.pactworld.org/galleries/default-file/Kolwezi_Economic_Development_and_Gov...Final.pdf (accessed 23 January 2010).

Radio Okapi. 2008a. 'Axe Kalemie-Nyunzu-Kongolo: la population se plaint des tracasseries des militaires non brasses' [Axis Kalemie-Nyunzu-Kongolo: the population complains about hassles of non integrated militaries]. Radio Okapi. 19 May. Online: http://radiookapi.net/sans-categorie/2008/05/19/axe-kalemie-nyunzu-kongolo-la-population-se-plaint-des-tracasseries-des-militaires-non-brasses/ (accessed 23 Janury 2010).

_____. 2008b. 'Mines : Manono-Kongolo-Bukavu, nouvel itinéraire de la cassitérite vers l'exportation' [Mines: Manono-Kongolo-Bukavu, new itinerary for cassiterite to export]. *Radio Okapi*. 28 August. Online: http://radiookapi.net/sans-categorie/2008/08/28/mines-manono-kongolo-bukavu-nouvel-itineraire-de-la-cassiterite-vers-lexportation/ (accessed 23 January 2010).

Réseau Ressources Naturelles. 2007. L'impact de l'exploitation minière sur l'environnement du Katanga. Summary of a roundtable organized by the Réseau Ressources Naturelles. Lubumbashi, 10 February. Online: http://www.copirep.org/.../séminaire%20sur%20l'exploitation%20minière%20au%20Katanga.pdf (accessed 21 January 2010).

Samset, Ingrid. 2002. 'Conflict of Interests or Interests in Conflict? Diamonds and War in the DRC'. *Review of African Political Economy* 29(93/94): 463–80.

SouthScan. 2005. 'China Scoops Up Minerals, Infrastructure Contracts'. SouthScan 20(11). Online: http://allafrica.com/stories/printable/200507060674.html (accessed 14 Febuary 2010).

Tull, Denis M. 2007. 'The Democratic Republic of Congo: Militarized Politics in a Failed State'. In Morten Bøås and Kevin C. Dunn (eds), *African Guerrillas: Raging Against the Machine*, 113–30. Boulder, CO: Lynne Rienner.

UNEP. 2009. *From Conflict to Peacebuilding: The Role of Natural Resources and the Environment*. Nairobi: United Nations Environmental Programme. Online: http://www.unep.org/pdf/pcdmb_policy_01.pdf (accessed 4 February 2010).

UN General Assembly. 2001. 'Role of Diamonds in Fuelling Conflict'. A/RES/55/56. United Nations. Online: http://www.un.org/depts/dhl/resguide/r55.htm (accessed 4 February 2010).

UN GoE. 2007. 'Interim Report of the Group of Experts on the Democratic Republic of the Congo'. S/2007/40. United Nations Group of Experts. Online: http://www.securitycouncilreport.org/atf/cf/%7B65BFCF9B-6D27-4E9C-8CD3-CF6E4FF96FF9%7D/DRC%20S200740.pdf   http://daccess-ods.un.org/access.nsf/Get?OpenAgent&DS=S/2007/40&Lang=E&Area=UNDOC (accessed 12 January 2010).

———. 2009. 'Interim Report of the Group of Experts on the Democratic Republic of the Congo'. S/2009/253. United Nations Group of Experts. Online: http://www.un.org/Docs/journal/asp/ws.asp?m=s/2009/253 (accessed 12 January 2009).

UNSC. 2008. UN Security Council Resolution 1857. 22 December 2008. United Nations Security Council. Online: http://www.undemocracy.com/S-RES-1857(2008).pdf (accessed 12 January 2010).

Vlassenroot, Koen and Timothy Raeymaekers. 2009. 'Kivu's Intractable Security Conundrum'. *African Affairs* 108 (432): 475–84.

World Bank. 2008. 'Democratic Republic of the Congo: Growth with Governance in the Mining Sector'. World Bank. Online: http://siteresources.worldbank.org/INTOGMC/Resources/336099-1156955107170/drcgrowthgovernanceenglish.pdf   (accessed 12 December 2009).

Chapter 10

WATER MANAGEMENT AND THE SECURITY-DEVELOPMENT NEXUS: THE GOVERNING OF LIFE IN THE eTHEKWINI MUNICIPALITY, SOUTH AFRICA

Sofie Hellberg

Introduction

During the last decades water has increasingly become a critical issue in global and local governance, raising questions about human and environmental security and about states' and individuals' right to freshwater and to development. Recently, after 15 years of debate, the United Nations assembly agreed to define access to clean water as a human right (UN 2010a).

The challenges in global water governance include a shrinking availability of water per capita due to pollution, population growth, urbanization and industrialization, a problem that is further amplified by the unpredictability of climate change. At the same time there is an urgent need to reduce the proportion of people living without access to safe drinking water. Water issues have increasingly been recognized as a global concern, and a consensus has emerged for a more conservationist approach in water management and for changing our perceptions and handling of water resources. These efforts are developed under the heading 'Integrated Water Resource Management' (IWRM) and are set to promote a management of water that is more efficient, equitable and sustainable – values that constitute the core of IWRM.

This chapter aims to discuss global water issues in relation to 'development', 'security', and the 'security-development nexus' and to explore, through a biopolitical lens, how water management in an IWRM regime can be understood as a technique of governing subjects, life and lifestyles. To illuminate this, I will draw on research findings from the eThekwini municipality in South Africa. Ultimately this chapter will provide a critical reading of efforts to create a 'water secure' world.

The chapter is organized in four parts. Following these introductory notes the first part will discuss water issues in relation to 'development', 'security', and the 'security-development nexus'. This part explores how the dominant discourse on water management (i.e., the IWRM approach) produces global water issues as a domain of security-development. In order to do this, I draw up some basic points on how we can understand and analyse this from a biopolitical perspective. The second part discusses South African water policies and goals, and the technologies of water service delivery in the eThekwini municipality. The third part explores, through a number of stories on water service delivery as told by the water users themselves, how these policies and technologies affect the lives of eThekwini citizens. In the fourth and final part, these narratives will be discussed in relation to the theoretical framework of the chapter as well as connected to the IWRM approach in terms of how we can understand the biopolitics of water management in a sustainable development regime.

Water, Development, Security

There are many stories about water in relation to 'development' and 'security' and 'security-development'. Below I will briefly pick up on a few of them. This sketch will draw on Stern and Öjendal's (2010) mapping of the security-development nexus.[1] Öjendal and Stern bring up well-known stories about development and security and map the nexus onto six common narratives: the security-development nexus as: 'Modern (Teleological) Narrative'; 'Deepened, Broadened and Humanized'; 'Impasse/Impossible'; 'Post–Security-Development'; 'Security-Development as Technique of Governmentality'; and lastly as 'Globalized Security-Development'. I will use these narratives as a backdrop for understanding the different positions that water occupies in research and policy contexts. I will then apply the specific perspective, 'Security-Development as a Technique of Governmentality'. This will allow an exploration of the ways in which lives and subjects are governed, in terms of water use, by policies guided by the concept of sustainable development. In the following section I will discuss a few common stories about water and development, and water and security.

Water and Development

Because of its importance in all aspects of human life (Strang 2004), water access is a central issue in the development field. It is now widely recognized that water is fundamental for economic growth and for supporting livelihoods, as well as in poverty reduction strategies. This is evident, for example, in water and sanitation supply services and in terms of water for food production and health benefits (UNWWDR-3 2009). In urban-based and manufacturing economies water is needed for almost all economic activities, and in rural and agricultural-based economies water is often the most important factor for agricultural production and other livelihood strategies. This makes water access an essential ingredient to growing different types of economies, and the lack of it becomes a constraint to development (ibid.). Water issues thus occupy important positions in stories about development that are state-centric and measured in terms of economic growth (development as a 'modern narrative'), as well as those focusing on human development (development as 'humanized'). Water issues have perhaps gained the most attention through the increasing focus on the environmental dimension of development through the concept of sustainable development.

Water and Sustainable Development

In the beginning of the 1990s, water issues and their importance for development and environment were brought to attention during the International Conference on Water and the Environment (ICWE) which took place in Dublin in 1992 and during the World Summit in Rio the same year.

During the ICWE meeting in Dublin, it was acknowledged that the situation for global water resources was critical and that water scarcity and misuse of the resource pose 'a serious and growing threat' (ICWE 1992), not only to sustainable development and the protection of the environment, but also to human health, welfare and survival, food security and industrial development (ICWE 1992). Water issues were thus understood as crucial in terms of reaching environmental sustainability, but also in relation to social and economic dimensions of development. Water issues were important components of the targets set out in the World Summit on Sustainable development (see Rio Declaration 1992 and Agenda 21 1992, sec. 2, chap. 18) and later became a target within the seventh goal (to ensure environmental sustainability) of the Millennium Development Goals. The target sets out to: 'halve, by 2015, the proportion of the population without sustainable access to safe drinking water' (UN 2010b).

Integrated Water Resources Management

The solutions proposed for dealing with this 'global water crisis' have included a shift from supply management to demand management and on managing water as an economic good. This is in order to achieve efficient and equitable water use at the same time as encouraging the protection of water resources, which is part of what is labelled 'Integrated Water Recourses Management' (IWRM). IWRM is supposed to promote 'the co-ordinated development and management of water, land and related resources, in order to maximize the resultant economic and social welfare in an equitable manner without compromising the sustainability of vital ecosystems' (GWP 2000, 22), which is the most quoted definition of the concept.

IWRM as an approach has been immensely influential and is subsequently seen as the way forward. Progress in water management, as formulated in global policy documents, is measured in relation to the success in complying with the stipulations of IWRM (see, for example, World Bank 2004; UN WWDR 2003; UN WWDR-2 2006), such as recognizing that water is a fundamental (human) right along with developing measures such as demand management and cost recovery. These measures are in line with managing water as an economic good, which is acknowledged in the so-called Dublin principles mentioned above. Here it is stated that 'managing water as an economic good is an important way of achieving efficient and equitable use, and of encouraging conservation and protection of water resources' (ICWE 1992). The principles have gained a broad global consensus and are embraced as important ingredients of the World Bank water resources strategies (see World Bank 2004) as well as UN policies (see UN WWDR-2 2006).[2]

The way the dominant discourse of water management presents water issues – in terms of the narratives presented above – can be placed in the narrative of 'globalized development' (Stern and Öjendal 2010). According to this way of looking at problems in the water sector, nation-states lack tools to overcome the 'global water crisis' and global networks and institutions are needed in order to create the conditions for truly integrated water management. To this we will return. First, however, water issues will be discussed in relation to 'security'.

Water and Security

Since the 1990s, water issues have also been increasingly discussed in terms of international security, both in the research community as well as in policy circles. Serageldin, the then vice president of the World Bank, said in 1995 that 'if the wars of this century were fought over oil, the wars of the next century will be fought over water' (Serageldin, quoted in Shiva 2002, preface). In academia, the publication of the article 'Water Wars' (Starr 1991) can be seen as a starting point of this debate. Mainly, the focus in relation to this has been on the implications of water scarcity and trans-boundary waters on conflict and cooperation between states. The discussion on the nexus between water and security has however been broadened and deepened to include concepts such as 'human security', 'environmental security' and 'water security'.

Water Scarcity and Conflict

The debate on water and security that took off during the 1990s was initially framed in line with the focus of traditional security studies, which take sovereign states as their referent object. In this line of thinking it was stipulated that future water scarcity would provoke conflict between states, i.e., 'water wars', an argument based on the assumption that there are causal relationships between resource scarcity and (armed) conflict (see, for example, Homer-Dixon 1991, 1994). Furthermore, water has also been discussed as an ingredient in conflicts where it becomes a tool for warfare, for example through controlling the accessibility of the resource for one or more parties in a conflict (ICRC 1995). The argument that water scarcity leads to conflict has, however, been contested by research pointing to the lack of empirical evidence of these stipulations and at the same time showing the amount of cooperation (in terms of agreements, for example) that has historically taken place over shared water resources (see, for example, Wolf 1998; Wolf et al. 2003).

During the course of time, focus has partly shifted from international water conflicts to regional and local ones. The report *The Water Security Nexus* (GTZ 2010) gives a few examples of what these conflicts can revolve around: farmers can for example disagree over irrigation practices, local communities can disagree with farmers over drinking water, or resist large infrastructural projects such as dams, etc. Furthermore, as has been brought up in relation to local conflicts over water, communities get into disputes with water utilities or private companies involved in service delivery over the way water is perceived and the way water service delivery is arranged (see Shiva 2002). The most well-known example of this is the so called 'water war' in Cochamamba, Bolivia (Shiva 2002) – and in relation to the focus of this text – another well-known example is the Johannesburg case regarding the pre-paid water meters (see Bond and Dugard 2008).

While there is a lack of evidence of international water wars, there is at the same time no comprehensive overview of local water conflicts. What can be concluded, according to the GTZ report, is that there are indications that restrained access to water does provoke conflict 'when it affects already marginalized groups' (GTZ 2010). This brings us to the next story about water in relation to the security concept.

Water Issues and a Deepened and a Broadened Security Concept

Water issues have also been discussed in terms of a broadened and deepened security concept – as part of 'environmental security' (see, for example, Barnett 2001; Dalb 2008), 'food security' and 'water security' (Brauch 2008).

It has been argued that the critical security problems in relation to water is that of human suffering due to the lack of clean water (Wolf 1999). Here, the negative impact of water scarcity on the human being is central, which places the individual in focus in relation to these 'new' security threats.[3] One statistic that illustrates this point: approximately 3 million people die every year from water-related diseases in developing countries (GTZ 2010; UN WWDR-3 2009).

But what does 'water security' mean? There is no definition around which there is a consensus, but Wouters suggests (drawing on the human security discourse) that water security is 'the state of having secure access to water; the assured freedom from poverty of, or want for, water for life' (Wouters 2005, quoted in Brauch 2008).

Water, Security-Development

Ending up in a story of security as 'broadened and deepened' (cf. Stern and Öjendal 2010) in relation to water issues, through the concept of 'water security', we can link up with the idea of IWRM and the concept of development. The IWRM 'community' is namely, to a large extent, using the concept and language of 'water security'. According to the Global Water Partnership[4] it is through an IWRM approach that we are to achieve a 'water secure world' (GWP 2009), which, in turn, is vital in order to realize sustainable development (GWP 2010b). In the GWP strategy for 2009–13 it is stated that:

> A water secure world is vital for a better future: a future in which there is enough water for social and economic development and for ecosystems. A water secure world integrates a concern for the intrinsic value of water together with its full range of uses for human survival and well-being. A water secure world harnesses water's productive power and minimises its destructive force. It is a world where every person has enough safe, affordable water to lead a clean, healthy and productive life […] Water security also means addressing environmental protection and the negative effects of poor management, which will become more challenging as climatic variability increases. A water secure world reduces poverty, advances education, and increases living standards. It is a world where there is an improved quality of life for all, especially for the most vulnerable – usually women and children – who benefit most from good water governance. GWP believes that an integrated approach to managing the world's water resources is the best way to pursue this vision – a vision that encompasses all of life. (GWP 2010b, 6)

On the basis of the above, one could conclude that water issues have been both 'securitized' and 'globalized'. At the same time as creating opportunities for economic development and well-being, water issues (and their poor management) pose a threat to growth, health, welfare and the survival of both humans and economies. Situated in this nexus between development and security, water – and its simultaneously productive and destructive power – thus becomes represented as one of the global human survival issues (cf. Stern and Öjendal 2010, 20). We can hence understand the efforts of IWRM as a domain of security-development within the field of environmental governance, which is manifested in the description of 'water security' above. What then are the effects of presenting global water challenges in this way? Who is doing what, and for whom, in the name of this water security-development nexus (cf. Stern and Öjendal 2010); and who is getting what, when, where and how (cf. Turton 2002) in relation to the water resource? In order to explore these questions I intend to read these efforts as a 'technique of governmentality' through a biopolitical lens. The 'securing' of water issues can, as seen from this perspective, be understood as a technique of governing danger and contingency (Stern and Öjendal 2010) which calls for the regulation, control and surveillance of water use and access in order to sustain and foster life.

Understanding Water Governance as Part of a Biopolitics of the Population

As discussed above, water is strongly connected to 'the problem of life' (Foucault 2003, 241), its survival and well-being. This, along with the efforts to ensure that everyone has enough water to lead 'clean, healthy and productive' lives, as stated in the GWP strategy, certainly places water issues at the centre of a 'biopolitics of the population' (Foucault 1976, 139). This kind of politics is concerned with matters of life and death, birth and propagation, health and illness (physical and mental) and 'with processes that sustain or retard the optimization of the life of a population' (Dean 1999, 99). As seen from this perspective, water issues can be placed in a nexus between security and development, where techniques of water management work to govern, regulate and improve life and life conditions (Foucault 1976, 139).

In an analysis of a management of water that is supposed to 'encompass all of life' there is, however, a need to problematize how challenges in environmental and water governance are presented as global or universal problems, and to look into how power is exercised differently over (and through) different populations and individuals. Mark Duffield (2007) argues that rather than understanding biopolitical technologies as acting at a universal or global level, we need to understand that biopolitical practices make *distinctions between different forms of life*. He states that, 'biopolitics is not a single strategization of power in the sense of a globalizing or universal disposition for acting on and promoting life at the level of world population', but rather as something that is supporting and distinguishing different forms of life internationally, and that 'development embodies the biopolitical division and separation of the human species into developed and underdeveloped species-life'(Duffield 2007, 217). According to Duffield, this division between 'developed and underdeveloped species-life' was established 'during the period of colonization' but was further *confirmed* and *deepened* when sustainable development was mainstreamed into the (development) debate (Duffield 2007, 68). The entry of sustainable development in development discourse has put an end to earlier assumptions that the underdeveloped world would at some point resemble the developed; the poor in a sustainable development regime are 'expected to live within the limits of their own powers of self-reliance' (Duffield 2007, 68) and to adjust their expectations to be content with satisfying their basic needs at the same time as improving their resilience (Duffield 2007, 68–70). According to this perspective, contemporary environmental discourse – these new 'eco-knowledges' and new 'truths' about economy and society (Luke 1999, chap. 6) – and the concern of how to manage population and resources in relation to their environments (cf. Foucault 1976, 140; Rutherford 1999), thus *contains* rather than *reduces* the 'life-chance gap between the developed and underdeveloped worlds' (Duffield 2007, 68).

Analysing the security-development nexus in water management from a biopolitical perspective is thus to ask questions about how people are (attempted to be) governed in their resource use, how this is done technically and practically in relation to different populations, and what the biopolitical effects might be.

The South African example will be connected to these prevailing global discourses on resource management below. The case of eThekwini will then be discussed in more detail in relation to this 'green governmentality', i.e., the attempts to establish 'the right disposition of things'[5] in water management (cf. Luke 1999).

South African Water Policies

South Africa has adopted ways of counteracting the challenges involved in the increasing problem of water (un)availability from an IWRM perspective. The need for such an approach is set out in the National Water Policy (NWP 1997). In the National Water Resources Strategy (NWRS 2004) it is stated that: 'there is increasing understanding internationally that water resources can be successfully managed only if the natural, social, economic and political environments in which water occurs and is used are taken fully into consideration' (NWRS 2004, 10).

According to global standards, South Africa is doing well. The country is seen as one of the most progressive countries in the world in terms of balancing the parameters of equity, sustainability and economic efficiency (see, for example, Ashton and Haasbroek 2002, 191), and is getting ovations for its changed attitudes towards water management (see UN WWDR-2 2006, 13) as well as for its legislation (see RSA 1996, 1997, 1998) and the development of water markets (see World Bank 2004 24; UN WWDR-3 2009, 65) as advised by the World Bank (see, for example, World Bank 1999, 54). Of fundamental importance in terms of legislation is that the Constitution of the Republic of South Africa (RSA 1996) defines water as a basic right. To meet the demands of the constitution there are, along with demand management and full cost recovery polices, attempts to provide water to vulnerable individuals through the policy of 25 L per person per day as a basic right (Free Basic Water, FBW), which is equivalent of 6 kL per month per household consisting of eight persons (McDonald and Pape 2002, 28; DWAF 2002).

Water Service Delivery in eThekwini

If South Africa is to be seen as the national success story in relation to global discourses of water management, the eThekwini municipality is its municipal counterpart. The municipality is seen as a pioneer in sustainable service delivery but at the same time faces big challenges. As seen from the perspective of the municipality, the key biopolitical problem in terms of water is to reach a 'balance', or 'homeostasis' (Foucault 2003, 246), in the relationship between resource availability and inhabitants (Foucault 1976, 140) and to adjust water use to water accessibility in an economically sound, environmentally sustainable and socially equitable manner. This in a context where many of its inhabitants, who have been underserved during the apartheid era, urgently need to get access to safe water at the same that the utilization of existing water resources is close to the maximum (interview, Head of EWS Neil Macleod 1 April 2009). With a shrinking availability and a growing demand, the situation in eThekwini resembles problems on the national as well as global scale.

In the context of the challenge of the great disparities between its people, the Water and Sanitation unit (EWS) is, with their own words, looking in 'innovative ways' to find solutions in order to service all its citizens. The municipality has been praised for its success in providing water for the poor while simultaneously being able to recover costs (Loftus 2005a), and it was here that the free basic water policy (FBW) was developed. Judging from the global recognition the municipality has received – among others the municipality has won the UN's public service award (eThekwini Online 2007) – it can be seen as a good example of the implementation of central ideas in global discussions of water management.

The municipality has, however, simultaneously been heavily criticized both by academics and activists. According to Alex Loftus, who has done extensive research in the municipality, the municipality's water policies are 'inhumane' (Loftus 2005b, 250). This 'inhumanity' is to be understood in (at least) two ways. Firstly it is about the cruelty of the water supply disconnections and people's fear of 'debt collectors, bailiffs and imposed droughts'(ibid.). It is, however, also an argument in relation to how water policy is increasingly wrested from the control of people through meters, flow restrictors and money; which results in what Loftus calls an 'alienated waterscape'(ibid.).

From a Foucauldian perspective, this focus on the repressive side of water governance raises questions about its productive aspects. This chapter therefore explores the governmentality of the different attempts at governing people in their resource use, as well as its productive effects in terms of how power relations shape subjects, their interests and lifestyles. Below follows a discussion of the goals and technologies of water service delivery and how we can understand them from a biopolitical perspective.

Goals and Technologies of Water Service Delivery

According to the Water Services Development Plan (WSDP), the goals of eThekwini water services are as follows:

> all citizens have access to an appropriate, acceptable, safe and affordable basic water supply and sanitation service. All citizens are educated in the healthy use of water and sanitation services and the wise use of water. Water and sanitation services are provided: equitably (adequate services are provided fairly to all people); affordably (no one is excluded from access to basic services because of their cost); effectively (the job is done well); efficiently (resources are not wasted); [and] sustainably (services are financially, environmentally, institutionally and socially sustainable). (WSDP 2004, 11)

To fulfil the stated goals of the water sector in the municipality and to redress the backlogs,[6] the municipality has adopted three levels of services offered to domestic costumers.

Poor rural areas, where water infrastructure is available nearby, have been provided with the *ground tank system*, which is a system that guarantees free basic water (FBW) fed daily into a tank in the yard (WSDP 2004). The other two service levels include the *semi pressure supply*, received by the household via a roof-tank, and the *full pressure water supply*, fed directly to the household from the city's supply network. Different tariffs are charged for domestic customers based on the type of water service they receive and the amount of water they use in a 30-day period (WSDP 2004, 22).[7] In informal settlements, water dispensers (or standpipes) are installed as an interim measure (ibid.) and, as is the case with the ground tanks, the water is free of charge. Initially the FBW amount was 200 L per household per day, equivalent to the FBW 6 kL per household per month, but in July 2008 this amount was raised to 300 L or corresponding 9 kL. Another technical device, installed in order to come to terms with non-payment of services, is the so-called flow limiter. It is a kind of meter that can be set to restrict water supply at certain amounts of water (for example at the FBW level) but can also allow a flow of an unrestricted amount of water. The installation of the flow limiter comes with the opportunity to apply for debt relief. This gives a person who has accumulated arrears an opportunity to write them off by signing a contract with the council which will enjoin the costumer to pay his or her water bill on time and in full over a period of 20 months (EMWP 2007–8, 5).

From a biopolitical perspective, this way of developing and applying different levels of services and technological devices (ground tanks in rural areas, flow restrictors in township areas where people have accumulated debts, regular meters in the townships and suburbs, and so on) appears to be a strategy of governance that is making distinctions between different populations and individuals. This 'will to divide' has been argued to be a central characteristic of governmentality in modern societies (Walters 2004, 249). In this case it works to separate between those who will have to live within the (knowable) limits of basic needs and those who can afford to pay for a higher standard of living; between those who are legal consumers and those who are illegal; and further between those who live in (rural) areas where infrastructure would be too costly to invest in[8] and those who live in urban areas, as well as between those who are informal dwellers (and therefore not eligible for individual access points) and those living in formal housing.

How then do people experience these policies and technologies put in place? In order to get close to the lives that are being lived within these hydropolitical relations of power, interviews[9] have been conducted using a narrative method (see, for example, Clandinin and Rosiek 2007; Elliott 2005; Hinchman and Hinchman 1997). This method puts emphasis on lived experiences and the meaning-creating activity that the telling of stories implies, and is used in order to find a way to represent individual perceptions and usage of water in particular local contexts through the telling of life stories in terms of water. Such life histories should be seen as constructive of reality rather than representing 'real life' (White 1987, ix), and additionally as a construction of both the interviewer and interviewee (Stern 2006, 185).

The six stories will be discussed in relation to themes of 'water security' as formulated by the Global Water Partnership. These themes, derived from the GWP quotation above and formulated in relation to the local water narratives are: *water for 'survival and well-being'; water for basic needs (improved life conditions and new vulnerabilities); and water, payment and different living standards.* In the conclusion I will then discuss the IWRM and its limitations as an approach that 'encompasses all of life'. I will start by presenting two narratives in relation to the attempts of providing water for all through the policy of FBW. These stories are from two different places in eThekwini: an informal settlement in Crossmoor, Chatsworth, which has recently received access to a standpipe, and the rural community Mzinyathi where ground tanks have been installed. This will be followed by a discussion of stories about water meters (both regular meters and the flow limiter) and how they affect the narrators in terms of limiting (or talking about limiting) their water use in three different contexts in the township Ntuzuma: a flat community in Crossmoor, Chatsworth, and in the middle-class suburb of Glenwood.

Water for Survival and Well-being

A starting point in relation to the stories as well as the concept of water security is that water is essential for sustaining life, but it is not only important in terms of survival; it is not only a question of life and death. Water and water access play a part in political, social, cultural, religious, spiritual, economic, environmental and geographic settings, as well as in relation to our feelings of well-being and the way we live. This is explicitly acknowledged in the understanding of water security that the global water partnership embraces. As stated above it includes 'a concern for the intrinsic value of water together with its full range of uses for human survival and well-being […] It is a world where every person has enough safe, affordable water to lead a clean, healthy and productive life' (GWP 2010b, 6). The narratives discussed in the next part all oscillate between water for survival and basic needs and water for well-being and pleasure, and as such tell us something about the lifestyles that are being produced in the hydropolitical power relations in eThekwini. The first story is a narrative about changes in an informal settlement in relation to the provision of free basic water.

Water for Basic Needs: Improved Life Conditions and New Vulnerabilities

The people living in the informal settlement of Crossmoor, in Chatsworth, have recently had a standpipe provided for them. It is situated on the road down the hill from the settlement. This has certainly improved their situation in terms of water access. Before, they had to rely on access from the private houses situated close by, and sometimes they had to wait for people to get home before they could access water, and occasionally they were even denied it. Now they do not have to rely on other people's good will in order to get water for their basics; for drinking, cooking, cleaning and bathing.

The location of the standpipe, however, is something of a concern for the people in the settlement. It is not only because it is difficult to get the heavy water up the hill to their shelters, especially when it has been raining, but also because there are other people using the water – taxi drivers as well as people from other settlements. This is especially concerning to them since the municipality has told them that water access is going to be cut off if they overuse it. Albert[10], who has been living in the settlement since it was established, is therefore worried about the community's lack of control over the standpipe. Attached to the standpipe is a meter, of which he is well aware; he says:

> One thing I am not happy about is the meter. It would be better if it [the standpipe] was in the land [inside the settlement] and had a meter to count the amount of water we all use here […] It is hurting because we are told that they will stop the water if we don't look after the standpipe […] Because this is counted on us, the meter is there and it is pointing to us […] It is our responsibility.

When I ask Albert what he thinks of the water meter, he replies: 'What I think is what they are doing with that meter is that they are monitoring the way water is being used but what I can say is that water is not being abused'. Here, disciplining measures are applied where the people affected do not have control over the water that is being used. The result is that the community members get into fights with the people who want to use the water, thinking it is free and available for everyone. 'That's why they hate us', Albert says, but the fear of being without water is greater than the inconvenience involved in going down the hill in order to chase away people using the water. He continues, 'That's why I don't have a problem [doing that]'. Albert thus takes on the responsibility of taking care of the standpipe in a context where the free basic water comes with worries and even conflicts.

Generally, however, people are happy to have received the new standpipe, as is Albert. Still, he is anything but satisfied with his water situation. He remembers a time when he had access to a shower and a flushing toilet. When comparing the situations he says,

> 'being here, you sometimes feel like you are an animal'; 'You can't freshen up'; 'There [when having access to the above mentioned facilities] I was feeling like a human being'; 'When we wash here I first have to go outside

[and fetch water, and then go inside my shelter] and nobody must come inside and the whole house becomes a toilet'; 'You see like what I saw [at the place with the facilities], that's a way of living'.

The connection between water and water facilities and what it is to live a dignified life is clear in Albert's story. The way of life and the material conditions in the settlement are to him undignified, as Albert does not even feel 'human'.

Another location within the municipality which has recently received access to piped water is the rural community Mzinyahti. The community was a pilot area for the water and sanitation project that involved the installation of tanks as well as urine diversion (UD) toilets. Many of the narrators tell me that they think their situation is better now compared to before when they had to walk to the river to fetch water. They can now drink clean water and they do not have to walk long distances carrying water on their heads. It is mainly women and children who bear the responsibility of fetching water in order to satisfy the needs in the households. In terms of workload, the fact that the tank enables the households to access water in the yard has meant more for women than for men in the community.

Mrs Mabuza[11], who lives in the community, seems to be happy with the change of not having to fetch and carry 'dirty water', that is 'tasting of salt', but she is worried about the interruptions she is experiencing with the tank system. The interruptions, she explains, normally start at the houses on top of the hill: 'We sometimes stay for days [without water] because it finishes first at the top and then we pass on water for one another and fill it up and keep it in dishes', she explains. Not knowing when and why water was going to be interrupted causes frustration and worry in the community. The convenience of having water accessible nearby in the yard has thus come along with a dependency on the municipality and a sense of helplessness when the water is not available in the tank, which causes another type of inconvenience than experienced in the past. Accessing water services is hence to enter into a relation of power and dependence, and the improvement of life conditions – through the availability of clean water for basic needs – has simultaneously created new vulnerabilities, similar to the dynamics experienced by Albert in the informal settlement.

Additionally, there are still households without access to water in their yard in Mzinyathi, namely, the people who have moved into the area after the programme was initiated and those who initially were left out because they could not pay the installation fee for the tank. According to the municipality this policy has now changed; those who are now being enrolled in the free basic water programmes in other communities do not have to pay this fee any longer.

However, for the people in Mzinyathi, it would require that the municipality restart enrolment to the programme, because if an individual household applies, it will still be charged for the installation. In some households where interviews were conducted, people were saving money in order to apply for the tank and their inability to pay the fee kept them from getting one.

Andile[12] was one of those who did not pay the initial fee and instead has done his 'own connection' to the municipality's network. He explains it as follows:

> I don't think it is an illegal connection because I couldn't manage to pay for the registration for accessing water. It is not an illegal connection it is just that they want us to do what they think is right they don't want to hear from us what we prefer in our lives: they always think for us, what is better for us.

Thus, for Andile his 'illegal' connection is part of a conscious resistance strategy against the municipality's water policies, and he refuses the logic of water management as he does not accept the idea of being an 'illegal' water user.[13]

Illegal connections and non-payment for water services are problems that are recognized by the municipality,[14] and they have been addressed through technologies such individual meters and flow limiters, and policies such as the debt relief scheme. Experiences of these technologies and policies will be discussed below.

Water, Payment and Different Living Standards

While stories in communities which were previously without water infrastructure revolve around the relatively easy access to clean water at present, water narratives in other locations centre rather on limiting or trying to limit water use.

Paying for water is a struggle for many of the municipality's poor households and 'payment' is a central theme in relation to water in many narratives. When I ask Mrs Bongani,[15] who lives in the township Ntuzuma to comment on the meter, she does so with the following: 'the mind is always thinking if you are wasting the water, the meter there […] It is saying what you are doing, you can see that how you are using water, now water you don't just use anyhow'.

It is apparent how Mrs Bongani feels supervised by the meter regarding her use of water. She can access as much she wants to but she risks a high water bill and therefore she has to adjust her behaviour, thinking always about how much she is using and for what. When I ask her about how much she pays, she knows the exact amounts of the bills that she has received during the time that she spent in her new house, and they are all around R 30 (around $3.33 US).[16]

Someone who has a more positive experience of the system of paying for water is Suleilah[17] who is 33 years old and lives in a flat community together with her mother and child in Chatsworth, where the flow limiter system has recently been implemented. Non-payment for services has been common in the community and the flow limiters are a way of addressing that. Many residents have accumulated large debts over the years, and along with the implementation of the flow limiter comes the possibility of applying for debt relief. When the flow limiters were installed, the members of the community were given choices in terms whether they wanted their water access to be restricted (at the FBW level or higher) or if they wanted to be able to access an unlimited supply. There are exceptions regarding who can choose, as for example for residents who are not legal tenants, but Suleilah's household had the option of themselves choosing whether to restrict water supply or go for the unlimited option. In relation to this she says: 'unlimited – I can use as much as I want but… yeah as long as you pay'. For many the installation of limiters means that they have to start paying regularly for water services. Despite this, Suleilah embraces the new system and says that it is good for the community. Her reasons are manifold. According to Suleilah, the new system has involved changes in terms of use and how people think about water, she says: 'we are very, very […] conscious now […] because we have this […] new system that we actually have to pay for water'. When relating the present situation to what was before she explains, 'we used to waste water a lot'; '[now] we don't waste water!' The new system has, according to Suleilah, involved the change that water use is now 'controlled' – something that she thinks is a good thing, because water is a basic need that is 'not to be wasted at all'. Suleilah tells me, with what appears to be satisfaction, that, 'we limit ourselves, we restrict ourselves'. She illustrates her point by bringing up the example of the small pools they used to fill for the children on hot days – so common in the Durbanite summer – and lets me know that people don't do that anymore. There are 'no more fun and games with water', she concludes. Suleilah knows exactly what her water bill amounts to every month, something that is simpler now that she gets a separate water bill, which in turn makes it easier for her to budget and keep an eye on the water use. Suleilah thus seems to accept the controlling effect of the new meters and embraces the changes they have brought about in people's behaviour – that they now restrict themselves and that they 'don't waste water'. This could possibly be explained by the fact that she now has a sense of being in control and choosing how she wants her water access and bills to be arranged. Suleilah also seems to have a central position in her neighbourhood, and the community members come for her to advise and help regarding the new system, she tells me. This might also be a factor in helping to create a positive picture of the new system and the understanding of herself as someone who is taking responsibility – both for water and for the community.

Additionally, at the time I visit Suleilah's apartment it has gone through renovations and the residents have been offered ownership of their apartments by the municipality. She brings this up when I ask her about what she means when she talks about 'The New South Africa', and she then goes on to talk about the FBW that everyone gets for free. We can read Suleilah's story as a story of someone who experiences that she is getting something from the state and/or the municipality (she differentiates between the two) in her capacity as a citizen in 'the New South Africa'. Through Suleilah's story we can thus see water access as a material expression of political inclusion (cf. Bakker 2010, 55) and which might be a reason for Suleilah to accept and embrace the idea of the payment and limitation of water use in the present, despite the negative effects it has on the possibilities of enjoying the pleasures of water. If the municipality succeeds in areas such as the one where Suleilah lives, where people have refused to pay for services for a long time, the municipality will consequently be able to turn individual, and perhaps collective, water stories of resistance into stories of acceptance.

The contrast is quite stark between the flat community where Suleilah lives and the suburbs situated closer to the city centre. Here a limitation of water use is rarely connected to economic necessities but rather to an 'environmental awareness'. Karen[18] lives in such a suburb, Glenwood. She is a 42-year-old teacher, who receives water through a full pressure system and, like Suleilah, she is also talking about limiting her water use. However, the use of relatively large quantities of water is important to her, as it is deeply connected to her way of life. She says: 'my way of life involves having water, coming out of taps in my house' She explains further:

> If I didn't get water coming into my house the way that we do […] I really would want to go live somewhere else […] that's how I feel, I feel very strongly that I could not personally, given my history at the age of 42, I could not live if they couldn't, if there wasn't water coming out of the tap.

At the same time water access is a worry for Karen. Karen's associations to the meter are first and foremost about what she refers to as 'the environmental crisis'. When I ask about what she thinks and feels about the meter she replies:

> it just goes [tjick-tjick-tjick-tjick-tjick] and […] I feel a bit of a panic and I suppose it is related to some kind of environmental sense of the water crisis that our world is in and […] worrying about that and worrying

what's gonna happen to our world because our water supply I think is finite and we don't treat it like that and so I do have a little bit of a panic about: ah! You are wasting water!

This worry is a recurrent theme in her talk about water and Karen is quite dramatic with what the ignorance of the water issue could involve: 'I think it might be in some ways kind of the end of our world as we know it, the water crises'. In Karen's narrative water issues are strongly associated with future threats to Karen's way of life.

In Karen's story this feeling of guilt also becomes blurred with fond water memories. Karen explains how she loves to swim, in the pool and in the ocean ('everywhere!') and that she loves to shower, something she does twice a day. However, she tells me how she feels about watching large amounts of water going down the drain, and explains: 'we don't bathe cause it just looks like it's so much water when you pull out the plug it becomes something hard to even watch you know so much water'. A big difference compared to the other narrators is that Karen does not know how much she pays for water. She has to look for the bills in order to find out and they show amounts of around R 500 (around $55.50 US).

Karen clearly associates her water situation with the legacy of the apartheid system and her privileged situation as a White South African. And when discussing the bills Karen explains why she doesn't think she is entitled to the FBW of 9 kl that every household gets free of charge: 'I think water is a right and people must pay for it if they are wealthy and if they are not wealthy then they shouldn't have pay for it'. But when I ask her about what she thinks *her* right is in terms of water as a South African citizen she answers that she thinks it is hard in 'context of the disparities' but that she thinks that 'it should be that everyone has the right to […] potable water inside their house'. When relating it to her own situation Karen says, 'I suppose in a way, the way that I'm talking it makes it sound like I think it's my right to have water coming out of my tap if I can pay for it […] and I do, hot and cold water'. Given Karen's background in the ANC, the struggle against apartheid and what she calls her former 'activist identity', it seems as if coming to this understanding whilst she is talking is painful.

In Karen's narrative it is clear how water and water service delivery is constitutive to her identity. How Karen accesses her water is one of the fundamentals in her life, she would leave her home and her country if she did not receive the service the way she does, ironically this comes in the context of a country where this level of service is not at all the reality that the majority of South Africans enjoy. Given Karen's background, she would clearly resist a way of life that many others have to accept because they lack Karen's resources. Obviously, the water bill and the ability to pay is not what keeps Karen looking after her water use. This is rather something that is motivated by her 'environmental consciousness', in turn informed by an environmental awareness discourse. Clearly Karen sees herself as someone who can and should take responsibility for issues relating to water and her subject positions in relation to the resource shifts from that of being a fortunate White South African who enjoys the pleasures of water to that of a middle class person with excessive use and irresponsible behaviour. Karen is thus at unease with the situation in her country but she could never imagine living at lower standards.

Concluding Comments: An Approach that 'Encompasses All of Life'?

In prevailing global discussions, water's productive and destructive power is acknowledged. The resource is understood to be central both to opportunities for economic development and well-being, while at the same time posing threats to growth, health, welfare and the survival of both humans and economies. Water issues are thus represented as one of the global survival issues and are produced as a domain of security-development. This is manifested in the description of 'water security', as phrased by the Global Water Partnership which states that 'a water secure world integrates a concern for the intrinsic value of water together with its full range of uses for human survival and well-being' (GWP 2010b, 6).

In this chapter, the attempt to come to terms with challenges in water management and to create a 'water secure world' through an IWRM has been analysed as part of a 'green governmentality' which aims at establishing 'the right disposition of things' between humans and their environment.

An analysis of the local context of the eThekwini municipality, which is seen as a pioneer in sustainable service provision, has put to light the different strategies of governance that are applied in relation to different populations. Different levels of services and technological devices have been developed and applied in order to provide the users with the level of service for which they are eligible or for which they can pay (ground tanks in rural areas, flow restrictors in township areas where people have accumulated debts, regular meters in the townships and suburbs and so on), and thus also different levels of service for *different populations*. From a biopolitics perspective one can understand these technologies of water management as instruments of a regulatory power with disciplining effects on the individual water user, and as instruments that play a part in producing boundaries between populations, for setting conditions for their livelihoods and identities, and thus as strategies that are making distinctions between different forms of life.

Through the water users' own stories in relation to themes of 'water security' we can learn that policies in line with an IWRM approach have improved life conditions, but at the same time have created new problems and vulnerabilities in communities that have recently received access to free basic water. The stories told by those who pay for water illustrate how strains are put on poor water users and households, while the more well-off can continue to use large quantities of water as part of a way of life. At the same time, the narratives provide us with text through which we can analyse how the water users themselves are made active in their own government to become sustainable and responsible water users. In order to be effective and accepted, regulatory mechanisms thus require (and produce) active citizens who conduct themselves in accordance with these norms. A biopolitics of water management thus assumes water users that have a will to be governed and to govern themselves.. This means that rather than understanding water policies in the municipality as 'inhumane' and 'alienating' we can understand them as becoming part of who people are, how they (do not) want to live and who they (do not) want to be as humans.

In prevailing global discussions on water management, an integrated approach to managing the world's water resources is seen as the best way to pursue a vision that *encompasses all of life* (GWP 2010b, 6). However, based on an analysis of the governmentality of water management and the stories of the water users themselves in the local context of eThekwini, this approach rather seems to work to *distinguish* between different forms of life and to promote and protect *certain* ways of lives. This in turn highlights the limitation of an IWRM approach in water management as a way of producing 'productive lives', 'raising living standards' and 'an improved quality of life for all' (GWP 2010b, 6) as it appears rather to be a strategy that is *containing* the gap between those who survive on a bare minimum of water and those who can pay for a higher standard of living.

Notes

1 See also Chapter 2, this volume.
2 The principles include that '1. Fresh water is a finite and vulnerable resource, essential to sustain life, development and the environment'; '2. Water development and management should be based on a participatory approach, involving users, planners and policy-makers at all levels'; '3. Women play a central part in the provision, management and safeguarding of water'; and '4. Water has an economic value in all its competing uses and should be recognized as an economic good'(ICWE 1992).
3 The first phases of research on 'environmental security' however remained state-centric (Brauch 2008, 32).

4 GWP is an international network of partners created in 1996 to foster the implementation of IWRM (GWP 2010a).
5 This refers to Foucault's perspective on 'government'; see Foucault (1979) 'Governmentality', *Ideology and Consciousness* 6: 5–21.
6 The backlog is defined as follows. *Rural*: number of households without a water supply via a ground tank, yard tap or direct supply to the house (whether the supply is by means of a connection to the municipality's water reticulation system or a borehole or a water harvesting scheme); or number of households greater than 200 metres from an outlet device (an EBU or water dispenser). *Non rural, formal*: number of households on properties greater than 200 metres from water reticulation infrastructure. *Non rural, informal*: number of households without a (minimum of) standpipe supply within 200 metres (WSDP 2004, 27).
7 The eThekwini municipality has progressive water tariffs (see EWS homepage 2011a).
8 This is known as the waterborne edge (see Gounden et al. 2006)
9 In this chapter only six interviews will be discussed in detail; in the thesis for which this material was collected, a total of 64 narrators were interviewed, of which the majority were interviewed twice. Pseudonyms are used.
10 Interviews with 'Dlamini, Albert' 20 November 2008 and 12 March 2009, Chatsworth, eThekwini municipality.
11 Interviews with 'Mabuza, Nonthandazo' 20 November 2008 and 10 March 2009, Mzinyathi, eThekwini municipality.
12 Interviews with 'Ndebele, Andile' 25 November 2008 and 13 March 2009, Mzinyathi, eThekwini municipality.
13 To have an illegal water connection means that the water user has connected to the municipality's water pipes without having permission to do so, or that the water user has tampered with the connection in order to bypass the water meter or flow limiters (in cases where the user has one).
14 Interview with Macleod, Neil, Head of Water and Sanitation, eThekwini Municipality, 1 April 2009, Durban.
15 Interviews with 'Bongani, Lungile' 2 December 2008 and 20 February 2009, Ntuzuma, eThekwini municipality.
16 All US dollar equivalents are figured as of 12 October 2011 and are meant only as a rough guide.
17 Interviews with 'Amad, Suleilah' 11 December 2008 and 16 March 2009, Chatsworth, eThekwini municipality.
18 Interviews with 'Scott, Karen' 17 December 2008 and 6 April 2009, Glenwood, eThekwini municipality.

References

Agenda 21. 1992. 'Agenda 21: The United Nations Programme of Action from Rio'. UN Department of Economic and Social Affairs, Division for Sustainable Development. Online: http://www.un.org/esa/dsd/agenda21/ (accessed 4 November 2010).
Ashton, Peter and Bennie Haasbroek. 2002. 'Water Demand Management and Social Adaptive Capacity: A South African Case'. In Anthony Turton and Roland Henwood (eds), *Hydropolitics in the Developing world: A Southern African Perspective*. Pretoria: African Water Research Unit.
Bakker, Karen. 2010. *Privatizing Water: Governance Failure and the World's Urban Water Crisis*. Ithaca and London: Cornell University Press.

Barnett, Jon. 2001. *The Meaning of Environmental Security: Ecological Politics and Policy in the New Security Era.* New York: Palgrave.

Bond, Patrick and Jackie Dugard. 2008. 'Water, Human Rights and Social Conflict: South African Experiences'. *Law, Social Justice and Global Development* 1.

Brauch, Hans Günter. 2008. 'Conceptualising the Environmental Dimension of Human Security in the UN'. In Moufida Goucha and John Crowley (eds), *Rethinking Human Security.* Chicester: UNESCO/John Wiley and Sons.

Clandinin and Rosiek. 2007. 'Mapping a Landscape of Narrative Inquiry: Borderlands Spaces and Tensions'. In Jean Clandinin (ed.), *Handbook of Narrative Inquiry: Mapping a Methodology.* London and New Dehli: Sage.

Dalby, Simon. 2008. 'Security and Environmental Linkages Revisited'. In Hans Günter Brauch, Ursula Oswald Spring, Czeslaw Mesjasz, John Grin, Pál Dunay, Navita Chadha Behera, Béchir Chourou, Patricia Kameri-Mbote and P. H. Liotta (eds), *Globalization and Environmental Challenges: Reconceptualizing Security in the 21st Century.* Berlin and Heidelberg: Springer.

Dean, Mitchell. 1999. *Power and Rule in Modern Society.* Los Angeles and London: Sage.

Duffield, Mark. 2007. *Development, Security and Unending War: Governing the World of Peoples.* Malden, MA and Cambridge: Polity Press.

DWAF. 2002. Water is life, sanitation is dignity. Draft White Paper on Water Services. Department of Water and Forestry Affairs: Pretoria.

Elliott, Jane. 2005. *Using Narrative in Social Research: Qualitative and Quantitative Approaches.* Los Angeles, London, New Dehli and Singapore: Sage.

EMWP. 2007–8. eThekwini water policy. eThkwini Municipality. Online: http://www.durban.gov.za/durban/services/water_and_sanitation/policies_and_guidelines/ethekwini_water_policy/WaterPolicy20072008Real%20PolicyEnglish.pdf (accessed 14 May 2009).

eThekwini Online. 2007. eThekwini to receive United Nations public service award. Press release, 7 August 2007. eThkwini Municipality. Online: http://www.durban.gov.za/durban/government/media/press/pressitem.2007-08-07.0111243590/view (accessed 13 March 2011).

EWS. n.d. eThekwini Water and Saniation home page. Online: http://www.durban.gov.za/durban/services/water_and_sanitation (accessed 13 May 2011).

Foucault, Michel. 2003. *Society Must Be Defended, Lectures at the Collège de France 1975–1976.* New York: Picador.

———. 1976. *The Will to Knowledge: History of Sexuality I.* London: Penguin Books.

Gounden, Teddy, Bill Pfaff, Neil Macleod and Chris Buckley. 2006. Provision of free sustainable basic sanitation: The Durban experience. 32nd WEDC International Conference. Colombo, Sri Lanka.

GTZ. 2010. 'The Water Security Nexus Challenges and Opportunities for Development Cooperation'. Deutsche Gesellschaft für Technische Zusammenarbeit. Eschborn.

GWP. 2000. *TAC Background Paper No.4: Integrated Water Resources Management.* Global Water Partnership: Stockholm.

———. 2009. *Background Paper No. 14 Water Management, Water Security and Climate Change Adaptation: Early Impacts and Essential Responses.* Global Water Partnership.

———. 2010a. Global Water Partnership homepage. Online: http://www.gwp.org/ (accessed 9 November 2010).

———. 2010b. 'Strategy 2009–2013'. Global Water Partnership. Online: http://www.gwp.org/Global/About%20GWP/Strategic%20documents/GWP_Strategy_2009-2013_final.pdf (accessed 6 November 2010).

Hinchman, Lewis P. and Sandra K. Hinchman (eds). 1997. *Memory, Identity, Community: The Idea of Narrative in Human Sciences*. State University of New York Press.

Homer-Dixon T. 1991. 'On the Threshold: Environmental Changes as Causes of Acute Conflict'. *International Security* 16(2): 76–116.

_____. 1994. 'Environmental Scarcities and Violent Conflict: Evidence from Cases'. *International Security* 19(1): 5–40.

ICRC. 1995. Water and war: symposium on water in armed conflicts. Conference report. International Committee of the Red Cross.

ICWE. 1992. 'The Dublin Statement on Water and Sustainable Development'. International Conference on Water and the Environment, Dublin.

Loftus, Alex. 2005a. '"Free Water" as Commodity: The Paradoxes of Durban's Water Service Transformations'. In David A. McDonald and Greg Ruiters (eds), *The Age of Commodity: Water Privatization in Southern Africa*. London and Sterling: Earthscan.

_____. 2005b. A political ecology of water struggles in Durban, South Africa. PhD diss. School of Geography and the Environment, University of Oxford, Oxford.

Luke, Timothy W. 1999. 'The Entry of Life into History'. In E. Darier (ed.), *Discourses of the Environment*. Malden, MA: Blackwell Publishers.

McDonald, David A. and John Pape. 2002. *Cost Recovery and the Crisis of Service Delivery in South Africa*. Cape Town and London: Zed Press and HCRS Publishers.

NWP. 1997. 'National Water Policy'. Department of Water and Forestry Affairs. Online: http://www.dwaf.gov.za/documents/Policies/nwpwp.pdf (accessed 6 October 2010).

NWRS. 2004. 'National Water Resources Strategy'. Department of Water and Forestry Affairs. Online: http://www.dwaf.gov.za/Documents/Policies/NWRS/Default.htm (accessed 6 October 2010).

Rio Declaration. 1992. 'The Rio Declaration'. United Nations Conference on Environment and Development. Online: http://www.un-documents.net/rio-dec.htm (accessed 4 November 2010).

RSA. 1996. *Constitution of the Republic of South Africa. Act 108 of 1996*. Republic of South Africa. Government Printer: Pretoria.

_____. 1997. *Water Services Act, no. 108 of 1997*. Republic of South Africa. Government Gazette: Pretoria.

_____. 1998. *National Water Act, no. 36 of 1998*. Republic of South Africa. Government Gazette: Pretoria.

Rutherford, Paul. 1999. 'The Entry of Life into History'. In E. Darier (ed.), *Discourses of the Environment*. Malden, MA: Blackwell.

Shiva, Vandana. 2002. *Water Wars: Privatisation, Pollution, Profit*. Cambridge, MA: South End Press.

Starr, Joyce R. 1991. 'Water Wars'. *Foreign Policy* 82 (Spring): 17–36.

Stern, Maria. 2006. 'Racism, Sexism, classism, and Much More: Reading Security-Identity in Marginalized Sites'. In Brooke A. Ackerly, Maria Stern and Jacqui True (eds), *Feminist Methodologies for International Relations*. Cambridge: Cambridge University Press.

Stern, Maria and Joakim Öjendal. 2010. 'Mapping the Security–Development Nexus: Conflict, Complexity, Cacaphony, Convergence?' *Security Dialouge* 41(1): 5–29.

Strang, Veronica. 2004. *The Meaning of Water*. Oxford and New York: Berg.

Turton, Anthony. 2002. 'Hydropolitics: The Concept and its Limitations'. In Anthony Turton and Roland Henwood (eds), *Hydropolitics in the Developing World: A Southern African Perspective*. African Water Research Unit: Pretoria.

UN. 2010a. The human right to water and sanitation. United Nations General Assembly, 64th session. A/64/L.63/REV.1. Online: http://www.unesco.org/water/wwap/news/archives/UNDecWaterHR_EN.pdf (accessed 6 November 2010).

UN. 2010b. 'Millennium Development Goals'. United Nations. Online: http://www.
 un.org/millenniumgoals/environ.shtml (accessed 6 November 2010).
UN-WWDR. 2003. *World Water Development Report: Water for People Water for Life*. World Water
 Assessment Programme. Paris and New York: UNESCO and Berghahn Books.
UN WWDR-2. 2006. *Water: A Shared Responsibility*. United Nations World Water Development
 Report 2. World Water Assessment Programme. Paris and New York: UNESCO and
 Berghahn Books.
UN WWDR-3. 2009. *Water in a Changing World*. United Nations World Water Development
 Report 3. World Water Assessment Programme. London: UNESCO and Earthscan.
Walters, William. 2004. 'Secure Borders, Safe Haven, Domopolitics'. *Citizenship Studies* 8(3):
 237–60.
White, Hayden. 1987. *The Content of the Form: Narrative Discourse and Historical*. Baltimore,
 MD: John Hopkins University Press.
World Bank. 1999. *South Africa Country Assistance Strategy: Building a Knowledge Partnership*.
 World Bank. Report no. 19665. Online: http://www-wds.worldbank.org/external/
 default/WDSContentServer/WDSP/IB/1999/10/07/000094946_9909231209021
 7/Rendered/PDF/multi_page.pdf (accessed 14 May 2008).
World Bank. 2004. *Water Resources Sector Strategy: Strategic Directions for World Bank Engagement*.
 Wold Bank. Report no. 28114. Online: http://www-wds.worldbank.org/external/
 default/WDSContentServer/IW3P/IB/2004/06/01/000090341_20040601150257/
 Rendered/PDF/28114.pdf (accessed 14 May 2008).
Wolf, Aaron T. 1998. 'Conflict and Cooperation along International Waterways'. *Water
 Policy* 1(2): 251–65.
_____. 1999. 'Water and Human Security'. *AVISO* 1999(3). Victoria, BC: The Global
 Environmental Change and Human Security Project.
Wolf, Aaron T., Shiba B. Youffe and Mark Giordano. 2003. 'International Waters:
 Identifying Basin at Risk'. *Water Policy* 5(1): 29–60.
Wouters, P. 2005. 'Water Security: What Role for International Water Law?' In F. Dodds
 and T. Pippard (eds), *Human and Environmental Security: An Agenda for Change*. London and
 Steling, VA: Earthscan.
WSDP. 2004. *Water Services Development Plan*. eThekwini Water and Sanitation Unit, 2.

List of Interviews

'Amad, Suleilah' interviews, 11 December 2008 and 16 March 2009, Chatsworth,
 eThekwini municipality.
'Bongani, Lungile' interviews, 2 December 2008 and 20 February 2009, Ntuzuma,
 eThekwini municipality.
'Dlamini, Albert' interviews, 20 November 2008 and 12 March 2009, Chatsworth,
 eThekwini municipality.
'Mabuza, Nonthandazo' interviews, 20 November 2008 and 10 March 2009, Mzinyathi,
 eThekwini municipality.
Macleod, Neil, Head of Water and Sanitation, eThekwini Municipality, interview 1 April
 2009, Durban.
'Ndebele, Andile' interviews 25 November 2008 and 13 March 2009, Mzinyathi, eThekwini
 municipality.
'Scott, Karen' interviews 17 December 2008 and 6 April 2009, Glenwood, eThekwini
 municipality.

www.ingramcontent.com/pod-product-compliance
Lightning Source LLC
Chambersburg PA
CBHW022354280326
41935CB00007B/180